W9-ADX-047

# COMMUNALISM AND THE POLITICAL PROCESS IN MALAYA

# COMMUNALISM AND THE POLITICAL PROCESS IN MALAYA

K. J. RATNAM

Published for the University of Singapore
by the
UNIVERSITY OF MALAYA PRESS
KUALA LUMPUR
1965

Sole Distributors:
*Oxford University Press, Amen House, London E.C.4*
GLASGOW NEW YORK TORONTO MELBOURNE WELLINGTON
BOMBAY CALCUTTA MADRAS KARACHI LAHORE DACCA
CAPE TOWN SALISBURY NAIROBI IBADAN ACCRA
KUALA LUMPUR HONG KONG



PRINTED AND BOUND IN ENGLAND BY
HAZELL WATSON AND VINEY LTD
AYLESBURY, BUCKS

# PREFACE

In this book I have tried to present the political consequences of communal divisions in the Federation of Malaya. I have concentrated on the post-war period[1] because it is only with the Second World War that the bulk of the non-Malay population in the country ceased to be transient and became a part of the settled population, demanding widely increased political rights and thereby threatening the privileged position of the Malays. Further, it is mainly as a result of the political advancement seen during the post-war period (such as the creation of Malayan citizenship, the introduction of elections, and the attainment of independence) that the problems inherent in a plural society have come to be really felt.

As can be seen from the chapter headings, I have approached the subject by selecting for discussion those topics and issues which form the basis of communal disagreement. As a result I have had to sacrifice a certain amount of historical continuity; but I find this approach more suitable for a detailed analysis of my main theme. However, within each chapter I have tried to preserve some sense of the sequence of events and the accompanying changes in attitudes. This may unfortunately have led to some repetition, although I have attempted to keep it to a minimum.

Perhaps I have not made any significant use of findings in related studies or, for that matter, of the more general contributions to theory in the social sciences in so far as they are relevant. I can explain this only in terms of my very modest objective, which is simply that of presenting the communal problem as it exists in the Federation of Malaya. I have neither set out to make any direct contribution to theory in political science nor tried explicitly to make use of current concepts and terminology. However, studies of this kind may not be without value as a basis for the general development of theory and in many ways may even be necessary for that development.

Many of the observations found in this book, particularly those pertaining to communal attitudes, are in the main projections of

1. Roughly up to 1961, when work was completed.

expressed *élite* opinions (of which there are examples in the text), newspaper comments and so on, and are no doubt also influenced by my own familiarity with the Malayan political scene and participation in that society. Some of these opinions have, subsequent to the writing of this book, been confirmed through lengthy interviews with officials of all the major political parties undertaken as part of a different project. There are, in addition, other general observations on the nature of communalism and its relation to politics (such as those found in the last chapter) for which no claim is made except that they either seem logical or appear to be reasonable in the light of what is said in other parts of the book.

In the absence of any extensive and carefully planned surveys, it would be impossible to make claims about the accuracy of statements on communal attitudes. It may, of course, be possible roughly to estimate the relative popularity of different viewpoints on the basis of support given to different political parties whose chief distinguishing feature is their stand on the communal problem.[2] But then the fortunes of these parties, because they are also influenced by other, often temporary, factors, can easily fluctuate without corresponding fluctuations in the popular appreciation of their respective platforms. It is also relevant that leaders often succeed in 'creating' the interests which they eventually seem to represent, a fact which limits the scope for generalizations on basic communal attitudes. It may of course also be argued that, given the existence of political propaganda, even opinion surveys are liable to the same limitations. At times, objective factors, e.g. the indebtedness of the members of one community who are mostly farmers to money-lenders who belong to another community, may account not only for the presence but also for the intensity of communal attitudes.

What is important, however, is that the country does not have a satisfactorily developed system of interest articulation with voluntary organizations performing a useful political role. This makes the testing of collective opinion extremely difficult, especially at the lower levels of political participation. Even organized labour, so prominent in the politics of Singapore, plays a relatively unimportant role in shaping and expressing political attitudes in the Federation.

2. In fact most political parties are classifiable by the positions they occupy in the Malay versus non-Malay continuum.

As in other 'developing' countries, the inadequacy of organized interests has resulted in a communications network which, to the observer, is uneven in that the volume and continuity of the flow of messages from authoritative channels (and from the political *élites* generally) to the society far outweigh the flow in the opposite direction. By and large, the interests which most clearly seem to act as pressure groups on the political system are those which, though appearing to be functional, are efficacious mainly because they operate within a communal framework and represent communally sensitive issues. In the case of the Chinese community, the best examples would be the various guilds, chambers of commerce and educational groups; among the Malays, teachers and religious leaders (between them representing the areas of Malay culture which are politically of most consequence today) are the ones with greatest political influence. But for these, there are few effective pressure groups in the country.

It may on the whole be quite reasonable to argue that the inadequate system of interest articulation is in many ways a product of the major and clear-cut communal divisions which discourage popular interest in functionally specific groups. In Malaya communal interests undoubtedly override economic interests. This has produced a situation where political parties have to be relied on to perform the task of articulating particularistic demands. There is thus no accurate and continuous indication of the policy preferences of organized interests except, of course, for those which are expressed by political parties and which therefore stand the risk of distortion both by the advocates and by the policy makers (in cases where the two are different). As for larger communal interests, those publicly known to be championed by communal bodies vying for popular support in the open political scene are naturally difficult of aggregation in a competitive process. Unfortunately, even in the urbanized modern sector one does not have the mitigating influence of politically significant functional groups.

Much of what I say in this book would indicate the predominance, in Malayan politics, of issues which in most Western democracies may be felt to be politically neutral. This feature, common to many Asian and African states, has often been taken to be a reflection of a tangled and confused political scene where issues are most imperfectly conceived even by the active participants. While there may doubtless be some justification for this view, it should not lead to assertions about the domination of 'political' by what are considered 'non-political' issues (e.g. religion, language)—except perhaps in cases where certain issues are patently 'manufactured' and, in one's opinion, would evoke no political feelings on their own. It would, on the whole, be more realistic simply to recognize that in many of these societies the political domain is much wider and that issues which in other countries may have little or no political significance do in fact have such significance to a point, in some cases, of constituting the central area of political controversy and determining, almost wholly, the selection of leaders. It is, after all, not surprising that issues which most clearly divide a society (whether caste, religion, language or anything else) should constitute an important theme in the politics of that society, with obvious implications for the attainment of basic political consensus.

Even in more general matters such as attitudes towards authority, methods of persuasion, and social restraints on political styles, one can justly make pronouncements only in terms of how they conflict with the established mores and the stated ambition of creating a 'rational' political process. One may, in addition, follow one's own preferences based on considerations of greater order and efficiency, provided these preferences and the goals which they are meant to attain do not remain unexplained. In the absence of any such standpoint a person undertaking a study of these aspects of politics may well be without respectable criteria for his work. It makes little sense to question the features of one political system simply because they differ from those of another which is felt or even known to be successful.

This book is a slightly amended version of a thesis submitted for the degree of Ph.D. at the University of London. I should like to thank Professor K. E. Robinson of the Institute of Commonwealth Studies, University of London, for his suggestions and criticisms both when this book was being written as a thesis and when it was being revised for publication. My thanks are also due to Professor K. B. Smellie and Sir Sydney Caine, who supervised my work at the London School of Economics and Political Science.

K. J. Ratnam.

# TABLE OF CONTENTS

# LIST OF TABLES

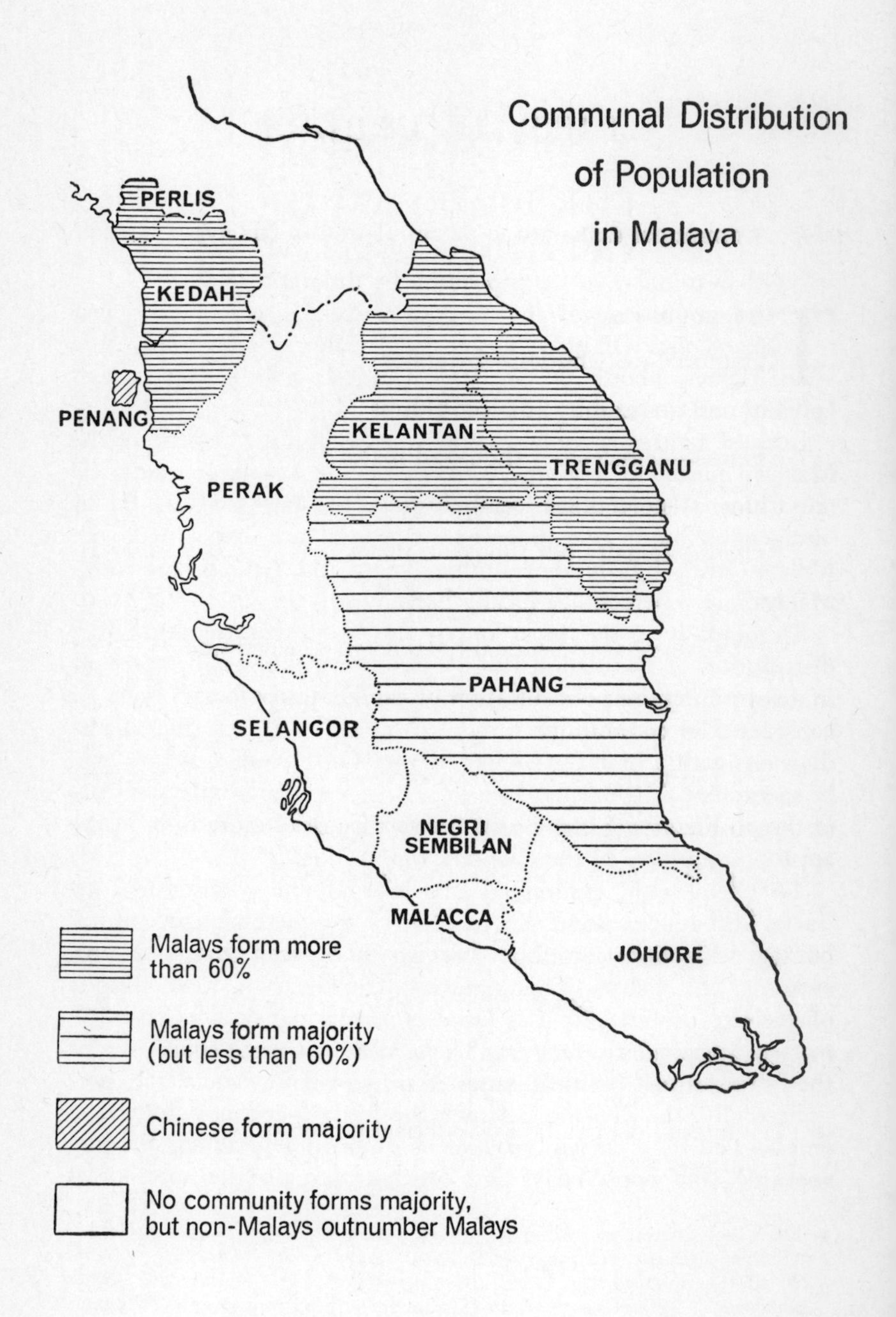
Communal Distribution of Population in Malaya
PERLIS
KEDAH
PENANG
PERAK
KELANTAN
TRENGGANU
PAHANG
SELANGOR
NEGRI SEMBILAN
MALACCA
JOHORE
Malays form more than 60%
Malays form majority (but less than 60%)
Chinese form majority
No community forms majority, but non-Malays outnumber Malays

## CHAPTER ONE

# THE PROBLEM OF NATIONAL UNITY

THE population of the Federation of Malaya in 1957 was 6,278,763. Of this figure, just under 50 per cent were Malays, about 37 per cent Chinese, about 12 per cent Indians, and about 0·2 per cent 'Others'.[1]

In these figures is contained the most significant feature of the Malayan plural society: the Malayan nation is one of numerical minorities. Also of vital importance is the fact that, as far as 'indigenous' and 'non-indigenous' groups are concerned, the Malays are slightly outnumbered by the immigrant non-Malays.

Although it is the most important single consideration, the distribution of population (by communities) is not all-important in determining the political process; certain other factors must be considered in order to get a more complete understanding of the divisions within Malayan society. Some of these 'other factors' will be mentioned only briefly here, so as to give a broad understanding of the problems at hand. They will be discussed more fully in the appropriate places in the chapters which follow.

To begin with, communal divisions are not determined by 'racial' differences alone. There is also a complete lack of cultural homogeneity, each community having its own religion, language, customs, and habits. This naturally constitutes a very serious obstacle to unification; it is also the reason why certain 'cultural' matters (particularly language) have come to constitute some of the most difficult political issues of present-day Malaya.

Secondly, the division between the Malays and non-Malays is emphasized by a certain amount of physical separation. Broadly speaking, the non-Malays are concentrated on the west coast

1. The exact figures, according to the *1957 Census Report*, were: Malays—3,126,706; Chinese—2,332,936; Indians—695,985; and 'Others'—123,136. No effort is made in this book to distinguish between 'Malays' and 'Other Malaysians'. Malays are treated as a category encompassing both. Pakistanis and Ceylonese are included under 'Others'.

and the Malays on the east coast and in the north.[2] To some extent, this quite effectively restricts contact between the two groups. Communal jealousies are also affected by the fact that the west coast is far more developed and enjoys a higher standard of living than the east coast and the north.

The urbanization pattern provides a valuable index of both physical separation and differing standards of living. Penang, Selangor, and Perak, all on the west coast, are the most urbanized while Kedah, Kelantan, Trengganu, Perlis, and Pahang are the least so. The first three have a Chinese majority, while the other five are predominantly Malay.[3]

TABLE 1

*Urban population—composition by different communities*[4]
(per cent)

| *Year* | *Malays* | *Chinese* | *Indians* | *Others* | *Total* |
|---|---|---|---|---|---|
| 1931 | 19·2 | 59·6 | 17·8 | 3·4 | 100·0 |
| 1947 | 21·1 | 62·3 | 13·8 | 2·8 | 100·0 |
| 1957 | 20·0 | 67·7 | 8·7 | 3·6 | 100·0 |

Thirdly, political and economic power are not both concentrated in the hands of any single community; political power is largely with the Malays and economic power with the Chinese.[5] This feature, together with the fact that no community is numerically dominant, has helped to make communal bargaining a very prominent feature of Malayan politics, by emphasizing interdependence.[6]

Fourthly, there is the conflict between the traditional claims of the Malays and the demands of the non-Malays, most of whom

2. See population map on p. xii and Table 2 on p. 4.
3. This reveals another interesting point, namely that the growth of cities in Malaya has not been the result of local rural-urban migration, but rather that of migration from outside, notably from China and India.
4. Figures for 1931 and 1947 are from the *1947 Census Report*, p. 46. Those for 1957 are compiled from the statistics given in the *1957 Census Report*, Report 1, Table III.
5. The Chinese are economically dominant only in relation to the other local communities. The very substantial economic strength of the Europeans is not taken into consideration here.
6. This will be discussed in greater detail in Chapter Two.

are locally born and have been accepted as Federal citizens. The Malays, by virtue of being the 'sons of the soil' (and also in view of the 'special position' which they enjoyed under British rule and which preserved their political supremacy *vis-à-vis* the other Asian communities), insist that their interests should be safeguarded through certain concessions and privileges. The non-Malays, however, while accepting some of these demands as being either fair or expedient, seek to ensure that the privileges given to the Malays are only temporary, and that their own rights as local citizens will be progressively increased. While some Malays campaign for an extension of the privileges now given to their community, there are also those non-Malays who seek an immediate withdrawal of all Malay privileges. In these claims is contained the central theme in Malay/non-Malay relations; and the political process in the Federation of Malaya may be said to consist largely of an attempt to establish and maintain a viable equilibrium between the different communities.

Finally, there is the conflict between Malay regionalism[7] and the necessity to have a strong central government. Even those Malays with strong regional sentiments realize that the 'communal problem' will have to be solved at the centre: should the States be allowed to determine their own policies in certain major fields (such as education, Malay rights and so on), it is possible that Malay interests will not be safeguarded in those States which are dominated by non-Malays; furthermore, the Federation as a whole will not be able to maintain and display the trappings of a Malay State, as the Malays themselves desire. While these considerations are understood, there is nevertheless some resentment among the Malays because administration and policies in predominantly Malay States cannot be more pro-Malay than general national policies permit; and national policies are becoming more and more conditioned by the fact of communal inter-dependence. The non-Malays, generally, have no regional loyalties, and concentrate on safeguarding their interests at the national level.[8]

7. State loyalty has constituted a very integral part of Malay politics. Though less significant when compared to the pre-war period, evidence of this can still be found today.
8. The Straits Chinese in Penang and Malacca may be considered an exception in certain respects. They have made attempts to set themselves apart from the rest of the population on certain matters. (See pp. 98–99.)

TABLE 2

*Communal distribution—by states*

| | *Malays* | *Chinese* | *Indians* | *Others* | *Total* |
|---|---|---|---|---|---|
| Johore | 444,907 | 392,425 | 71,002 | 19,231 | 927,565 |
| Kedah | 475,747 | 143,833 | 66,986 | 15,077 | 701,643 |
| Kelantan | 463,292 | 28,816 | 5,642 | 7,835 | 505,585 |
| Malacca | 743,252 | 120,690 | 23,248 | 4,056 | 291,246 |
| Negri Sembilan | 151,426 | 149,911 | 54,428 | 8,566 | 364,331 |
| Pahang | 179,113 | 108,140 | 21,832 | 3,864 | 312,949 |
| Penang | 165,081 | 327,287 | 69,031 | 10,733 | 572,132 |
| Perak | 484,878 | 539,368 | 178,480 | 18,664 | 1,221,390 |
| Perlis | 71,268 | 15,763 | 1,547 | 2,288 | 90,866 |
| Selangor | 291,393 | 488,634 | 201,047 | 31,817 | 1,012,891 |
| Trengganu | 256,349 | 18,069 | 2,742 | 1,005 | 278,165 |
| Total | 3,726,706 | 2,332,936 | 695,985 | 123,136 | 6,278,763 |

Before proceeding any further, it is worth noting that none of the major communities in fact constitutes a totally distinct and homogeneous unit. A substantial portion of the country's three million-odd 'Malaysians', for example, are immigrants from Indonesia. From a purely legal standpoint, it may be argued that these immigrants are in fact as much aliens as the Chinese and the Indians. In practice, however, they have easily and rapidly become assimilated into the ranks of the general Malay population, enjoying the same rights and privileges as the Malays. Assimilation has been easy not only because they are Muslims (like the Malays), but also because they share a common area of culture with the local Malays.[9]

The Chinese and the Indians, while remaining categories quite distinct from the Malays, are themselves not culturally homogeneous. Among the Chinese, for example, there are several dialect-groups each with different traditions; these groups tend to have different occupational preferences, and are concentrated in different parts of the country.[10] The following table enumerates

9. It is, however, relatively easy to distinguish recent arrivals.
10. For further elaboration, see V. Purcell, *The Position of the Chinese in South-east Asia*, p. 33.

them, and gives the numerical strength of each for the years 1921, 1931, and 1947.[11]

TABLE 3

*Chinese community: dialect groups*

| *Dialect Group* | *1921* | *1931* | *1947* |
|---|---|---|---|
| Hokkien | 379,028 | 538,852 | 827,411 |
| Cantonese | 331,757 | 417,516 | 641,945 |
| Hakka (Kheh) | 217,697 | 317,506 | 437,407 |
| Tiechew (Teochiu) | 130,026 | 208,681 | 364,232 |
| Hainanese (Hailam) | 68,200 | 97,568 | 157,649 |
| Kwongsai | 998 | 46,095 | 71,850 |
| Hokchiu | 13,821 | 31,908 | 48,094 |
| Hokchia | 4,058 | 15,301 | 12,754 |
| Henghwa (Hinhoa) | 1,659 | {31,025} | 17,065 |
| Other Tribes | 24,496 | | 36,260 |
| Total | 1,171,740 | 1,704,452 | 2,614,667 |

There are, needless to say, other divisions as well, such as those between the local-born and the China-born, the English-speaking and the non English-speaking.

Like the Chinese, the Indians are also divided by linguistic differences, determined by their places of origin in India. Also as in the case of the Chinese, these differences are usually accompanied by varying occupational preferences. Class and social status are other dividing factors.[12]

While in themselves significant, these internal divisions of the different communities will not be discussed in any detail in the present study. What is of direct concern here are the divisions which exist between the different communities, and which make communalism the most significant factor in the country's political process; furthermore, such divisions as exist within the different communities have tended to be largely overshadowed in a context where far more striking differences (i.e. those between the different communities) are only too obvious.

When divided into Malay and non-Malay categories, one of the

11. M. V. del Tufo, *1947 Census Report*, p. 75. No breakdown (by dialect groups) was attempted in the 1957 census.

12. Prior to partition in India, the 'Indian' category in Malaya was further divided between Hindus and Muslims. 'Pakistanis' have now become a separate category.

most significant features of the Malayan society is that the former has a cultural and institutional continuity in the local context while the latter lacks a Malayan traditional past. The fact that they are now settled is certainly a most vital feature of the non-Malay communities; but also important is the fact that they are only recent settlers. In view of their numerical strength, this makes their assimilation a problem of the very first magnitude.

Considering that it is non-Malay immigration which has been responsible for creating the Malayan plural society, a few comments need to be made on some of the main features of this immigration and the settlement which followed.

It has been observed that the Chinese and the Indians, the former in particular, provided Malaya with 'the energy, industry and adaptability without which British ambitions could never have been realized.'[13] As for the political implications of their immigration, however, it is sufficient to say that most Chinese and Indians who came to Malaya during the first three decades of the twentieth century[14] (and, by and large, right up to the Second World War) were little more than 'birds of passage': they left once they had made their money. Fluctuations in the country's economic well-being were always accompanied by corresponding fluctuations in the inflow and outflow of Chinese and Indians into and out of Malaya.[15] Being primarily of a transient nature, these communities did not generally interest themselves in gaining local political rights. Thus, although there were large numbers of Chinese and Indians in the country,[16] the political problems of a plural society were not strongly felt.

With these general observations in mind, a separate study of Chinese and Indian immigration may now be undertaken, with comments on some of the main features of these communities.

13. 'Races and Parties in Malaya', *Round Table*, Vol. 42 (1951–2), p. 238.

14. It should be realized that the mass immigration of Chinese and Indians into Malaya is essentially a twentieth-century occurrence.

15. In this connexion, the *Federated Malay States Annual Report for 1933* observed: 'Malaya . . . is subject to somewhat sharp fluctuations in respect of the number of the non-Malay inhabitants. The total population is swelled by immigration in times of prosperity and shrinks through emigration during a period of economic stress such as has ruled for the past two or three years.' (pp. 7–8.)

16. In 1921, 29·4 per cent of the population were Chinese and 15·1 per cent Indians in the mainland; in 1931, 33·9 per cent were Chinese and 15·1 per cent Indians; in 1947, 38·4 per cent were Chinese and 10·8 per cent Indians. *1947 Census Report*, p. 40.

The Chinese originally ventured to Malaya in search of trade; soon they began to take an active interest in mining the peninsula's rich tin deposits. The establishment of British authority and the subsequent opening up of the country for economic exploitation did a great deal to encourage mass immigration; but it was some time before Chinese immigration was brought under control. Furthermore, no effort was made to orientate the increasing numbers of Chinese towards local institutions: for the most part, they were administered independently.[17] Socially and culturally, no effort was made even to acquaint them with local traditions. In view of the common assumption at the time that the Chinese were only a transient community, this state of affairs is understandable. But, as will be seen later in the study, the fact that they were allowed to lead a very independent existence for a considerable period of time has been of some significance in determining some of the current attitudes of the Chinese community.

As already mentioned, the depression of 1931–3 caused a great outflow of Chinese from Malaya. This soon resulted in a move to control their future inflow: it was felt that some measure of stability had to be introduced into the immigration system if steady economic development were ever to be made possible. An effort had already been made in 1928, through the Immigration Restriction Ordinance, to give the local authorities the right to restrict or prohibit the landing of immigrant labourers at times of emergency. It was now thought that the provisions of this Ordinance had to be made more permanent so that an efficient system of control would be in operation even in times of prosperity.[18] In moving the new Aliens Bill in the Straits Settlements Legislative Council, the Secretary for Chinese Affairs explained: '. . . in times of prosperity, alien immigrants swarm into Malaya in very large numbers, but, unless those times of prosperity continue, sooner or later we are faced with the situation that we have today, where there is widespread unemployment not only among the alien

17. Prior to the advent of British authority, the Malay Rulers (who had troubles of their own) were only too glad to let the Chinese rule themselves. Thus, both before British intervention and during the early stages of British control, Chinese secret societies continued to flourish. These societies were built mainly on clan foundations, and it was through them that each group sought to protect its own interests against rival organizations.

18. *Proceedings of the Legislative Council of the Straits Settlements for the Year 1932* (Singapore, Government Printing Office, 1933), p. B 78.

population but also among the Malayan born for whose welfare we have a growing responsibility.'[19] The Ordinance which resulted (the Aliens Ordinance of 1933) had the effect of limiting the monthly inflow of alien deck passengers into the country.[20] Up to 1938, this law was used only against male passengers, the effect being to stabilize the Chinese community by improving its ratio of females to males. The war in China (against Japan) further encouraged female immigration into Malaya.[21]

TABLE 4

*Chinese—females per thousand males*[22]

| Year | Females per thousand males |
|---|---|
| 1911 | 215 |
| 1921 | 371 |
| 1931 | 486 |
| 1947 | 815 |
| 1957 | 926 |

Aided by the Sino-Japanese War which preceded it, the Pacific War encouraged most Chinese in Malaya to remain for a longer period than planned. Since they now had their women with them, they soon found it possible to have a full social and family life. Furthermore, the earlier Revolution in China (1911) had produced an upsurge in education among the Chinese in Malaya, with several schools being built in the country, thus they now also had facilities for educating their children. As a result the end of the Pacific War found the Chinese community in Malaya a part of the settled population, with an interest in local political rights.[23]

19. Loc. cit.
20. The Chinese were almost exclusively the ones affected by this Ordinance, since the Bill defined an 'alien' as 'any person not being either a British subject or the subject of a state under His Majesty's protection or the subject of a state in respect of which a mandate on behalf of the League of Nations had been accepted by His Majesty'. *Straits Settlements Legislative Council Proceedings for the Year 1932*, pp. B 78–79.
21. It is interesting to speculate on what might have happened to the Chinese community in Malaya had no concession been made as regards female immigration. It is certainly possible that the community might then have failed to strike any permanent roots in the country.
22. Figures for 1911–47 obtained from the *1947 Census Report*, p. 57; 1957 figure derived from *1957 Census Report*, Report 1, p. 1.
23. The consequences of this transformation are discussed in greater detail in Chapter Two. The unsettled political situation in China might also have discouraged many Chinese from returning after the war.

The fact that the Chinese have become more and more settled is shown by the changing percentage of those locally born. While in 1921 only 20·9 per cent of the community was born locally, the figure for 1957 was as high as 74·5 per cent. This means that a very substantial portion of all Chinese in the Federation today have few real ties with China. In terms of the need for non-Malays to become more conscious of their local identity, this is no doubt very encouraging.

TABLE 5

*Chinese—locally born*[24]

| | (*per cent*) |
|---|---|
| 1921 | 20·9 |
| 1931 | 29·9 |
| 1947 | 63·5 |
| 1957 | 74·5 |

Unlike their Chinese counterparts, the Indian immigrants did not generally settle down to an independent existence after their arrival in Malaya. Brought in largely for employment in rubber estates, they were, for some time, treated like an ordinary economic commodity by the local employing authorities: they were imported at times of need and shipped back when their presence was not profitable. As a result of serious protests from official quarters in India against this practice, the Indian labour force in Malaya was eventually brought under the joint supervision of the Malayan Controller of Labour and the Indian Agent appointed by the Government of India. In 1938, the Indian Government made a final move and terminated the emigration of unskilled labour to Malaya.

If the average Chinese immigrant was independent, resourceful, and ambitious, the Indian estate labourer was, as a rule, satisfied to have his interests looked after by the paternal figure of the Indian Agent; neither did he make a reasonable effort to seek alternative employment so as to improve his social and economic status. Social stratification has been very much a feature of the entire Indian community; it is precisely for this reason that its

24. Percentages for 1921–47 obtained from the *1947 Census Report*, p. 58; percentage for 1957 derived from the total figures (of local born) given in each State Report of the 1957 Census.

middle and upper classes, unlike their corresponding categories in the Chinese community, have been almost entirely imported, and not recruited from the ranks of the lower classes.[25]

As in the case of the Chinese, the changes which have taken place in the sex-ratio and percentage of locally-born in the Indian community give some indication of the degree of settlement.

TABLE 6

*Indians—females per thousand males*[26]

|  | |
|---|---|
| 1911 | 320 |
| 1921 | 424 |
| 1931 | 514 |
| 1947 | 687 |
| 1957 | 746 |

TABLE 7

*Indians—locally born*[27]

|  | (*per cent*) |
|---|---|
| 1921 | 12·1 |
| 1931 | 21·4 |
| 1947 | 51·6 |
| 1957 | 64·5 |

Having briefly looked at the origins of and divisions within the Malayan plural society, one might now proceed to analyse the problem of national unity from the point of view of the emergence and growth of nationalism. To begin with, it must be noted that such unity as may be found in the country today is essentially a post-war phenomenon.

It has been observed that, prior to the Second World War, Malaya, unlike India and Ceylon, was a 'country with no politics', displaying a 'tranquil and complacent atmosphere of public life'.[28]

25. T. H. Silcock and A. Aziz, 'Nationalism in Malaya', in W. L. Holland (ed.), *Asian Nationalism and the West*, pp. 275–6.
26. Figures for 1911–47 obtained from the *1947 Census Report*, p. 58; 1957 figure derived from *1957 Census Report*, Report 1, p. 1.
27. Percentages for 1921–47 obtained from *1947 Census Report*, p. 85; percentage for 1957 derived from the total figures (of locally born) given in each State Report of the 1957 Census.
28. G. L. Peet, *Political Questions of Malaya*, p. 3.

If 'politics' is taken to mean a local nationalist movement based on local constitutional objectives, this observation is largely true: the Malays, still very much under the influence of regional loyalties, had not evolved a sense of common nationhood; the non-Malays were not sufficiently 'Malayan' to be concerned with local constitutional advancement. Despite this, traces of political consciousness were by no means totally lacking, but this consciousness was, by and large, the direct by-product of and response to the rising nationalist movements in China, India, and Indonesia.

The Chinese in Malaya contributed their share towards helping the 1911 Revolution in their motherland, mostly by way of financial contributions. In December 1912 the Kuomintang established a branch in the Straits Settlements, under the Societies Ordinance. Registration of this branch was permitted by the Government, not only because the activities of the Kuomintang in Malaya were not at this time anti-government, but also because the authorities realized that, by registering the organization, they would have better information on its activities. Two years later, however, certain difficulties led to the closing down of this branch;[29] subsequently, other branches in the Federated Malay States either dissolved themselves or went underground. Despite this, Kuomintang efforts in Malaya were not ended, the party's reorganization in China (1919–24) being a strong rejuvenating factor. After 1923 the organization fell under strong Communist influence and this, together with the various civil disturbances attributed to its members and the fact that it was becoming increasingly anti-British, led to the party's suppression in 1925 as a subversive element. The movement was still unbeaten, and continued functioning under various other titles such as labour unions and educational associations. Following the achievement of greater power by the Chinese Kuomintang in 1926, the volume of revolutionary propaganda in Malaya was considerably increased.

A very significant feature of Kuomintang activies in Malaya was

29. President Yuan Shih Kai had outlawed the Kuomintang in China in 1913, thereby incurring the hostility of the organization's branches in Malaya. Since Britain was then on friendly terms with the Chinese Government, a close watch was kept on the Kuomintang's activities in Malaya. When, in 1914, the Registrar of Societies demanded the full list of the organization's members, many decided to discontinue their connexions, probably in fear of endangering their local interests.

the striking extent to which they faithfully reflected developments in China.

The triumph of 1926 put the Malayan Governments in a dilemma. The British Government had by now recognized the organization's unquestioned leadership in China, and the Foreign Office must have been aware that its non-recognition in Malaya would indeed appear anomalous. The Malayan Governments, however, were not only concerned about the Kuomintang's subversive activities, but also realized that its recognition would legalize in Malaya an *imperium in imperio*.[30]

For its part, the Malayan Kuomintang argued strongly to have the ban lifted. Saying that there was a general sympathy among the Chinese in the country for its nationalist cause, its spokesmen pointed out that there was no inclination on the part of its headquarters to accept the extremist branches. It was also argued that the Chinese middle class and skilled labour class were disinclined to support the leftist faction's professed desire to back Dr. Sun Yat-Sen's proposal to unite the interests of China with those of the Soviet Union.

The year 1927 saw Chiang Kai-shek purge the Communist elements from the ranks of the Kuomintang in China.[31] This led the extremists in Malaya to break away from the central body and to form an organization of their own, this step being an important landmark in the development of the Chinese-dominated Communist Party in Malaya. Despite this break, the Malayan Governments initially remained adamant in refusing to lift the ban on the Kuomintang. In 1930, however, following persistent requests from China, a compromise was effected whereby membership of the Kuomintang in China ceased to be illegal; but this did not enable the organization to re-establish branches in Malaya. When, with the outbreak of Sino-Japanese hostilities, efforts were made in Malaya to consolidate the nationalist sentiments of the Chinese community, the Malayan Governments displayed a sympathetic attitude and allowed substantial sums of money to be remitted to China as contributions to the war effort.

The above account gives some indication of Chinese nationalism in pre-war Malaya. One is struck by the complete domination of the community's political life by external issues.

30. V. Purcell, *The Position of the Chinese in Southeast Asia*, p. 46.
31. The Kuomintang had officially opened its doors to Communists in 1924.

Malay nationalism before the War was neither very popular nor very effective. However, it is possible to speak of a growing political awareness among the Malays and of the development of a nationalist cause.

The reformist movement in Islam,[32] which reached Malaya during the early years of the twentieth century, was probably the first factor to influence the rise of Malay nationalism. During the first quarter of the century, this movement provided the main stimulus for political awakening among the Malays; it did not, however, go so far as to produce any well-defined political attitudes. Those who came under its influence also became familiar with its role in the rising nationalist movements of the Middle-East, notably Egypt.[33]

In Malaya, the spread of this movement not only produced a new interest in political matters but also led to a serious split within the Malay community, between the *Kaum Muda* (the modernists) and the *Kaum Tua* (the traditionalists). The conflict between these two groups in itself produced in the Malays a new understanding of their place in the fast-changing Malayan context.

With their political awakening, the Malays became increasingly conscious of the adverse economic position of their community. They realised that conditions now made it necessary for them to compete with the others in a political and economic world which they themselves had not created but which was rapidly transforming the administration and the face of their country. Urbanization and the growth of a complex economy had caused many of them to drift into this new world; but they found that theirs was essentially a subordinate role. And they realized that their participation in the process of development and modernization was characterized by a growing political and economic dependence. While they were protected by a special political status (e.g. non-Malays were

32. Having started with the Wahhabi movement in Arabia during the late eighteenth century, this reformist movement was carried to other Muslim areas by pilgrims who had visited Mecca. Its modernizing influence was the result of its efforts at doing away with the 'false traditions' which had accumulated and which did not originate from the Koran—e.g. the veneration of graves and saints.

33. The small group of Malays (mostly sons of aristocrats), who had gone to Cairo and Mecca for their higher education, was particularly influenced by developments in the Middle-East.

excluded from Civil Service appointments in the Malay states) and by a land reservation policy—and they certainly could not have been very happy at having to shelter under such protection—they also found that they were not only the employees of well-to-do non-Malays who were rapidly constituting the growing middle and upper classes, but were also generally in debt to Chinese and Indian middlemen and money-lenders. It was the circumstances governing their relations with the other communities which made their position look particularly unfavourable. As stated by one writer, 'they used to be poor men in a poor country, and now they were poor men in a rich country'.[34]

Due probably to the Malays' adverse economic position, pre-war Malay nationalism was in part a reaction against the presumptions and the growing demands of the non-Malay communities. The Straits Chinese, for example, had begun to contest some of the special rights given to the Malays, insisting that they themselves should be given local rights and privileges since they were also a part of the local population, and because they had contributed substantially to the economic development of the country. To the Malays, this clearly indicated an effort gradually to push their own community into the background. Especially during the 1930s, this resentment towards non-Malay ambitions played a decisive role in shaping the activities of the Malay nationalist intelligentsia. Even such opposition as had existed to the policies of the Colonial Government became overshadowed by efforts to combat the 'non-Malay threat'.

The 1930s witnessed another important development: several Malay nationalists became strongly influenced by the rising nationalism in Indonesia. This group of Indonesian-inspired nationalists looked to the *Partai National Indonesia* (led by Soekarno) for inspiration and leadership; and many of them found it attractive to think in terms of an independent Indonesia of which Malaya would be a part.[35] Led for the most part by the left-wing *Kesatuan Melayu Muda* (Union of Malay Youths), this movement for the joint independence of Indonesia and Malaya reached its peak when, during the closing stages of the Japanese régime, discussions were held both with the Japanese as well as with the leaders of the

34. L. A. Mills, *Malaya: A Political and Economic Appraisal*, p. 5.

35. It is possible that fear of non-Malay domination was partly responsible for this desire to unite with Indonesia.

Indonesian nationalist movement to finalize the details of the independent Indonesian-Malayan union.[36]

Despite the advanced stages of planning which its leaders reached, this movement had very little support. Two reasons may be given for this. First, its leaders did not really 'go to the masses' with a view to stirring widespread enthusiasm for their proposed scheme. This was so not only because (before the War at any rate) the mass of the population was not politically active, but also because these leaders had easy access to top-level discussions without having to prove or rely upon the strength of their following. Secondly, it is possible that the loyalty of the average Malay for his traditional institutions and forms of authority (e.g. the sultanate) acted against the popular acceptance of a movement which, by virtue of what it hoped to achieve, was too radical. There can be little doubt that the indigenous political and social structure of the Malays would have been substantially altered, or possibly even destroyed, in the event of union with an independent Indonesia.

Resentment towards British policies, although in many ways overshadowed by the other factors just mentioned, constituted yet another specific aspect of pre-war Malay nationalism. The trend towards administrative centralization, for example, was a constant source of dissatisfaction because it caused the Sultans and the state councils to become less and less effective. There was also considerable dissatisfaction over the increasing authority of British officials, and the failure to absorb Malays in larger numbers and on better terms into the expanding bureaucracy.

Finally, the Malay nationalist intelligentsia also began to doubt whether the culture of their own community could survive unaided in an increasingly heterogeneous environment.[37] Influenced by Arab pan-Islamism, Indonesian nationalism, and Japanese pan-Asianism, 'they nevertheless saw their own political awakening not as any brave new world, but as a tardy recognition of dangers threatening to convert their race into an "aboriginal stock" and their culture into a museum piece'.[38]

36. When, in mid-1945, the fall of Malaya and Indonesia seemed imminent, the Japanese acceded to this request for independence.

37. The *Persaudaraan Sahabat Pena* (Brotherhood of Pen Friends) founded in the 1930s, for example, was dedicated to raising the standards of the Malay language and safeguarding Malay culture from extinction.

38. Silcock and Aziz, op. cit., p. 286.

From the above account it is quite clear that pre-war Malay nationalism, though strongly influenced by external forces, had a definite local relevance.

Political consciousness among the Indian community was almost negligible in the years before the War; most of the Indians were imported labourers with little interest in political issues. Such political feeling as existed was largely determined by three different influences. First, there was the direct influence exerted by the Indian Agent. As part of his duties, the Agent made periodic visits to the rubber estates, inquiring into the living conditions of Indian labourers and generally showing a paternal interest in their welfare. To the labourers, his presence was in some measure symbolic of the allegiance they owed to India, and in him they saw a figure who reminded them of their non-local identity.

Secondly, one may mention the influence exerted by the Central Indian Association, an organization founded in Kuala Lumpur in 1937 following Mr. Nehru's first visit to Malaya. Compared to that of the Kuomintang, the political influence of this body was indeed very small; it was nevertheless the most outstanding example of Indian political consciousness in pre-war Malaya. Having gathered into its organization representatives from the different Indian associations in the country, the Central Indian Association played an important role in the formation of the Indian Independence League during the period of Japanese occupation.

Finally, there was the role played by Indian journalism. This, however, did not involve a conscious effort to spread Indian nationalist propaganda in Malaya; it was only that the journalists concerned were largely Indian nationalists themselves, and their interpretation of news from India helped to stimulate a certain amount of nationalist feeling among their readers.

It will thus be clearly seen that such nationalist movements as existed in Malaya before the War were communally isolated. There was no common inspiration and there were no common goals. Nationalism thus failed to unite the people in a common cause[39]; it also failed to produce any appreciable effects on the political process within the country. In the absence of any major demands for constitutional advancement, the British continued to maintain unquestioned authority. Representation by election was

39. It should also be pointed out that despite the presence of different nationalist movements, the mass of the people remained quite unaffected.

totally unknown, public representation at the different levels being determined by Government nomination.[40] In each legislature there always existed a fixed majority of Government officials.

It was against this setting that the occupation of Malaya by the Japanese took place. While communal antagonisms had remained somewhat dormant during the pre-war years, the years of occupation witnessed a tragic deterioration in inter-communal relations. It was also during these three-and-a-half years that the 'country with no politics' ceased to exist, giving way to one with an active political life. For these reasons, the impact of the occupation on the different communities may now be briefly examined.

Due largely to their long-standing enmity with China, one of the first things the Japanese sought to do on occupying Malaya was to try to frighten the Chinese community into submission.[41] Those suspected of being Communist or nationalist agents were promptly executed; the community as a whole was blamed for being unco-operative, and the calibre of its leadership was condemned as poor. Generally, the Chinese were accused of being undesirable elements, and their actions were alleged to be detrimental to the maintenance of peace and order in the country. Commenting on this, one writer observes:

> In so far as this list of 'undesirables' was meant as a euphemism for guerrillas it was substantially correct for guerrilla activity in Malaya was all but exclusively the role of the Chinese.[42]

While Malay and Indian support for the resistance movement was totally insignificant, the Japanese in fact succeeded in using these two communities to fight the guerrilla forces. Thus the resistance movement and the opposition that was formed to meet it became, in effect, a communal war. Led by the Japanese, Malay (and some Indian) units launched attacks against Chinese guerrilla forces; in retaliation, the latter began attacking Malay villages. So proceeded the unhappy deterioration in Sino-Malay relations,

40. There was, however, one notable exception. The British Chambers of Commerce in Singapore and Penang were given the right to elect members to the Straits Settlements Legislative Council. This privilege was denied to the Chinese and Indian Chambers of Commerce.
41. In this they failed because their actions in fact produced the opposite effect: the Chinese retaliated instead of being cowed into submission.
42. W. H. Elsbree, *Japan's Role in Southeast Asian Nationalist Movements*, p. 147.

reaching a climax in the outburst of bitter (but isolated) intercommunal clashes in the days immediately following the surrender of the Japanese.

While these events could not but produce undesirable consequences, part of the reason for the hardening of communal tensions during the occupation probably lay in the fact that, at times of widespread insecurity, people tend to believe that they are safest among members of their own community.

The absence of Indian opposition to the Japanese régime is easily understandable. While to the Chinese the Japanese were the invaders of their homeland, they appeared to the Malayan Indians as the potential liberators of their own mother-country. At a time of aroused nationalism, the Indians felt that they could make common cause with the Japanese because Britain, Japan's opponent in the War, was in many ways their enemy too. The Japanese had effectively challenged British authority in Malaya; should they not be helped to do the same in India?[43] It was mostly on this reasoning that Indian support for the Japanese was based.[44]

From a purely political standpoint, the Indians were probably the ones most substantially affected by the Japanese régime; their interest in the Indian independence movement was indeed in striking contrast to their political apathy before the War.

The occupation had a mixed impact on the Malay community. While some (especially the younger Malays) became convinced that Malay political dominance could be achieved and maintained without much difficulty or complication, there were others who came to believe the exact opposite, being convinced that non-Malay co-operation would be vital in the future administration of

43. The Indian Independence League was organized in Malaya with Japanese support and encouragement, and branches were set up throughout the country. The ambitions of the Indian National Army, however, never reached any fruition. Its defeat was decisive, and with the arrival of the British it was soon forgotten. As suddenly as it had sprung up, this new wave of Indian nationalism lost all its prominence in the Malayan political scene.

It is possible that the size of the Indian National Army in Malaya was to some extent influenced by the considerable unemployment among the Indians during the occupation, caused largely by the closing down of rubber estates.

44. It should, however, be realized that the intentions of the Japanese did not coincide with those of the Indians. While the former regarded the Indian Independence Movement merely in terms of their own pan-Asian ambitions, the latter, on the other hand, were interested only in the liberation of India. Thus, what to the Japanese was merely a means to a more elaborate end, was the end itself to the Indians. Each found the other useful for different reasons.

the country.[45] The views of the former group were considerably influenced by the fact that Japanese administration had been carried out without Chinese support, with the Malays as the chief local participants.[46] To the latter group, however, the occupation revealed the political potential of the Chinese and Indian communities; they realized that these communities would soon channel their energies towards local ends. Thus they either had to co-operate with them or continue to rely on British protection indefinitely; by themselves they certainly could not run the entire government of the country.

In summing up the reactions of the different communities to Japanese rule, it is important to emphasize that common interests were absent. The Chinese fought their own war against the Japanese; the Indians were concerned only about the liberation of India; and those Malays who supported the Japanese thought only in terms of the possible restoration of Malay political supremacy in the country.

The dividing effects of the occupation were fortunately not very enduring and it was not long before the deep animosities which emerged during this period gave way to a conscious effort at co-operation. It should, however, be noted that the first developments after the War did not in any way help the process of unification. By seeking to withdraw Malay privileges, the Malayan Union proposals of 1946 resulted in the rise of Malay nationalism on an unprecedented scale. Thus Malay unification was the only unification which initially took place.

In contrast, the Federation scheme which replaced the Malayan Union displeased the non-Malay communities, and led them to view the Malays with certain misgivings. However, once the first impact of these constitutional changes was over, efforts began to be made, through co-operation, towards nation-building. The factors which encouraged this may now be considered.

The outbreak of Communist terrorism, followed by the Emergency, was the first factor which urgently necessitated the projection of the idea of a common national identity. In the face of the Communist insurrection, it was realized that all sections of the

45. Silcock and Aziz, op. cit., pp. 290–1.
46. Among the rural Malays, the experience of having defended themselves against Chinese guerrillas produced a similar feeling of independence and self-confidence, not to mention antagonism, towards the Chinese.

population had to be welded into a single Malayan nation if apathy were to be overcome and if potential sympathizers and supporters were to be lured away from the Communist force. Generally speaking, the Malays were always regarded as a 'safe' community in this respect since the Malayan Communist Party, being a predominantly Chinese organization, could not win their sympathy. It was the Chinese who presented the real difficulty. They had to be convinced that the Communist Party consisted mainly of China-born Chinese whose actions were in no way connected with the welfare of the locally-born.[47] Thus, while a general effort had to be made to foster a common national consciousness among all the communities, special attention had to be given to the Chinese (and non-Malays generally) to give them a convincing picture of their local identity and future well-being.[48] Ever since the beginning of the Emergency, all the means of mass-communication have been extensively used, both by the Government as well as by certain political parties, to propagate the concept of a Malayan nation embracing all the communities.

While this propaganda did much to encourage such national unity as exists today, success was by no means immediate. When national service was introduced (in 1950), for example, considerable numbers of Chinese and Indians sought to leave the country. It was reported that ships going to India had become fuller, and that about 6,000 Chinese of call-up age had applied for visas to return to China.

Although the reasons for this were obvious, Chinese and Indian newspapers only tried to give excuses: they argued that these departures were motivated by such things as disturbance to studies, desire to visit families at home, and so on. In commenting on this, Silcock and Aziz observe: 'There is some feeling that those who ran away to escape national service were bringing shame to their own community, but in every case the sense of racial origin appears

47. This was made considerably easier by the fact that the nature of civilian casualties gave clear proof that the Communists were neither local nationalist nor champions of the Chinese community. During the first eight years of the Emergency, of a total of 2,504 civilians killed, 1,685 were Chinese. (Great Britain, Central Office of Information, *Malayan Record*, 1957, p. 11.)

48. It was largely to these ends that the officially-sponsored Communities Liaison Committee (see footnote 48 on p. 84) was founded in 1948. The Malayan Chinese Association, which emerged the following year, was strongly dedicated to organizing the Chinese community against the Communists.

to have been stronger than the sense of national opposition to Communist aggression.'[49]

The unenthusiastic response of the Chinese to the Government's call for help did not fail to attract official comment and criticism. A report put out by the Information Department on *Communist Terrorism in Malaya* observed: 'The lack of Chinese recruits to the Security Forces has been a disappointing feature of the Emergency. Chinese applied in large numbers for posts as Liaison Officers and Assistant Resettlement Officers, but few have been willing to serve in the regular Security Forces.'[50] The late Sir Henry Gurney (High Commissioner from 1948 to 1951) was more critical of the situation. Saying that it was necessary for the Communists to be opposed by a Chinese effort if the whole of the Chinese rural population were to be prevented from falling under Communist influence, he observed:

> A feeling of resentment is growing among all the other communities at the apparent reluctance of the Chinese to help. These people [the Chinese] live comfortably and devote themselves wholly to making money. . . . Leading Chinese have contented themselves with living in luxury in Singapore and criticising the Police and security forces for causing injustices. These injustices are deplorable but are the fault not of the Police but of those Chinese who know the truth and will not tell it. The longer this goes on, the more injustices there will be and the greater the opening to Communist propaganda.[51]

Despite these discouraging beginnings, the non-Malays have, in recent years, come to think more and more in terms of their local identity. Broadly speaking, their change of attitude has been encouraged by two main factors: citizenship concessions and national constitutional progress.[52] As far as the former is concerned, it is important to realize that although citizenship concessions might have been used partly to induce the non-Malays to become locally-oriented by giving them a local status, efforts were

49. Silcock and Aziz, op. cit., pp. 343–4.
50. Federation of Malaya, Department of Information, *Communist Terrorism in Malaya*, p. 28.
51. Tan Cheng Lock, *The Reorganization of the Malayan Chinese Association* (1951), section (2): 'A note in the handwriting of the late Sir Henry Gurney recently found amongst his private papers and known to have been written two days before his death.'
52. To this must be added the fact that they have become increasingly conscious of the permanent roots which they have established in the country.

also made to ensure that those who were made eligible to become citizens would in fact help to consolidate the image of the Malayan nation. To this end, a clear statement was made as regards the privileges and obligations of local citizens. As the doors of citizenship were opened wider to them, the non-Malays became increasingly aware of their local identity, rights, and responsibilities.

As regards the second factor (national constitutional advancement), the approach of independence may be singled out as having been of outstanding significance. In 1952, the Colonial Secretary had stated that Malaya was unfit to receive any major political concessions, and that independence would not be forthcoming until unity between the different communities had been achieved. This no doubt provided a strong incentive for influential politicians to think in terms of co-operation;[53] and non-Malay leaders became fully aware that, for co-operation to be effective (and for the Malays to be willing to co-operate), the general ranks of their own communities had to be persuaded to think of themselves essentially as Malayans, participating in a common national movement with the other communities.[54] The fact that the Alliance Party (which is an inter-communal organization embracing all the three major communities) has succeeded in establishing and maintaining a position of dominance in the political arena in the face of opposition from communal bodies may be regarded as a testimony to the success of these efforts. In this connexion Malaya has been somewhat fortunate in that, unlike the experience in British India, efforts to encourage co-operation have not been hampered by any bitter middle-class competition for government appointments. This has been so not only because there has been room enough for everybody, but also because the different communities have stood in complementary rather than competitive relations to one another: educated Malays largely join the bureaucracy while non-Malays tend to go into business and the professions.

It may be argued that the late introduction of elections[55] helped to 'conceal' communal rivalries and divisions before independence,

53. It should be remembered that co-operation was also rendered necessary by the relative numerical strength of the different communities.

54. In this connexion, the successful effort made by the Malayan Chinese Association (M.C.A.) to help Chinese to apply for citizenship and register as voters is particularly outstanding.

55. There was only one national election (in 1955) before independence was achieved in 1957.

thus making it possible for a picture of unity to be presented, and facilitating a peaceful transfer of power.[56] The force of this consideration may be apparent in the fact that 'independence' was by far the most outstanding issue during the 1955 elections. The fact that the Alliance lost some of its support in the 1959 elections to communal parties like the Pan-Malayan Islamic Party and the People's Progressive Party tends to reinforce this view.

While it is possible that the above argument is correct, the reverse possibility should by no means be overlooked. Bearing in mind the facts of population distribution, it is conceivable that, had many more elections been held, the need for inter-communal co-operation might have become more widely appreciated: people might have come to realize that no amount of communal solidarity can produce Malay or non-Malay political domination. Thus, while the results of the 1959 elections may lend support to the first view, it is possible that succeeding elections may prove the second.[57]

Finally, developments since independence may briefly be looked into. Even to those most dedicated to a programme of inter-communal co-operation (such as the partners of the Alliance), the difficulties of establishing a generally acceptable balance between the different communities have proved to be far too enduring; present difficulties are all the more exasperating when viewed in contrast to the sanguine expectations of the immediate pre-independence period.[58]

Perhaps the most disturbing development in post-independence Malaya, in terms of national unity, has been the resurgence of Malay nationalism.[59] There has been a growing tendency for

56. The approach of independence also had an entirely different effect in certain respects, in that it caused a scramble for rights, privileges, and safeguards. This will be discussed in later parts of the book.

57. This second view is no doubt considerably weakened by the fact that it assumes the continued (and perhaps smooth) functioning of parliamentary democracy; the possibilities of deadlock, violence, and so on have been overlooked.

58. Within the Alliance itself, differences over general policy matters (e.g. education policy) are by no means the only difficulties. Disagreements over the allocation of seats (as between the different partners) at elections constitute another major source of conflict.

59. The term 'Malay nationalism' is used here in a rather wide sense; in certain cases, 'Malay communalism' or 'Malay regionalism' may be more appropriate. The choice of 'nationalism' may be justified on the grounds that there is a common tendency among communalists and regionalists alike to believe that they are fighting a nationalist cause, because they still feel that Malaya is a Malay country.

Malays to assert their superior claims in the country. This development was in fact indicated during the months immediately preceding independence. For example, a Malay Congress was convened, comprising all those bodies which considered the constitutional proposals to be a 'sell-out' of Malay interests. When the Malayan Chinese Association accused the participants of this Congress of being 'disloyal' to the country[60] in that they sought to exert sectional over national interests, a Malay newspaper replied: 'It should be noted that the "spongers" [meaning the non-Malays] are only staying in other people's home and there will be a time when they will have to quit when the owners claim it back. It must not be thought that the Malay States have been "surrendered" until doomsday to those people who pretend to love Malaya and who ignore the Malays.'[61]

The post-independence period has also witnessed considerable activity on the part of non-Malay communalists. Dissatisfaction has been expressed over those sections of the Constitution which give Malays certain preferences and privileges in the country. Furthermore, despite the acceptance of Malay as the national language, there has been some insistence that multi-lingualism should be accepted for all practical purposes. There has also been considerable opposition to the trend towards a Malay-oriented educational policy.

60. This accusation was made in the editorial of the party's official organ, the *Malayan Mirror*, of 20 June 1957.

61. Federation of Malaya, Department of Information, *Daily Press Summary of Vernacular Papers*, 26 July 1957, p. 2 (from the editorial of the *Kritik*—a Kuala Lumpur Malay weekly—20 July 1957).

# CHAPTER TWO

# CONSTITUTIONAL GOVERNMENT

THIS chapter is divided into two sections. The first deals with the more general aspects of constitutional government in the Federation of Malaya. The second comprises a general survey of constitutional development in the country, with emphasis on the degree to which communal considerations have conditioned political change.

## SECTION 1

The nature of constitutional government in any country must be strongly dependent on whether the people to be governed are relatively homogeneous or belong to different communal groups with differing interests. In a relatively homogeneous society, constitutional provisions usually reflect certain generally accepted values while at the same time giving sufficient scope for efficiency in administration. No doubt the degree to which the values reflected are 'generally acceptable' may be open to dispute; but agreement with, and opposition to, constitutional provisions in such a society are not generally the outcome of rigidly divided attitudes. Consequently, it is possible to rely on such a thing as 'popular opinion'.

In a plural society, however, constitutional government draws its character more from the need to provide safeguards for the different communities than from the desirability of serving 'popular opinion'. Thus, while it may be possible in a relatively homogeneous society for a constitution to function successfully even when opposed by, say, 10 per cent of the population, the chances of similar success are much less in a 'plural' context. Here political behaviour tends to be determined by communal considerations, and communal considerations tend to penetrate almost all political issues, a tendency which usually becomes exaggerated when economic roles follow communal lines. For this reason, if a constitutional provision in such a society were opposed by 10 per cent of the total population, it is quite likely that this opposition would stem from disagreement on communal lines. In view of the fact that communal groups are more readily organized for political action (since they seem to maintain a state of 'organization' even if physically scattered), and are capable of more sustained effort than other forms of pressure groups, the opposition of this 10 per cent invariably becomes a more serious matter than it would in a relatively homogeneous society. This is particularly true in the case of countries like Malaya where, as mentioned earlier, no community forms a numerical majority.

In a plural society, a constitution is faced with the task of convincing each community that it can be assured of a certain minimum for itself, and that other communities will be prevented from going beyond a certain maximum. The real difficulty, however, rests not on this alone but on the fact that the 'minimums' and 'maximums' demanded by the different communities seldom if ever coincide. In fact, it is possible that certain communities may be interested only in safeguards while others may concentrate on the opportunities provided for advancement, and perhaps domination.

In discussing the nature of constitutional government in a plural society, it is necessary initially to understand the prevailing political aspirations in that society. What is the constitution intended to do: strengthen the position of one community at the expense of others, or lessen communal tension by providing adequate safeguards for all the communities? The former policy, in its pure and simple form (the best example of which is perhaps the policy of continued subjugation followed in South Africa), is of no direct relevance in discussing the Federation of Malaya: the way in which the Malayan society is divided does not provide any scope for its successful execution.

In so far as the latter policy is concerned, two major approaches may clearly be discerned: 'assimilation' and 'accommodation'.[1] The choice between the two may admittedly be an arbitrary one, but the influence exerted by factors such as the numerical strength of minorities, their degrees of distinctiveness, rates of immigration

1. 'Assimilation' depends on two main factors: the willingness of minorities to lose their special identity, and the willingness of majority groups to accept others into their fold. 'Accommodation', as used here, refers to situations where each community in a society, while seeking to preserve its own special characteristics, is willing to respect those of others. It should be noted that when members of minority groups are coerced into abandoning their individuality for the supposed benefit of the State, 'assimilation' can constitute one of the 'hostile' policies adopted by dominant groups.

(in the case of immigrant minorities), and so on should not be overlooked.[2] As will be seen later in this book, constitutional development in the Federation of Malaya seems to indicate a certain conditional acceptance of both policies (that is, 'assimilation' and 'accommodation') by the different communities. The fact that Malay has been established as the national language is in a way indicative of an assimilationist policy;[3] but allowances made for the preservation of non-Malay cultures and ways of life reflect the degree to which 'accommodation' is accepted.

It would be unrealistic to assume that the present Constitution has solved all the problems of inter-communal relations in the Federation of Malaya, or that its basic principles will prove acceptable for all time. Experience shows that respect for minority interests (and, in the case of minorities, for the claims of dominant groups) is seldom if ever based on a sense of justice alone: convenience and adjustment play a crucial role. It is precisely for this reason that dominant groups do not grudge being liberal in their treatment of groups whom they have no cause to fear, while they resent making concessions to groups which threaten their superiority. Similarly, the demands of minorities are quite often determined by the amount of support which they can muster, and the degree to which their services are indispensable to the society to which they belong. Turning directly to the Malayan situation, the Malays fear any increase in Chinese power; this means that they would always want any 'adjustment' to be in their own favour and at the expense of the Chinese. The Chinese, on the other hand, are only too aware of their numerical strength and of their indispensability as far as the country's economy is concerned; this means that they will continue to press for further 'adjustment' in their own favour.

Basically, the attitude of the Malay community towards constitutional government is compounded of three main factors: a heightened awareness of the legitimacy of its own position in the country; fear of non-Malay dominance; and suspicion regarding

2. It may, for example, be observed that smaller minorities tend to assimilate more readily than larger minorities; that minorities which have very distinctive qualities and long-standing traditions refuse to assimilate, and that immigrant minorities which arrive in small numbers and at rare intervals are more easily assimilated than those which arrive *en masse*.

3. In the event of full 'accommodation', there would have been at least some effort at multi-lingualism.

the sincerity of the non-Malay communities. Very broadly, the claims of the non-Malays may be said to rest on a negation of these factors. They claim that the settled non-Malays who regard the country as their only home and as the object of their undivided loyalty should also have a legitimate position in the country; that they only ask for what they consider to be justly their due (and that they are not interested in dominating the Malays); and that the sincerity of their loyalty is beyond question.

It is only natural that the non-Malays should want to allay the suspicions of the Malay community, but it is quite likely that they do not sufficiently recognize the difference between their loyalty and the loyalty which the Malays have for the State. The essence of this difference lies in the fact that the loyalty of the non-Malays is more particularly political in nature, while the Malays have an added feeling of cultural belonging. For the non-Malays, the community continues to be the basis of social identity, while political identity is inspired by the State in varying degrees.[4] By and large, these two identities continue to exist somewhat independently of one another. For the Malays, on the other hand, there is a close link between the two: the Sultanate, the Malay aristocracy in the states, Islam's acceptance as the State religion, the recognition of Malay as the national language—all these have more than a merely political implication for them. They have a direct bearing on their social existence as well.[5]

These considerations would suggest that, owing to the buttressing influence of social considerations, the loyalty of the Malays is more 'natural' than that of the non-Malays, that non-Malay loyalty is in many ways 'artificial'. A host of factors will have to be considered if the validity of this inference is to be ascertained. First of all, it will have to be recognized that the loyalty of the non-Malay communities is indeed an open question; it would be quite impossible to estimate how many of them are in fact loyal, and to what degree. It would, at the same time, be quite unjust if their loyalty were questioned merely because they were not Malays.

Even if it were taken for granted that Malay loyalty is 'genuine' in the sense that the Malays cannot, as a community, be suspected

4. It must be realized that the communal feelings of the non-Malays is extra-national both in origin and content.

5. This could explain the 'emotional' content in Malay nationalism made manifest in various political campaigns.

of loyalty to another state, the question remains as to how adequate this is in a plural society. As mentioned above, the Malays expect their political life to be kept in tune with their social life; they continue to regard their own community as the 'natural' political society in the Malayan State. They think more in terms of the need for the other communities to adjust themselves to a Malay environment than in terms of the need for their own community to abandon some of its special claims in the interests of a common 'Malayan' society.[6]

To the non-Malays, this form of reasoning would no doubt appear to be a far cry from what the Malays themselves demand from the others in the country. If the non-Malays are to consider themselves as being 'Malayans' first and foremost, and consequently regard the social allegiance which they owe to their respective communities as being subordinate to the political allegiance which they owe to the country, should not the Malays do likewise and make a definite effort to dilute their conception of Malay nationality so as to make it less significant in 'Malayan' terms? Indeed, it might even be considered that while the non-Malays learn the Malay language, live under a constitution which preserves the trappings of a Malay state, consider their social identity as being politically irrelevant, and thereby attempt to become true 'Malayans', the Malays, by continuing to learn their own language and by continuing to preserve the 'social' element in their loyalty towards the State, might very well remain Malays. But this is probably what the Malays actually want, that is, to bring the others closer to themselves while they remain where they are.

From a more academic point of view, however, this explanation is not satisfactory. If the Malays have the right to continue being Malays first and foremost, what use is there for the term 'Malayan'? Is the term meant only for non-Malays or is a Malay, by definition, automatically a 'Malayan' as well? In attempting an answer, one should first recognize that the term 'Malayan' serves purely to connote political identity; this means that it embraces the Malays as well. At the same time, it should also be noted that

6. It would follow from this that Malay loyalty is not strictly owed to the 'Federation of Malaya' in so far as the latter appears an 'artificial' construction. To put it simply, large numbers of Malays continue to have love and loyalty for 'their country', a Malay country.

the term would not have come into use had it not been for the presence of non-Malays who had to be classified as politically belonging to Malaya. (Otherwise the term 'Malay' would have been sufficient to connote political identity as well, just like 'Chinese' in the case of China.) This implies that the term is redundant in so far as the political status of the Malays is concerned.

These arguments suggest that the term 'Malayan' applies more particularly to the non-Malays; only in their case is it of any descriptive value. But the Malays are also free to use it, and if they do use it freely the term might cease to be merely descriptive and in fact connote a single nationality.[7]

Before discussing the actual constitutional evolution of the Federation of Malaya, an account of the manner in which the Malay and the non-Malay communities regard their respective positions in the country may be helpful.

To the Malays, the main consideration revolves around the fact that they were in the country before any of the other major communities. They had had their own system of government, and were not responsible for the arrival of large numbers of Chinese and Indians who, together, outnumber them today; the sole responsibility for this lay with the British who, from the beginning, had undertaken to protect the interests of their community. Now that the British have left, the Malays realize that they have to hold their own in a plural society which they did not create. In view of all these considerations they claim that, although they are a numerical minority (but the most numerous of all the groups), they should continue to have a controlling say in the manner in which the country is run. Concerning the adverse economic position of their community, they are of the opinion that the other communities should co-operate in facilitating the necessary improvement, stating that such improvement is a prerequisite for harmonious inter-communal relations.

Despite the country's transition from the indigenous political systems of the pre-British era (based on sultanate authority, where

7. Admittedly, the term is being used quite often to indicate a common nationality, but the fact remains that the average Malay does not consider its use necessary in his case. The situation is made none the better by the fact that many non-Malays, while being aware of the necessity of the term in their case, do not commonly think of themselves as Malayans.

all allegiance was due to the respective States alone and not to any common nation) to the present federal form of government fashioned on Western lines, the Malays have not undergone a full change in the basis of their loyalty. This is mainly because many of the old institutions have been preserved, and the creation of a new state has not implied the wholesale substitution of the Sultanate and the aristocracy by other forms of authority arising from a 'streamlined' administration. Although their authority has been made less absolute, the Sultans still retain considerable prestige. As far as the influence of the administration along Western lines is concerned, many traditional aristocrats have successfully taken on the duties of government on the state as well as the national level. The average rural Malay has not felt the full force of the transformation. This makes his continued adherence to some of the aristocratic traditions of the past, and some of his traditional ways of thinking, more understandable.

The arguments of the non-Malays, on the other hand, stem primarily from the claim that they did not ever force themselves on the country, and that their immigration into Malaya was, in their eyes, something that was more encouraged than discouraged. They emphasize that the contribution they have made towards the development of the country is unparalleled. The vital point, however, is that they now claim Malaya to be their only home. As Malayans they do not consider themselves inferior to the Malays, only different. Under these circumstances, they are convinced that the Malays are 'un-Malayan' to confuse race and religion with political identity.

One thing so far is clear, that a very significant feature of communal politics in the Federation of Malaya is the quest for legitimacy. Each community seems preoccupied with the idea of convincing the others that its own claims are natural and legitimate, and that its presence is most vital to the welfare of the country. For most practical purposes, the two communities which really matter in this dispute are the Malays and the Chinese. As already mentioned, Malay power is basically political and Chinese power economic.

Had the Malays been both politically and economically dominant, constitutional progress (such as the transition to representative government) would have only tended to confirm their superiority, in that they could have afforded to dismiss some of the claims of the other communities such as those pertaining to citizenship, administrative appointments, and so on. As it is, however, the situation is quite different and they have had to give some recognition to the economic and numerical strength of the Chinese community. But there is no guarantee that the Chinese are satisfied; neither is it obvious that the concessions made by the Malays have been made without reluctance.

The lines of reasoning followed by the two communities in their constitutional claims may be briefly mentioned. While the Malays appear to be of the opinion that the economic power in their hands should be increased as soon as possible in order to lessen dangers of political dilution (and perhaps to obviate the need for it), the Chinese seem to feel that the amount of political power now available to them should as soon as possible be sufficiently increased to do justice to their economic and numerical strength. Thus while the Malays need political authority to increase their economic power and need that economic power to preserve their political authority, the Chinese, on the other hand, are relying on their economic power to support their claims for increased political authority, and perhaps also feel that they need more political authority to safeguard their economic position. In other words, while the Malays want to 'mark time' until their political power is given economic justification (thereby also reducing the legitimacy of Chinese claims for political power), the Chinese want to 'cash in' while the going is in their favour.

This situation could well have resulted in a serious conflict had not common goals been recognized and the urgent need for unity understood. Fortunately, the leaders of both communities have shown a willingness to solve these problems sensibly, by relying on a policy of 'give and take'. Mr. Tan Siew Sin (the present Minister for Finance), for example, reflected this common willingness when he said, during the Legislative Council debates on the 1957 Constitution: 'In the last analysis, the pillar of Malayan independence is communal unity and understanding in general, and Sino-Malay unity and understanding in particular. Without it no constitution will work whether written or unwritten, perfect or imperfect.'[8]

It should, however, not be overlooked that economic con-

8. Federation of Malaya, Legislative Council, *Official Report of the Second Legislative Council* (for the period October 1956 to August 1957), col. 2872.

siderations constitute a very strong basis for Sino-Malay tensions. Malays generally tend to regard the Chinese as 'exploiters', having a firm grip on the country's economy. They are very conscious of the Chinese (and, to a lesser extent, Indian) predominance in trade and small business; they find the Chinese materialistic, hard-working, thrifty, and too keen on 'making a fast dollar'. They also find that it would be difficult for them to reduce Chinese dominance of the country's business life since the wholesalers, on whom retail business is so dependent especially for its credit, are also mostly Chinese. And it is very difficult for a Malay to enter a Chinese business because, among the Chinese, personal and family connexions play a dominant role in the choice of business associates. There is not sufficient social contact between the two communities to facilitate partnership on this basis.

As a general rule, it is inevitable that communalism should tend to complicate national issues. It is perhaps with this in mind that Martin Wight wrote: 'In a plural society everything makes for constitutional retardation. In a homogeneous society progress comes through pressure by the community upon the government; in a plural society such pressure tends to be dissipated between the different sections.'[9] This statement, while being quite true in itself, overlooks another equally important aspect of the relationship between social plurality and constitutional progress in colonial dependencies, namely that the prospect of certain forms of constitutional advancement (particularly independence), by emphasizing the need for concerted effort, often proves a valuable stimulus in encouraging inter-communal co-operation and understanding. In the face of communal politics, it may be necessary to 'create' a nation which can effectively campaign for independence, and to which independence can be granted. The Malayan example, as shown in the last chapter, clearly bears out this observation. As stated by Dr. Ismail, the Minister for Internal Security (then the Minister for Commerce and Industry), during the constitutional debates, 'This burning desire for independence which surges throughout South-East Asia has been buried in Malaya by a thin crust of communal distrust and inter-communal tension. What the Alliance has done was to scrape off this thin

9. M. Wight, *The Development of the Legislative Council; 1606–1945*, p. 89.

crust and let the powerful force of independence have free play.'[10]

Turning from the implications of constitutional progress to the actual drawing up and working of the constitutions themselves one notices that, in a plural society, the central problem arises from the need to establish and maintain a reasonable compromise between the general welfare of the nation and the particular demands of the different communities. In the face of communal politics suspicion tends to be rife, and accusations of partiality thereby become frequent. This no doubt hampers the smooth working of any constitution. In the words of Mr. Foster Sutton, a past Attorney General of the Federation Government, 'It is not enough in drawing up a constitution to attain a degree of precision which a person reading in good faith can understand, but it is necessary to attain, if possible, to a degree of precision which a person reading in bad faith cannot misunderstand.'[11]

Finally, some reference will have to be made to the implications of a federal form of government in Malaya. To begin with, one thing seems clear: that a 'pure' form of federalism cannot provide a clear-cut solution to the communal problem in the country, as there is not a general division of the different communities into states. This is particularly true in the case of the non-Malay communities. There are only four states (Kelantan, Trengganu, Kedah, and Perlis) where a single community (the Malays) forms more than 60 per cent of the population; in five of the remaining seven, no community forms a majority.

In so far as the solving of the communal problem is concerned, this distribution does not favour the reservation of substantial powers for the state governments, as has been done in Canada where Quebec remains a 'stronghold' of the French-speaking population. Thus the decision to establish a strong central government in Malaya is decidedly a good one, especially since, due to the over-all inter-dependence of the different groups, representation at the national level is bound to be influenced by the need for communal co-operation. In fact, communalism has had little to do with the establishment of federal government in the country.

If one is to look for the real roots of federal government in

10. *Legislative Council Debates* (October 1956–August 1957), col. 2950.

11. Federation of Malaya, Public Relations Dept., *How the Constitution Works* (a series of talks broadcast by Radio Malaya), p. 9.

Malaya, one will find that the Malays are solely responsible for its adoption. As mentioned earlier, until very recent times the loyalty of the Malay population was directed to the individual States and their respective Sultans. As will be seen in the following part of this chapter, the advent of the British, followed by the rapid development of the country, rendered necessary a certain measure of uniform administration. The position of the Sultans, however (coupled with the presence of state loyalty among the Malays), necessitated the preservation of a certain degree of regional autonomy.

## SECTION II

A brief survey of constitutional development in the Federation of Malaya might help considerably in facilitating a better understanding of the present study. This survey will not be undertaken from the point of view of general constitutional history; attention will be focused primarily on the manner in which communal considerations have influenced major political developments in the country. The more detailed aspects of these developments, in so far as they pertain to the main theme of the present study, will be taken up for discussion in the two following chapters.

As mentioned earlier, Sultanate authority was supreme in the Malay States prior to the advent of the British. By the nineteenth century, however, due largely to court intrigues and the activities of Chinese secret societies, the country was thrown into political chaos. Mid-nineteenth century Malaya was a picture of disintregrating government and explosive civil wars.

It was in the midst of this turmoil that the British decided officially to intervene in the country's internal politics. Such a step had already been requested a little earlier by Chinese merchants and miners (who were apprehensive of their future in the country) on the one hand, and harassed Malay chieftains on the other. The first step was taken in Perak, where one of the would-be Sultans had requested the British Governor's help in restoring law and order, stating: '. . . if all these dissensions are brought to an end, and the country is restored to peace, we and our great men desire to settle under the British flag.'[12] In answer to this request, a meeting was called at Pangkor in January 1874, resulting in the negotiation of the Pangkor Agreement of that year. The most

12. R. Emerson, *Malaysia: A Study in Direct and Indirect Rule*, p. 119.

important outcome of this Agreement was the acceptance, by the Sultan, of a British Resident who was to advise him on all matters except those pertaining to the religion and customs of the Malays. Such advice was always to be accepted and acted upon. Thus was set the pattern for the ensuing expansion of British influence in Malaya, giving authority over Malays and Chinese alike, and destined to bring into the country vast numbers of Indians to provide cheap labour.

The establishment of the Residential system in Perak was followed by the drawing up of agreements leading to the implementation of similar steps in Selangor (1874), Sungei Ujong, one of the nine territories constituting Negri Sembilan (1874), and Pahang (1888). This eventually led to the formation of the Federated Malay States, comprising Perak, Selangor, Negri Sembilan, and Pahang, in 1895.

As the result of a treaty concluded with Siam in 1909, the four northern States of Kedah, Kelantan, Perlis, and Trengganu were brought under the general suzerainty of the British. With Johore in the south, these formed the Unfederated Malay States. As compared to the Federated States, these five were less directly under the control of the British.

Thus the country was thrown into three different political groupings—the Federated Malay States, the Unfederated Malay States, and the Straits Settlements (which, comprising Penang, Malacca, and Singapore, had become a Crown colony in 1867). Since the Malay States still retained a certain amount of autonomy, it may be said that there were no less than ten separate governments in the country—the nine State governments and the government of the Straits Settlements. In a sense, this anomaly was truly reflective of the absence of political unity which may be attributed to the population itself during these early years. The Malays, as already mentioned, were still very much under the influence of regional loyalties, and had not as yet developed a common national spirit: the main preoccupation of the Chinese was the improvement of facilities for economic penetration; and the Indians, who were the last to arrive, were mainly labourers whose one ambition was to eke out a living for themselves and, if possible, to remit savings to their relatives at home.

Turning to administration, the upper Civil Service in the Straits Settlements was a field reserved for Europeans. Admission into the junior administrative service, however, was open to everyone, and selection was carried out on a competitive basis. The Malays were overshadowed in this field by the Chinese, Indians, and Eurasians, probably due to a lack of interest and enthusiasm (particularly since they were not given any priorities in these territories) and also because a greater number of non-Malays went in for English education.

The administration of the Federated Malay States, while being nominally left in the hands of the Sultans, was in fact subject to overwhelming control by British officials. As far as the Asian communities were concerned, Malay supremacy was maintained in the political field, non-Malays being ineligible for appointment to the Civil Service. In the Unfederated Malay States, on the other hand, rule by the Sultans was more direct, though even here the part played by the British was very significant.

This raises the question of indirect rule, and an effort will now be made to examine its application in Malaya.

The theory of indirect rule, providing for the superimposition of colonial administrations on existing indigenous institutions, has been applied with varying degrees of success by the British in their dependent territories. Its merits and demerits depend very much on specific local conditions, and if generalization on such a matter is possible, it may perhaps be observed that a policy of indirect rule is more suited to a relatively homogeneous dependency than to a 'plural' one. The Malayan example would perhaps bear out this observation. In Malaya, as implied earlier, the Sultanate provided the intermediary authority through which British policies could be implemented. From a purely institutional point of view, the position of the Sultans proved ideal for this purpose. As in most other dependencies where the policy has been attempted, indirect rule in Malaya at first somewhat mitigated the direct impact of British colonial administration on the traditional (Malay) society. Subsequent developments, however, clearly revealed the disruptive influence of the presence of non-indigenous communities which, when compared to the Malays, had different ambitions and a different level of economic advancement.

Unlike the Malays, the Chinese and the Indians (whose numerical and economic strength must be remembered) did not have any innate sense of respect and loyalty for the Sultans. To them there was nothing wrong in curtailing the powers and privileges of the Sultans, in so far as these conflicted with the efficiency to be derived from a more centralized administration. While British commercial interests were of the same opinion, the official policy of the British Government was largely determined by treaty obligations towards the Malays, whereby the institutions and the special position of that community were guaranteed. From the official British point of view, herein lay the setting of the problem: they had to maintain the old form of government and the old ruling body while a very significant portion of those governed (that is, the non-Malays) did not identify themselves with that form, and rejected the effective authority of that ruling body. This inevitably meant that almost every major decision made by the British had to breast the difficult and dangerous cross-currents of communal differences.

Objection to indirect rule was by no means restricted to the non-Malay communities. The Malays had grievances too, but for a different reason. While the Chinese and the Indians were averse to the very idea of indirect rule in Malaya, on the ground that it tended to impair the efficiency and uniformity of policy to be derived from centralized government, the Malays were more unhappy about the manner in which some of the definite requirements of indirect rule were gradually being disregarded. Their main grievance rested not in the manner in which Sultanate authority tended to impede centralized policy-making, but rather in the manner in which the trend towards centralization acted to the detriment of Sultanate authority.

Having briefly considered the different communities in Malaya in relation to the constitutional history of the country, we may now survey some of the major events and issues which have shaped the country's constitutional progress. The first such issue was the question of decentralization.

A direct outcome of increased British participation in Malaya's political life around the turn of the century was the growing movement towards centralized government. The motives behind this were mainly economic and political: centralized government would make possible the application of a more consistent economic policy; it would also rule out the need for duplication in administrative matters. In the words of Brigadier-General Sir Samuel Wilson (the Permanent Under-Secretary of State for the Colonies, who visited Malaya in 1932 to look into the problem of decentralization), the British were faced with 'the delicate problem of reconciling the natural political aspirations of the Rulers with the practical difficulties, economic and administrative, of decentralizing a system of government in a territory the size of Malaya.'[13]

To the Malays in general, and the Malay Sultans in particular, increased centralization tended to obliterate the States by destroying their individuality and by divesting them of what power they had left in their hands after the signing of the Treaty of Federation in 1895. By that Treaty, a substantial amount of power had been transferred from the hands of the State Residents to the Federal Secretariat under a Resident-General, a move which had considerably diminished contact with the Sultans. The rapidly expanding finances of the States, for example, were now brought under the complete supervision of the Resident-General.[14] While this form of unified control provided a great stimulus to commerce and development and hence undoubtedly found favour with the non-Malay communities, the Malays were becoming increasingly alarmed by the fact that the Sultans and the States were fast being pushed into the background by the large and efficient central administration which had evolved. Consequently, at the Second Conference of Malay Rulers[15] held in Kuala Lumpur in 1903, the question of increasing centralization was introduced for discussion by the Sultan of Perak. Although Sir Samuel Wilson, in his Report mentioned above, had seen fit to describe the period as one where there could have been 'little doubt that there was general acquiescence in the Federal system, where there was not wholehearted approval',[16] the Sultans were becoming increasingly apprehensive of the trend whereby the centre of administration had gradually drifted away from them, their Residents, and their States, to the Resident-General and his Secretariat at Kuala Lumpur.[17] Legis-

13. Great Britain, Colonial Office, *Report of Brigadier-General Sir Samuel Wilson, G.C.M.G., K.C.B., K.B.E., Permanent Under-Secretary of State for the Colonies on His Visit to Malaya, 1932*, Cmd. 4276, p. 3.
14. Ibid., p. 6.
15. In addition to the Rulers, the Conference also included Malay Chiefs and members of the State Councils. It was presided over by the High Commissioner.
16. Cmd. 4276, op. cit., p. 7.
17. After all, it was as a result of this apprehension that the Sultan of Perak had brought up the matter of over-centralization for discussion at the 1903 Conference of Rulers.

Sir Samuel Wilson himself observes in his Report: 'The first attempt to modify the [Federal] system was made by Sir John Anderson in 1909, because

lative authority had undergone a similar fate. Kuala Lumpur was thus becoming the focus of bureaucratic centralization at the expense of the Sultans and the State Councils.

As Malay dissatisfaction became more apparent, so did the need for administrative change. In 1909 an Agreement was concluded with the Rulers of the four Federated States providing, among other things, for the establishment of a Federal Council which was to be the main legislative and financial authority in the Federated Malay States.[18] With the High Commissioner as President, the Council included the Rulers and their Residents as members. Although the Agreement made vague references to some distinction between the powers of the State and Central Governments, the Sultans found what actually followed most disheartening. The State Councils were in fact left with little more than a few petty affairs to handle, and the position of the Rulers in the Federal Council was hardly distinguished, to say the least.

Having been briefly forgotten during the boom years which followed, the question of decentralization was once again introduced for discussion in the 1920s and 1930s, largely as a result of the efforts of two Governors, Sir Lawrence Guillemard and Sir Cecil Clementi. Up to this time, the non-Malay communities had not been particularly vocal with regard to this issue. Now, however, it became clear that they (the Chinese and European business circles, in particular) intended to put up a much stronger opposition to the Sultans' demand for decentralized government.

The year 1932 saw the adoption of a scheme which was aimed at maintaining the legitimate status and authority of the Malay Rulers and which, by encouraging a 'purer' form of indirect rule, hoped to prevent the political submersion of the Malays which would have resulted had the development of popular government on Western lines been permitted. It was also hoped that such a move, by virtue of its promise of greater autonomy for the States, would be instrumental in attracting the Unfederated States to join the Federation, thereby facilitating the ultimate formation of some kind of Malayan Union.[19] Although the arrival of the Japanese deprived the scheme of sufficient time to prove its worth, the

at that date he considered there was a strong feeling on the part of the Malay Rulers against the loss of authority by the State Governments.' (Cmd. 4276, op. cit., p. 7.)

18. Loc. cit.

19. E. E. Dodd, *The New Malaya*, p. 18.

initial stages did not suggest much promise. To begin with, the tendency towards bureaucratic centralization was not sufficiently checked since the Federal Government at Kuala Lumpur was merely shifted, to a large extent, to the High Commissioner in Singapore. Furthermore, the Unfederated States failed to show the anticipated enthusiasm for centripetal movement.

Generally speaking, the reactions of the Chinese and European business classes may safely be attributed to economic motives. To them, a greater degree of centralization meant a proportionately greater degree of convenience and security: centralized administration would have given them a single authority with which their dealings could have been conducted; it would also have rendered them less dependent on the varying and possibly inconsistent regulations imposed by the individual state governments.[20] In addition, the non-Malay communities may also have been of the opinion that the British would be more sympathetic towards economic advancement (in which the non-Malays would invariably have played a major role) than the Malay Sultans who, understandably, might have been expected to view anything which appeared to increase the economic gap between the Malays and the non-Malays with a certain amount of disfavour.

Although both the Malays and the Chinese had sufficient grounds to justify their respective attitudes in this matter, there is little doubt that the interests of the two communities stood diametrically opposed. While the former fought against the lowering of their economic status *vis-à-vis* the other communities (not to mention the possible extinction of their political status in the country), the latter were mainly preoccupied with the question of economic security: reduced Federal powers might very well have exposed them to discriminatory treatment in the hands of the Malay authorities. But there was another consideration as well. At a time of growing interest in their nationalist movement, the Chinese were considerably disturbed by the Government's hostile attitude towards the Kuomintang in Malaya, which they thought indicated an anti-Chinese bias.[21] This automatically put them on their guard, and they now became suspicious of every move which

20. British and Chinese undertakings were mainly centred in the Federated Malay States and in the Colony. This naturally made decentralization a move filled with adverse possibilities.

21. R. Emerson, op. cit., p. 322.

seemed to imply an improvement in the status of the Malays. Added to this, no doubt, was the fact that, unlike the British, the Chinese had no reason whatsoever to feel morally responsible for the future well-being of the Malay community.

Thus the question of decentralization cut right across the field of Sino-Malay interests. The British were left to compromise, and compromise they did. Faced with a situation where the Malays seemed as determined on decentralization as the Chinese were on a more centralized government, they decided to steer a middle course, and proposed to bring about decentralization—but by a gradual process. The policy was to be established in three stages, the first dating from 1935 to 1939. The Chief Secretary (who had replaced the Resident-General) was in turn replaced by a Federal Secretary, who was purely an administrative officer directly under the High Commissioner[22]; certain departments (such as Education, Health, and Public Works) were handed over to the States; and the States were given bloc grants, to be used under supervision.[23]

The decentralization issue was thus instrumental in introducing a very specific basis for inter-communal rivalry. Up to this time, Sino-Malay relations had been fairly satisfactory; but this does not mean that each community was constantly making friendly overtures to the other. The absence of animosity had been due to two quite different factors. First, there was their mutual submission to *pax Britannica.* This did not completely overrule the possibility of an inter-communal clash, but rather postponed the day of its arrival. Secondly, up to this time neither community had had any reason to 'step on the other's toes'. Their ambitions were different, and so were their fields of interest: they stood in complementary and not conflicting relations to one another. But, all the time, there were the few Malays who, as they gained experience in the Government Service, could not but view the

22. It had become evident that far too much executive authority rested with the Chief Secretary, impeding decentralization. Sir Lawrence Guillemard, for example, had stated that for decentralization to be possible, there had to be 'such gradual devolution of the Chief Secretary's powers to State Councils, Residents, and if necessary to Federal Heads of Departments, as will in effect amount to abolition of the office of Chief Secretary as at present constituted'. (L. A. Mills, *British Rule in Eastern Asia*, p. 52.)

Under the new scheme, the powers of the Chief Secretary were transferred to the Sultans in Council in state matters, and to the High Commissioner or Federal Secretary in federal matters.

23. The central control of finance was nevertheless maintained.

activities of the Chinese as increasingly bold and presumptuous. And there were also those Chinese who resented the practice of reserving Civil Service appointments for Malays alone among the Asian communities. This was broadly the situation at the outbreak of the Second World War.

Politically, the most outstanding effect of the Japanese occupation was the vast transformation in the political behaviour and aspirations of the people. Broadly speaking, this was due to two main factors. First, the years of occupation changed the non-Malay population from being basically transient to being largely settled. Secondly, the Malay population ceased to be politically depressed and complacent as it had been before the War, having acquired a new sense of its own importance and abilities. This was no doubt partly due to the fact that the Japanese had, in their own way, disregarded the non-Malay communities and shown that they did not have to be treated as indispensable to the welfare of the country.[24]

The first major constitutional step after the War was taken on 1 April 1946, when the British Military Administration was replaced by the Malayan Union. The new proposals embodied a fresh set of arrangements which clearly indicated an attempt at political experimentation by the British Government. Although the new scheme in fact proved abortive, it succeeded in intensifying the already present Sino-Malay tension.[25] It is also significant for having inspired an unprecedented interest in politics and administration among the Malays and, consequently, for having produced the first chapter in organized communal agitation, for constitutional ends, in Malayan history.

Britain's basic motive in introducing the Malayan Union scheme appears to have been greater simplicity and efficiency in administration, to be effected through centralization and direct rule. As mentioned earlier, the British had never before possessed direct jurisdiction over the Malay States by the treaties concluded with the Sultans. The situation had merely been one whereby the Malay Rulers had been obliged to accept the advice given to them on all matters except those pertaining to the religion and customs of the Malays, while continuing to act in their own name. The

24. The expense at which this point was proved is quite another matter.
25. It will be remembered that the years of occupation, and the period immediately following, had witnessed a deterioration in communal relations.

administrative advantages to be derived from centralization must always have been known to the British; but, before the War, they were restrained from attempting such a policy. Two reasons may be given for this. First, they were conscious of their treaty obligations towards the Malays and were probably apprehensive of the reactions of that community should its privileged position have been sacrificed in the interests of administrative unity. Secondly, the inter-war years were the heyday of indirect rule, considered an essential requirement of trusteeship. This was partly the result of an empirical attitude and partly that of a belief that Western institutions were not necessarily applicable in all colonial territories.

After the Second World War, however, emphasis was shifted to the creation of 'modern' states; and this implied more efficient administrations, rapid social and economic development by state action, and a more 'positive' approach to the question of eventual self-government. The colonial ideas of the Labour Party, furthermore, did not generally favour indirect rule which radical opinion has always considered reactionary. In the case of Malaya, it must also have been felt that the pro-Malay policy of the pre-war period had been largely discredited by the war-time record.

Saying that the divided nature of the country which had characterized the political structure of pre-war Malaya was not compatible with the need for national progress, the British Government proposed, through the new scheme, to give top priority to administrative unity. The White Paper explained: 'A stage has now been reached when the system of government should be simplified and reformed. International relations as well as the security and other interests of the British Commonwealth require that Malaya should be able to exercise an influence as a united and enlightened country appropriate to her economic and strategic importance.'[26] Consequently, it was decided to bring the Malay States under the jurisdiction of the British Crown, which was to be enabled to carry out a policy of uniform legislation for all the States under the Foreign Jurisdiction Act.[27] It was with this in mind that Sir Harold MacMichael, a Special Representative of His Majesty's Government, was sent to Malaya for the purpose of getting the approval of Their Highnesses the Sultans by concluding

26. Great Britain, Colonial Office, *Malayan Union and Singapore: A Statement of Policy on Future Constitution*, Cmd. 6724, 1946, p. 2.
27. Ibid., p. 3.

'with each ruler on behalf of His Majesty's Government a formal Agreement by which he [would] cede full jurisdiction to His Majesty in his State', and abrogating existing agreements that were in any way repugnant to the new proposals.[28]

Two vital changes highlighted the new scheme. First, the administrative structure of the country was to be readjusted whereby Singapore was to be established as a separate colony while the two other Settlements (Penang and Malacca), together with the nine Malay States, were to constitute a single political entity to be known as the Malayan Union. Secondly, communal preferences were to be abolished in so far as citizenship privileges were concerned, so that everyone (except Japanese nationals), regardless of race, born and resident in the Malayan Union or Singapore, would belong to a common political category, enjoying equal rights.[29]

In view of the fact that Singapore had a strong concentration of Chinese, the first change (the exclusion of Singapore from the Union) offset some of the advantages which that community gained as a result of the equal citizenship rights given to it. An examination of the 1947 census figures (reduced here to the nearest 5,000) proves most enlightening in this respect.[30] At a time when the population of Malaya as a whole (that is, including Singapore) was 5,845,000 of which 2,610,000 were Chinese, Singapore alone accounted for 935,000, including 725,000 Chinese. Thus, by excluding Singapore from the Union, the number of Chinese in the country was reduced to 1,885,000 out of a total population of 4,910,000. This move gave the Malays approximately 48 per cent of the population and a numerical superiority over the Chinese who, without Singapore, constituted only about 38 per cent of the total population. Although the White Paper made no direct reference to this particular aspect of the separation,[31] the above

28. Ibid., p. 4. 29. Cmd. 6724, op. cit., p. 2.

30. Although the proposals now under discussion were introduced in 1946, the population figures for 1947 are being used since the first census after the War was taken in that year. It may be assumed that the difference between these and the actual figures for 1946 could only have been slight.

31. The explanation actually given was: 'In considering the need for close political integration in Malaya, His Majesty's Government consider that, at least for the time being, Singapore requires special treatment. It is a centre of entrepôt trade on a very large scale and has economic and social interests distinct from the mainland.' (Cmd. 6724, op. cit., p. 3.) The reference to distinct 'social interests' is perhaps revealing to some extent.

consideration must have played a major role in deciding the new policy. The Colonial Office must have been well aware that, for the time being at least, the separation of Singapore would act as a guarantee that democratization could be effected without any immediate danger of the Malays being politically submerged by the Chinese.

The second major change (the abolition of citizenship privileges) was very definitely to the disadvantage of the Malay community. Despite the exclusion of Singapore from the Union, there was little doubt that the very roots of Malay political superiority were now severely threatened. Once the proposals were made known, the Malays showed every intention of opposing them to the bitter end, and indeed it was the sustained pressure applied by them which eventually resulted in the scheme's withdrawal. The main factors which inspired Malay opposition to the new scheme may now be discussed briefly.

To begin with, the Malays did not expect this sudden reversal of policy on the part of the British Government. To them the liberation, followed so soon by the new proposals, represented a deterioration in British intentions from the sublime to the very ridiculous. Their 'special position' was suddenly to be ended, particularly as a result of the new citizenship proposals; their Rulers were made nothing more than mere 'stuffed shirts', endowed with powers which, for all practical purposes, were grossly inadequate.[32] The principle of decentralization, to which the British seemed to have adhered so resolutely in pre-war years, was now to be abandoned, and the old treaty relations were now to be made invalid, discarded in favour of a scheme which placed their community on a political parity with the Chinese and Indians, in whose intentions and loyalty they had little faith and with whom they could not compete favourably, given equal opportunities.

The Malays realized that the general character of the new scheme pointed the way to a democratic electorate in the not-too-distant future. To them this meant that Chinese and Indian immigrants, with inadequate residential qualifications and an artificial loyalty towards the country, would be given a substantial say in the policies of government. As if adding salt to the wound,

32. In each State, the main body of law now ceased to require the assent of the Ruler; it was now the Governor whose approval was required for any legislation.

the British had also seen fit to introduce the scheme in an arbitrary and high-handed manner, without consultation and without regard for the opinions of the Sultans—a 'lump it and take it' attitude, as Lord Elibank put it in the House of Lords.[33] British policy had, up to this time, been dictated by

> a conscientious regard for the binding qualities of treaties, a recognition that its economic policies had flooded the country with aliens, and a realization that without protection Malaya would soon cease to be a country of the Malays and would in fact become, what casual observation had mockingly called it, another province of China. There was the rub.[34]

Under these circumstances, it appeared that the British had broken faith in bringing about this complete *volte-face* in their policy towards Malaya.

But the fundamental issue was not the merely legal rights of the Sultans or the questionable methods adopted by Sir Harold MacMichael in procuring the signatures of the various Rulers,[35]

33. Great Britain Parliament, House of Lords, *Official Report of Debates*, Second Volume of Session 1945–1946, col. 934.

34. S. W. Jones, *Public Administration in Malaya*, p. 137. Some Chinese leaders did not take too kindly to the observation that their community was attempting to turn Malaya into another province of China. Mr. Tan Cheng Lock, for example, observed in rather caustic terms:

'This myth, for which the Chinese are not responsible and which was originally concocted in the imaginative brain of some European writer of the globe-trotter type, has since been used as a weapon with which to attack the Chinese. I affirm that it is a lie and a slander reiterated maliciously to injure the Chinese out of jealousy and envy for Chinese economic success in Malaya, which has been won by sheer dint of hard work, by their industry, enterprise and initiative as well as by untold sufferings endured by them in the past, without any outside help and without any protection or aid from the Chinese Government throughout the whole period of Malayan history.'

(Tan Cheng Lock, *Malayan Problems*, p. 116.)

35. In letters written to Capt. Gammans (Conservative Member in the British House of Commons who visited Malaya during the Malayan Union Crisis) many of the Sultans complained of the unfortunate circumstances under which their signatures had been procured. The Sultan of Kedah, for example, wrote:

'I was presented with a verbal ultimatum with a time limit, and in the event of my refusing to sign the new agreement, which I call the Instrument of Surrender, a successor, who would sign it, would be appointed Sultan. Members of the State Council were compelled to sign an undertaking that they would advise me to sign it. I was told that this matter was personal and confidential, and was not allowed to tell my people what had taken place.'

The Sultans of Johore, Perak, Selangor, and Negri Sembilan lodged similar complaints. (*Straits Times*, 29 March 1946, p. 2.)

although these no doubt were of some consequence. The main question was whether or not Britain would continue to consider Malaya as primarily a Malay country. The Malays clearly did not want to see their country transformed into another Palestine where they would lose their special identity in a common citizenship embracing all communities. It is quite likely that their opposition to the Union proposals would not have been quite as intense as it turned out to be had they been the only people in the country, or had they formed a large majority therein. As it was, it seems clear that their opposition was very much the product of considerations regarding their status *vis-à-vis* the non-Malays, the Chinese in particular.

Despite their initial complaisance (which, it was claimed, was due to duress on the one hand and faith in British intentions on the other) the Sultans soon added their voices to the general Malay outcry. While echoing some of the objections raised by the Malay community in general, they were more categoric in their demands, giving individual attention to matters such as citizenship (stating, for example, that since Singapore was not to form a part of the Malayan Union, residents in Singapore should not qualify for Malayan Union citizenship—a proposal clearly aimed at reducing Chinese political strength), the alienation of State land (stating that this should be left in the hands of the State Councils), finance (proposing that State Councils should control their own finances), and so on. Their protests were motivated by three important considerations: they wanted to restore the prestige which they themselves had lost; they wanted the States to retain a greater measure of sovereignty; and, finally, they wanted to see the Malay community back in the privileged position it had occupied before the War.

In summing up Malay opinion in general, three main political groupings are discernible within the community. First, there were the Malay Sultans who, in addition to demanding greater authority for themselves, also felt obliged to support those who were mainly preoccupied with the question of preserving the special position of the Malays. In addition to the objections already mentioned, the Sultans also maintained that it was quite ridiculous for the Governor to be associated with legislation concerning matters primarily related to the Mohammedan religion. The second group were the upper class local officials and members of the aristocracy.

Despite the fact that they held a position of leadership in their comparatively limited Malay circles, these men now found themselves faced with a situation which made it necessary for them to compete with members of other communal groups in a broader field of political activity. Finally, there were the ordinary people, inspired and led by politicians (notably Dato' Onn), and mainly preoccupied with the preservation of their community's traditional institutions and the continuation of their privileged position.

The reactions of the non-Malay communities did not in any way equal those of the Malay community, either in intensity or in the extent of popular support. By and large, those non-Malays who supported the proposals did not make much effort to meet Malay opposition; those who opposed them did not bother very much with mass support, and mostly belonged to the left-wing intelligentsia.

The arguments put forward by those non-Malays who voiced their opposition to the scheme were quite different from those on which Malay opposition was based. While the Malays deplored the manner in which the Sultans had not been consulted, and questioned the equal status given to the non-Malays by the new proposals, the non-Malays in question seemed to take their new status for granted, and consequently deplored the manner in which they themselves had not been consulted; convinced that they belonged to the country as much as anyone else, they maintained that their views necessarily formed an integral part of Malayan opinion. According to Mr. H. B. Lim, the Secretary of the Malayan Democratic Union, the people as a whole were the most important factor in the issue especially because, as a result of the Pangkor Agreement of 1874 and all the subsequent treaties, the Sultans had, in actual fact, ceded their sovereignty.[36] This had made the Malayan Union Agreement nothing unusual as far as the Sultans were concerned.[37] Mr. Lim referred to Captain Gammans' attempt to represent the constitutional crisis as a product of the violation of the Sultans' sovereignty as 'both factually and chronologically incorrect'. His main objection was that the people had not been consulted; Sir Harold MacMichael

36. H. B. Lim, 'Malaya's "Constitution"', *Labour Monthly*, Vol. 28 (1946), p. 381.

37. It is interesting to note here the difference between Malay and non-Malay opinion with regard to the position of the Sultans.

and the Sultans had had no right to agree on the White Paper *in toto* on behalf of the people. With regard to the consequences of the proposals, Mr. Lim asserted: 'The aggregate result of this constitutional swindle is that all popular Malay, Chinese, Indian and Eurasian organizations are being antagonized.'[38]

To sum up, it appears that the roots of the conflict lay in a single issue: were the British going to recognize the *de facto* position of the non-Malay communities who now claimed to regard Malaya as their only home and hence considered themselves eligible for widely increased political rights, or were they going to continue recognizing Malaya as essentially a Malay country? To a certain extent, the Malays appeared to be willing to give increased rights to the other communities; but at the same time they insisted on the maintenance of their privileged position.

The British realized that, with the upsurge of Malay nationalism on an unexpected and totally unprecedented scale,[39] urgent re-thinking was necessary in their policy for Malaya. It was imperative for them to abandon the Malayan Union, set up a federal form of government, and give the Sultans a greater measure of autonomy.

With regard to their main objectives (namely, the establishment of a strong and effective central government and the creation of some form of common citizenship), the British refused completely to abandon their stand. But now, however, they were willing to consult Malay opinion, knowing full well that such a move would be vital in permitting the successful implementation of new policies.

As a first step in drawing up a new Constitution for the country, a Working Committee was appointed comprising Government

38. H. B. Lim, op. cit., p. 382.

39. The political awakening of the Malays was indeed striking. As observed by one writer, from being 'sleepy beneficiaries of a privileged position', they now became 'champions of their own rights and critics of those who tried to destroy them'. (S. W. Jones, *Public Administration in Malaya*, p. 139.) Mass rallies and processions became quite common, and there were slogans like 'Malaya for the Malays', 'Down with the Malayan Union', 'We will fight for our rights and our country', and 'Has our benign protector turned bully?' (L. D. Gammans, M.P. 'Crisis in Malaya', *The Spectator*, Vol. 176 (1946), p. 601, and *Malay Mail*, 30 May 1946.) Even the women came out to lead processions and address public meetings. It was clear that the entire Malay community ('From padi-planters to Sultan', as Mr. Gammans put it) became strongly united in opposing the Malayan Union.

representatives on the one hand and the Rulers, together with representatives of the United Malays' National Organization,[40] on the other. This Committee was given the task of drawing up a Draft Constitution, and the very fact that it had representatives from the Government and the Rulers as its members tended to give its report an aura of authority. Although the proposals made by this Committee were subsequently forwarded to a Consultative Committee (which was to represent the views of the non-Malay communities) for its consideration, the non-Malays, judging from some of the memoranda submitted to the latter Committee, very much resented the fact that they were not consulted in the first instance. The decision to include the U.M.N.O. in the Working Committee constituted another point of grievance, particularly among the other Malay political organizations.

The proposals made by the Working Committee left no doubt that the intention was now to re-establish Malaya as a Malay country. It was made possible for non-Malays to become citizens, but the regulations governing their eligibility were undoubtedly stringent; the Sultans were to be given more authority, and the Malays were to receive 'special treatment' in certain vital fields.

In an effort to reflect popular opinion, the Consultative Committee invited (and received) memoranda and oral evidence from all sections of the public. Most of the opinions submitted to it indicated that citizenship regulations and representation in the Legislative Council were the main points of grievance, and it was on these matters that the Committee laid emphasis in submitting its recommendations.

The task facing the Consultative Committee was by no means a simple one, particularly since the non-Malay communities did not present a common front. Admittedly, there was a common request for a strong central government and a reduction in Malay privileges, but the specific claims made both by individuals and by organizations were mostly communal in character. Each community sought to assert the legitimacy of its own position in the country. The following extracts, taken from some of the memoranda submitted to the Committee, are most indicative in this respect:

40. The United Malays' National Organization (hereinafter referred to as the U.M.N.O.) was formed in 1946 to help organize Malay opposition to the Malayan Union proposals. It was included in the Working Committee to represent moderate Malay opinion.

(Malay) This is a Malay country, which has been acknowledged to belong to the Malays from time immemorial. . . . It is necessary that the Malays should be given more votes than the other races . . . the Malays must . . . give priority to the people of their own race no matter what countries or government they may come from, as long as they are Malays. (Memorandum from *Persatuan Melayu*, Trengganu.)[41]

(Chinese) . . . we and those before us have lived and toiled in this country and have contributed in a very large measure towards the development and progess of Malaya. . . . The Chinese should have the same representation as the Malays for they have contributed the most in the development of this country and have to pay the greatest share of the taxes and rates.[42] (Selangor Chinese Chamber of Commerce.)

(Indian) Men's memories are very short and hence the tendency to regard Indians as unwelcome intruders whose contribution to Malayan economy is nil. . . . The Malay community may be excused for short memories, but the Raj [meaning, the British] cannot dispute the contributions of India and Indians to the extension of its influence in this part of the world from the founding of Singapore in the early part of the nineteenth century to the liberation of Malaya a few months ago. (Memorandum from the Indian Association, Trengganu.)[43]

(Ceylonese) A significant feature has been that Ceylonese with traditional loyalty and conservatism have given their entire lives exclusively to the service of Their Highnesses and the British Administrators, while other races ventured into vocations of great gain. . . . (Memorandum from the Ceylon Federation of Malaya.)[44]

(Eurasian) The Eurasian is the son of the soil and we in Malaya have no other country which we can regard as our homeland. (Memorandum from the Eurasian Union.)[45]

(Indian Muslim) The Indian Muslims of Malaya wish to have a separate existence not only because of their religion but also on account of the fact that the Indian Muslims differ from the rest of the Indians in matters of culture, religion, history, names and civilization. (Memorandum from the Penang Indian Muslim League.)[46]

(Sikh) . . . The Sikhs are recognized as a separate entity among the peoples of India and stand as a powerful minority that steadies the extreme views of the major races in India. Likewise, in Malaya, the

41. Federation of Malaya, *Report of the Consultative Committee*, 1947, pp. 116–17.
42. Ibid., pp. 141 and 143.
43. Ibid., p. 114.
44. Ibid., p. 123.
45. Ibid., p. 138.
46. Ibid., p. 93.

Sikhs claim that their peculiar position to the domiciled Indian races makes them a powerful minority whose recognition would ensure the equipoise that is needed for the adequate representation of Indians in the Councils of the country. (Memorandum from the Malayan Sikh Union).[47]

To confuse the issue further, the British community entered the picture as well, urging wider representation for its own interests. Indeed, one man went to the point of asserting that:

. . . most Asiatic races require to be ruled by a benign autocracy and are incapable of ruling themselves on account of suspicion or envy of others. . . . Malaya must not become a colony of either the Chinese or the Indians, as these two races seem to desire. . . . The popular saying that the Chinese have made Malaya is a fallacy. . . . Malaya was made by the British benign Rule by giving good advice to the Rulers, by the introduction of the Hevea tree and by qualified or trained mining engineers. The English made Malaya.[48]

The recommendations of the Consultative Committee did not meet the wishes of all its members. In this respect, it is significant to note that its two Chinese members (Col. H. S. Lee and Mr. Leong Yew Koh) were at variance with the others over the question of citizenship and representation in the Legislative Council.[49] This is interesting when one considers that the Committee was in fact meant to represent non-Malay opinion;[50] and the Chinese form such a large part of the non-Malay population. Regarding citizenship, Col. Lee and Mr. Leong were of the opinion that the principle of *jus soli* should be accepted, and that the recommendations, as they stood, were 'grossly unfair';[51] concerning representation in the Legislative Council, they demanded an increased share for the Chinese, stating that this was necessary in view of the community's numerical strength, its long association with the country, its vast economic undertakings, and the fact that it contributed about 70 per cent of the total taxes.[52] In the face of these considerations, they 'reluctantly agreed to the ratio of 100 to 75 of

47. Ibid., p. 161.
48. Ibid, p. 103 (letter from Mr. H. W. Reid).
49. Ibid., pp. 181–2.
50. The composition of the Committee, however, failed to ensure this, the nine members being made up of five Europeans, two Chinese, and two Indians.
51. *Report of the Consultative Committee*, p. 182. For committee's citizenship proposals, see Chapter Three.
52. Ibid., pp. 181–2.

Malay and Chinese representation in the Federal Legislative Council'.[53]

The recommendations of the Consultative Committee were sent back to the Working Committee for study, and the proposals which finally emerged were submitted for consideration by a Plenary Conference of the Governor, the Rulers, and other Malay representatives. The scheme which emerged out of these discussions (aimed, as suggested by the procedure, at granting some recognition to communal demands) was accepted by the British Government as being adequate to meet the political exigencies of the time.

The new proposals provided for a Federation Agreement between the Crown and the Malay Rulers; each Ruler was to conclude a further Agreement with the Crown concerning his own State. Each State was subsequently to ratify both the Federation and State Agreements. The net result of the new Constitution was the restoration of Malaya as a primarily Malay country. The Sultans were to enjoy the 'prerogatives, power and jurisdiction which they enjoyed prior to the Japanese occupation';[54] the State Agreements were to provide for special facilities as regards the education and training of the Malays; and the High Commissioner's responsibilities were to include 'the safeguarding of the special position of the Malays and the legitimate interests of the other communities'.[55] In addition, the Councils of State were now empowered to legislate independently on matters pertaining to the religion and custom of the Malay inhabitants.

Taken in its entirety, the Federal Constitution was far from democratic when compared to post-war Constitutions in India, Ceylon, and the Philippines. It did, however, constitute a definite improvement on the pre-war situation; contrary to the tendency then, the British and the Malays now found it no longer possible to ignore the fact that the non-Malay segments of the settled population had become a most vital element in the country's life and hence had to be given certain citizenship rights equal to those of the Malays themselves. To put it simply, this was largely due to the fact that the non-Malays now formed a substantially increased percentage of the settled population.

53. Ibid., p. 182.

54. Great Britain, Colonial Office, *Federation of Malaya—Summary of Revised Constitutional Proposals*, Cmd. 7171, p. 5.

55. Loc. cit.

As one might have expected in view of the conflicting claims of the day, the Federation scheme failed to satisfy either the Malays or the non-Malays. If they had compared the new proposals with the Malayan Union scheme, the Malays would undoubtedly have had cause to be satisfied with them; compared to the pre-war situation, however, the new scheme looked unsatisfactory. The non-Malays, on the other hand, might have been happy had they judged the new Federal Constitution in terms of the constitutional set-up in pre-war Malaya; but it was the Malayan Union scheme which was now used for purposes of comparison.

By and large, the non-Malays appeared to be the more disappointed, for in a sense the Federation scheme was a reversal of the Malayan Union proposals which had been so much to their advantage. In protest, the Chinese community held a *hartal* throughout the country on 20 October (1947), the move being sponsored by the Pan-Malayan Council of Joint Action (led by Mr. Tan Cheng Lock) and supported by the Associated Chinese Chambers of Commerce, the Malayan Trade Unions, and the Malayan Communist Party.

In view of the dissatisfaction aroused by the new proposals, it is worth considering the alternatives which might have been adopted by the British Government in deciding the constitutional future of the Malay Peninsula. In this way the Federation Agreement can be placed in its most appropriate perspective.

To begin with, there was the possibility of following a policy aimed at gradually reducing two of the three main communities to considerably less significant minorities—a policy which, if implemented successfully, might have meant the termination of the communal problem. On closer examination, however, one finds that such a policy would invariably have been both too radical and too dangerous to be considered as being practicable in any respect. The communities in question would undoubtedly have had to be the Chinese and the Indian, and though the policy might have been welcomed by some of the more extreme Malay nationalists, practical economic and political considerations would have rendered its implementation most unwise. The impracticability of such a policy was perhaps best assessed by Professor Silcock: 'So long as Malaya remains politically unsophisticated and is firmly controlled by British administrators backed by British troops, it is possible to call it a Malay country and assume that Chinese and Indians are aliens without implying any intention to take drastic action against them. But anyone with even a rudimentary sense of political possibilities must realize that a self-governing Malay Malaya is an impossibility unless most drastic action is taken against the other two races over a period of years.'[56]

From an economic standpoint, such a policy would not have been feasible because, for it to be successfully implemented, the country's distributive trade, large mining concerns, and other important fields of economic activity, mainly held by the Chinese, would have had to be transferred to the Malays who, for all practical purposes, would have been unable to take over and carry on independently. By alienating the sympathies of the Chinese population this policy, if adopted, could also have been instrumental in turning large parts of that community into active supporters of Communist terrorism.

As a second alternative, the British could have ignored all obligations to the Malay community and consequently withdrawn all the restrictions which, up to that time, had prevented the other communities from acquiring a position of dominance. A policy of this nature might have resulted in unrestricted immigration from China (at least prior to the establishment of the Communist régime there, but nevertheless involving great numbers in view of the exodus of refugees), and a natural consequence of this might have been the submersion of the other two communities by the Chinese. It is also possible that, with the influx of immigrants from China, ties with that country would have been considerably strengthened, resulting in serious complications in the political life of Malaya. However, as indicated by the opposition which followed the attempt to establish the Malayan Union, there is no doubt that the Malays would have used all the political weapons available in combating the implementation of such a policy.[57]

Although the Federation Agreement left much to be desired both from the Malay as well as the non-Malay point of view, it cannot be denied that, when compared to the alternatives discussed above, it was a product of good sense. Its most outstanding shortcoming was the failure to emphasize adequately that the differences

56. T. H. Silcock, 'Forces for Unity in Malaya', *International Affairs*, Vol. 25 (1949), pp. 455–6.

57. Considering the opposition which the Malayan Union scheme faced in Britain, it is very unlikely that such a policy could ever have been seriously contemplated.

in interests between citizens and immigrants (of the same racial group) were far greater than those between the different communities residing in the country. As it was, the citizenship issue in particular brought to the forefront several aspects of Sino-Malay conflict.

The Federation Agreement of 1948 was not left unaltered until its replacement by the Constitution of 1957. The most important changes were related to citizenship and the composition of the Legislative Council, and will be discussed in some detail in Chapters Three and Five. In so far as the present survey of general constitutional development is concerned, it now remains briefly to discuss the country's transition from dependent to independent status.

More than any of the previous Constitutions, that drawn up for the independent Federation of Malaya in 1957 was a product of consultation and compromise. As a first step, an independent Constitutional Commission [58] was set up, for the purpose of drawing up a Draft Constitution. The recommendations made by this Commission were very largely the product of the testimony provided by the people in the country. Saying that various recommendations had been received by them in the form of memoranda, the Commission declared:

> We have come to the conclusion that the best proposals for dealing fairly with the present constitution are those put forward by the Alliance. The parties of the Alliance have given full consideration to this matter and apart from a few minor points they have reached agreement. We are satisfied that this agreement is a reasonable and proper compromise between the views of the parties, each of which has the most widespread support from the race which it represents, and we are further satisfied that this agreement is a better way of doing justice between the races than any other that has been suggested or occurred to us.[59]

The contradictions inherent in the Commission's terms of reference give some indication of the peculiarities of constitutional government in Malaya: the Commissioners were asked

58. The Commission was made up entirely of non-Malayans. It was headed by Lord Reid, the other members being Mr. W. J. McKell (Australia), Mr. B. Malik (India), Mr. Justice Abdul Hamid (Pakistan), and Sir Ivor Jennings (U.K.).

59. Great Britain, Colonial Office, *Report of the Federation of Malaya Constitutional Commission, 1957*, Colonial No. 330, p. 16.

to create a strong central government while at the same time providing for the maintenance of States' rights and the safeguarding of the position of the Sultans; they were asked to draw up a Constitution based on democratic ideals while at the same time preserving the 'special position' of a single community, the Malays; and they were asked to draft proposals for a common nationality, and at the same time give assurance to the Rulers that this would not be interpreted 'in a strictly legal sense'.[60]

Such were the problems facing the authors of the Draft Constitution. Two of the most vital aspects of constitutional government pertaining to the definition of the State and its nationals, remained vague: on what concept of the State was the Federation of Malaya to be established, and what was to be the basis of nationality? On the one hand the trappings of a Malay state had to be preserved and the Malays had to be given priority over the others; this would have reflected some of the qualities of a national state. On the other hand, however, citizenship had to be open to everyone irrespective of race, and a strong central government had to be established where authority would be non-communal. Although definitions and explanations have frequently been attempted, these ambiguities have persisted to the present day.

The recommendations made by the Commission proved to be slightly weighted in favour of the non-Malays.[61] This was indicated by decisions such as the refusal to establish Islam as the State religion contrary to the request made by the Alliance, the (limited) acceptance of multi-lingualism in the Legislative Council,[62] and the introduction of a time-limit (fifteen years) after which the question of the special position of the Malays was to be reconsidered. One of the Commissioners, Mr Justice Abdul Hamid, disagreed with the majority opinion on these issues, and supported the recommendations submitted by the Alliance.

The Malayan public received the Draft Constitution with mixed feelings, there being a definite line of distinction between Malay

60. *Report of the Federation of Malaya Constitutional Commission, 1957*, p. 6.

61. This does not mean that the non-Malays were given a superior position as compared to the Malays; it is just that the position of the Malays was made less exclusive than one might have expected.

62. Members of the Legislative Council were to be given a limited right to speak in a Chinese or Indian language, and no language qualifications were recommended for candidates wishing to stand for election.

and non-Malay opinion. The *Straits Times* of 21 February 1957 said: 'It is not an ideal solution that the five wise men of the Commission have devised, in the sense that it does not promise all things to all the interests affected. But the perfectionist approach was ruled out by a host of factors; by the problems inherent in a plural society, by the resistance of the past to the claims of the present, by the existence of uneven economic conditions, by the forced pace of political transformation, and by the very nature of the task the Commission was set,'[63] adding later: 'It is the recommendations on citizenship, special Malay rights and on the question of State religion that will command wide attention.'[64]

Chinese and Indian leaders were generally enthusiastic in their first reactions to the Draft Constitution. Most of them found it either 'reasonable' or 'broad-minded', but there were also those who felt that it could hardly have been better. The Penang Straits Chinese British Association, for example, went to the extent of saying 'this is what we had prayed for'.[65] The China-born Chinese welcomed the proposal which gave non-Malay members of the Legislative Council a limited right to speak in their own language for a period of ten years from *Merdeka* (Independence) Day.

The Malays, on the other hand, showed considerable dissatisfaction over some of the provisions contained in the Draft Constitution, particularly those pertaining to language, State religion, and the special position of their community. This was clearly indicated by the stand taken by the U.M.N.O. Tengku Abdul Rahman said: 'The report has overlooked provisions for the Malays, but the Alliance Government has not.'[66] Some of the other leaders (Dato' Onn, for example) expressed great concern over the future voting strength of the Malay community, in view of the liberal provisions which now governed citizenship qualifications.[67] With regard to the proposal that the special position of the Malays be reviewed after fifteen years, it was felt that, in the absence of more permanent safeguards regarding land holdings, the Malays would eventually be driven out of the better areas.[68] The general opinion seemed to be that the Malays had been badly let down by the Commission.

63. *Straits Budget*, Singapore, 28 February 1957, p. 2.
64. Ibid., p. 3. 65. Ibid., p. 16.
66. Ibid., 21 March 1957, p. 14. 67. Ibid., 7 March 1957, p. 13.
68. Loc. cit.

Considering the reactions in general, the most outstanding feature was the Malay community's efforts to improve its status under the new Constitution. The more moderate elements within the non-Malay communities accepted the validity of some of the demands made by the Malays; but there were also many with far less moderate views. Given intemperate leadership, the situation could easily have produced an impasse; fortunately, there was accommodation on both sides. Tengku Abdul Rahman, for example, in speaking to the U.M.N.O. General Assembly, emphasized that while there was decidedly a need to preserve the rights of the Malays, those of the non-Malay communities should not be made to suffer in an independent Malaya.[69] To those Malays who were unwilling to compromise with the other communities, the Tengku said that the history and racial make-up of Malaya should be borne in mind while studying the Commission's report, and asked: 'How can we seize all rights for ourselves alone? Will the other races keep quiet? Will the world allow us to make the other races suffer? Will the British then free our country?'[70] It was statesmanship of this calibre which saved the U.M.N.O. from a serious rift within itself, arising from the question of whether or not the Report of the Constitutional Commission was adequate as a basis for the future Constitution of the country. Despite opposition, the Tengku and his Executive Council were given a vote of confidence at a General Meeting of the party; they now had the 'complete authority' to make the Commission's Report the foundation on which the new Constitution would be constructed.[71] The meeting in question was most important in that, had the Tengku and his Executive Council been denied the vote of confidence, the Alliance Government might have been forced to resign.

The M.C.A. (Malayan Chinese Association), too, did its share in this campaign for moderation. The central Working Committee of the Association unanimously agreed not to press for those recommendations of the Constitutional Commission which had gone beyond the proposals submitted by the Alliance, although these were essentially to the advantage of the non-Malay communities.[72]

Knowing very well the urgent need for solidarity and mutual tolerance, the three parties of the Alliance now presented a united front with regard to the four main issues at hand—State religion,

69. Ibid., 4 April 1957, p. 9. 70. Loc. cit.
71. Ibid., p. 8. 72. Ibid., 11 April 1957, p. 14.

the special position of the Malays, citizenship, and national language. It seems apparent that the leaders of these parties, while recognizing the desirability of unity within their respective communities, did not overlook the deeper implications of a wider unity embracing all the communities. That this unity was essential for national progress was only too obvious; that it also suited communal interests must have been known: the Malays and the Chinese had to accommodate each other not just because the welfare of the country demanded it, but also because neither had the power to 'go it alone'. Consequently, while the leaders of the U.M.N.O. emphasized that it was not the intention of the Malays to establish themselves at the expense of the others, those of the M.C.A. and the M.I.C. (Malayan Indian Congress) reciprocated by acknowledging that it would have been wrong, at that moment, to confront the Malays with the possibility of change, or substantially to weaken the safeguards which that community already had.

The Draft Constitution was submitted for scrutiny by Her Majesty's Government in the United Kingdom and by the Working Party[73] in the Federation. When the latter had agreed on its recommendations, a delegation comprising the High Commissioner, the Chief Minister, the Attorney-General, and representatives of Their Highnesses the Rulers and the Government of the Federation went to London for the purpose of discussing the Report and the amendments which they considered necessary with Her Majesty's Government. Having lasted from 13 to 21 May, the talks resulted in agreement being reached 'between all parties on all points of principle'.[74] When the amendments proposed by the Working Party were incorporated into the original draft, the revised version was sent back for consideration at meetings of the Working Party in the Federation, at which officials of the United Kingdom were present. Although the revised draft differed from the Constitutional Commission's recommendations on certain vital matters, the basic framework was largely left unchanged.

73. The Working Party consisted of the High Commissioner, 4 representatives of Their Highnesses the Rulers, 4 representatives of the Government of the Federation, the Chief Secretary, and the Attorney-General. It held twenty-three meetings between 22 February and 27 April, and reported to the Conference of Rulers on 14 March, 10 April, and 7 May, and to the Federal Executive Council on 3 and 6 May.

74. Great Britain, Colonial Office, *Constitutional Proposals for the Federation of Malaya*, Cmnd. 210, pp. 3–4.

The Commission, in making its recommendations, had attempted to effect a compromise between all the demands which, in its opinion, had been justifiable. The Constitution which now emerged was a compromise between the Commission's compromise and the Malay opposition which had followed the publication of the Draft. As opposed to the recommendations of an independent body (the Commission), and in the sense that past experience had shown Malay approval to be most vital, the final proposals were more clearly geared to suit local political realities.

Taken as a whole, the Constitution appears to have done justice to all sections of the population—'justice' not in the more abstract sense of the term or in the sense that no community is given any priority, but rather in the sense that the privileges and restrictions inherent in it are not out of tune with political needs in the country. In short, the emphasis has not been on complete equalization, but rather on giving the Malays and the non-Malays an approximation of what they expect.

The establishment of Islam as the State religion, the preservation of the special position of the Malays, and the refusal to permit the use of Chinese and Indian languages in the Legislative Council, have definitely helped to preserve the Malay identity of the State. This has satisfied the Malays. At the same time, the non-Malay communities have not been really offended: despite opposition from certain Chinese quarters, the citizenship regulations, for example, do not give the Malays any permanent advantage. Neither does the preservation of the special position of the Malay community (and, for that matter, the establishment of Islam as the State religion, and the refusal to accept multi-lingualism) really undermine the 'legitimate interests' of the non-Malays.[75] Finally, the Rulers have been given their due: in addition to maintaining their traditional positions, they have also been given residual powers—and this despite the Alliance's request to the contrary.[76]

75. It is, however, vital that the 'special position' of the Malays be interpreted judiciously. Promotions in the Government services, for example, should continue to be based on seniority and qualifications; otherwise non-Malay Government servants are bound to get somewhat disaffected.

76. The granting of residual powers to the Sultans is actually of little practical consequence, since the elaborate enumeration of Federal and State powers, and the unqualified generality of some of the former, reduces the possibility of residual legislation to a minimum.

The most significant aspect of the present Constitution probably lies in the degree to which it regulates plural democracy,[77] so as to ensure that the ultimate values of political democracy are not endangered. In this respect, despite the preservation of certain special rights for the Malays, no visible efforts have been made permanently to foster the interests of one community alone. This means that the demands of plural democracy have not been given any unconditional precedence. The general character of the Constitution appears to indicate an effort ultimately to link the demands of plural democracy with those of political democracy, in the sense that provisions have been made to ensure that the latter would be accepted in its full form only when its acceptance would not endanger the needs of the former.

It may be argued that the establishment of Islam as the State religion is contrary to the demands of political democracy in a society where only about 50 per cent of the population belongs to the Muslim faith. This may be true in terms of a purely theoretical interpretation of democratic ideals, but practical considerations should not be completely overlooked. For all intents and purposes, the provision in question is indeed innocuous. The position of other faiths has not been really affected, and religious qualifications have not been given any political significance. The recognition of Malay as the national language may be defended on somewhat similar grounds. The need for an official language cannot be disputed, and there can be little doubt that Malay has a far superior claim in this respect than any other language. No doubt there may be a case for multi-lingualism, but democracy does not necessarily have to imply a complete disregard for traditional claims.[78] As far as the dictates of democracy are in question, the important thing is that everyone is given the

77. The term 'plural democracy' is used here to mean a system which, while allowing for popular participation in politics, nevertheless recognizes each communal group as a distinct entity, and thereby provides certain privileges and guarantees in the interests of maintaining some balance.

'Political democracy', on the other hand, makes no such provisions and ignores the presence of communal divisions by placing everyone on an equal footing.

78. It should also be noted that multi-lingual government could lead to a host of complications and unnecessary expenditure, and would only perpetuate the cultural diversities within the Malayan society.

opportunity, and the encouragement, to learn the Malay language.[79]

Reactions to the new Constitution were, once again, somewhat mixed. In commenting on the document the *Straits Times* of 12 July stated: 'It is a workable constitution, the best that honest patience and goodwill could devise. It draws its essential strength from the unity of the Alliance partners whose memorandum became the broad basis of the Reid Commission's proposals. The agreement on citizenship is the main pillar, buttressed by democratic institutions which can make Malaya the envy of her neighbours.'[80] While this might largely be true, there was nevertheless a certain amount of opposition from the more communally-oriented quarters both among the Malays and the non-Malays. While the former insisted that independence, by forcing the Malays to fend for themselves, should be accompanied by more substantial safeguards for their community, the latter (as represented by the Chinese Guilds and Chambers of Commerce in particular) interpreted independence as implying a 'clean start', whereby all priorities had to be terminated. The arguments put forward by the spokesmen of the latter group centred around four major claims: citizenship by birth; equality of all citizens; a multi-lingual Legislative Council; and the easing of residential requirements for those wishing to become citizens by registration.

The Alliance, however, remained united. With the exception of the speech made by Mr. S. M. Yong (who, referring to a press headline: 'Alliance told: Don't Argue', said that he was ready to 'argue and take the consequences', and went on to champion the claims of the Chinese Guilds), the opinions expressed in the Legislative Council when it met to debate the Constitutional Proposals clearly indicated a well-disciplined party bloc. Speaker after speaker explained that no constitution could satisfy all sections of the population, and that no constitution could provide absolute safeguards. Said Mr. Tan Siew Sin: 'The draft Constitution has not satisfied any community completely. No single community has obtained all that it has asked for or what it thinks it should get . . . but at the same time I humbly suggest that no

79. The continued recognition of English as an official language is undoubtedly of great help to the non-Malay communities. It is to be hoped that the use of this language is maintained until such time as Malay can be used exclusively without implying a lowering of educational standards.

80. *Straits Budget*, 18 July 1957, p. 3.

community will be adversely affected by this Constitution or by its implementation.'[81] Speaking on behalf of the Settlement Chinese, the representative for Penang made a complementary statement when he observed: '. . . if we understand that what we want must be measured in terms of what other people want, I think there is a great future for this country.'[82]

There was, however, an unhealthy aspect to the unity which seemed so evident during the debates. Only too frequently was the plea heard that the Bill should be passed at all costs since the fate of *Merdeka* depended on it and since there were adequate provisions for amendments later. In short, acceptance without approval was requested of those who were not satisfied with the proposals; at the same time, an effort was made to convince the unconvinced that 'things were bound to work out'. As far as the intra-party discussions of the Alliance[83] were concerned, it seems likely that agreement was often reached in the interests of convenience. Present disagreements within the party (which will be discussed in the chapter on *Party Politics*) give some indication of this.

81. Federation of Malaya, Legislative Council, *Official Report of the Second Legislative Council* (for the period October 1956 to August 1957), col. 2868.
82. Ibid., col. 2972.
83. It should be remembered that all major issues were thrashed out within the party before an official stand was taken.

## CHAPTER THREE

# CITIZENSHIP

IN discussing citizenship legislation in the Federation of Malaya, it is important to bear in mind that this legislation has had to be designed to serve two purposes: legal and socio-political. In the first place, it has been found necessary to define the country's own nationals; as stated by one authority, 'Federal citizenship was an attempt to narrow down the Malayan population to a specific Malayan political community.'[1] Secondly, it has been hoped that this definition would lead to the emergence of a united and well-integrated Malayan society, in which communal sympathies would be replaced by a rising national spirit. The full significance of these two purposes can be understood only when one recognizes that the most urgent political consideration in the country for the best part of the last two decades has been the need for some device which can stimulate a common Malayan consciousness and the concept of a Malayan nation.

The realization of these aims, however, has been complicated by a host of factors. Most important of these is the fact that, while the desired emergence of a common political community has called for a certain liberalization of citizenship qualifications so that all the communities are given an equal opportunity to find their common Malayan identity, there has been no guarantee that the basis of political power would become effectively decommunalized in the event of such liberalization. In other words, while liberal citizenship regulations might very well create an enlarged Malayan community with loyalty focused on the Federation of Malaya rather than, say, China or India, the emergence of such a community does not necessarily presuppose a corresponding trend towards non-communal politics within the country.[2] However, although a common basis of eligibility for citizenship does not guarantee the immediate birth of non-communal politics, it is an

1. F. G. Carnell, 'Malayan Citizenship Legislation', Oxford University, Institute of Colonial Studies, Reprint Series No. 7, p. 517 (reprinted from the *International and Comparative Law Quarterly*, October 1952).
2. In the case of the Malays, for example, liberalization could very well provide the motive for increasing and sustaining communal solidarity.

undoubted prerequisite for the eventual demise of communalism as a compelling political force.

The difficulties surrounding citizenship legislation arise from a conflict between Malay and non-Malay interests. The former are reluctant to dilute their political identity in a common 'Malayan' fold, and fear the implications of placing the Chinese and the Indians on an equal footing with themselves. The non-Malays, on the other hand, remain convinced that they should be given an equal share in the country's political life. A more detailed study of the arguments put forward by the two groups will perhaps produce a better understanding of the issue.

The Malays fully realize that, in a truly 'Malayan' society, the word 'Malay' will have to become politically irrelevant. Already their main grievance is that their status has fallen from that of a nation to that of a mere community. The liberalizing trend in citizenship has produced two fears in their minds. First, they still have very strong doubts regarding the professed loyalty of the non-Malay communities; for this reason they consider liberalization to be a political risk of the first magnitude. Secondly, they realize that since the non-Malays are now admitted to citizenship on a large scale, their own community will, as a matter of course, have to relinquish gradually all the privileges which it has hitherto enjoyed.

Thus the Malays have tended to emphasize that citizenship qualifications should never be more liberal than is necessary to guarantee a person's assimilation to the country's way of life, meaning, more specifically, his familiarity with and sympathy for Malay culture—language in particular—and his undivided loyalty towards the Malayan nation. Some of the practical considerations underlying this attitude have already been discussed in the previous chapter.

It may be added here that, to the Malays, the acceptance of citizenship as a mark of assimilation is vital in the sense that, while admitting only the 'desirable' elements into the legally defined 'Malayan' fold, such a policy would also greatly enhance the prestige of their own cultural traditions. If assimilation were accepted as the essential citizenship qualification, this would not only strengthen the emergence of a common nationality, but would also serve progressively to weaken all opposition to the continued preservation of the Malay character of the country. Such considerations are only to be expected from the Malays, since it is quite natural for any distinct indigenous group, especially when it finds itself a numerical minority living with other distinct groups, to desire that every form of political change should carry with it conditions which confirm its own position of superiority.

While it may be possible to generalize about the Malays and say that, as a community, they resent some of the claims made by the non-Malays (such as the demand that Chinese be established as an official language), it should not be overlooked that many of the community's leaders have a keen understanding of political possibilities and recognize that practical considerations require a broad base for the Malayan political community, embracing Malays and non-Malays alike. It is only the more traditional Malay nationalist who still maintains that the Malay community and the Malayan political community should broadly be one and the same. Ignoring some of the realities of politics in a plural context, he has a simple and straightforward explanation for his attitude: politically he finds in the non-Malays a strong threat to his own privileged position; economically he finds them prospering in his own country while his people lag behind; and culturally he finds them largely unassimilated. He is yet to be convinced that the non-Malay settlers are not aliens in the full sense of the term.

The non-Malays, on the other hand, maintain that the traditional claims of the Malay community are both irrelevant and obstructive in the modern context. Their arguments have mainly revolved around the demand for *jus soli*, that every person born in the country should be made a citizen by operation of law.[3]

Besides making this claim, the non-Malays (particularly the Chinese) have also tended to emphasize certain practical considerations such as their economic and numerical strength which, in their opinion, necessitate their unrestricted acceptance as Federal citizens. In countering the Malay assertion that the non-Malay communities have not generally shown an allegiance sufficiently strong to warrant an unreserved grant of citizenship privileges, they point out that it is difficult for them to exhibit the faith worthy

3. As mentioned in the last chapter, this principle (*jus soli*) was recognized by the Malayan Union proposals but withdrawn when the scheme was replaced by the Federation Agreement of 1948. Since that date, however, the non-Malays have, in progressive measures, received concessions in the same direction, culminating in the recognition of *jus soli* (but not retrospectively) in the 1957 Constitution.

of citizens as long as the Malays continue to regard them as aliens. Indicative of this attitude are the words of Dato' Sir Cheng-lock Tan, the most prominent Chinese leader to date, who, in criticizing the provisions of the 1948 Agreement, observed:

The only way to cure the China-born Chinese of their obsession with Chinese national politics is to make them a generous offer (as was done under the original Malayan Union Scheme) of Malayan citizenship, which alone can reconcile them to their loss of interest or participation in Chinese politics. The best method of detaching the affections of an immigrant population from the country of its origin is to afford adequate facilities for the transfer of such affections to the land of its adoption. As long as an immigrant population is treated as alien, for so long will it necessarily turn towards its motherland and thus constitute a potential danger to the land in which it is permanently settled.[4]

While admitting that there may be some truth in the above argument, it cannot be denied that the writer is guilty of over-simplification. To begin with, where a non-indigenous population is substantial (particularly where, as in Malaya, it constitutes a numerical majority), loyalty to the country of adoption cannot be easily aroused by the mere granting of citizenship rights. This is particularly so when, encouraged by the comfort of numbers, such non-indigenous sections possess ample facilities to perpetuate their own ways of life and to foster their own interests while overtly professing an attachment to the country of adoption. Under these circumstances, the indigenous population would be justified in maintaining that citizenship rights, if given too freely, might not inspire the definite feeling of affinity which a citizen is expected to have towards the State to which he belongs.

In so far as the Federation of Malaya is concerned, this attitude among the Malays is made particularly relevant by the fact that a substantial portion of the immigrant population considers its own culture, economic status, and general capacity for progress to be superior to those of the Malays. Thus, if respect for the way of life to be adopted is taken as a factor which encourages assimilation, one can understand why the Malays have had difficulty in setting a common pattern for all to follow. This, no doubt, has put them on their guard. While the non-Malays might love Malaya enough to make it their permanent home, it is also possible that, given the opportunity, they might very well establish a political and

4. Institute of Pacific Relations, *Three Reports on the Malayan Problem*, p. 19.

cultural order which is aimed primarily at serving their own interests.

The citizenship issue in the Federation raises three vital questions, which may be found relevant wherever social plurality has a direct bearing on the political process.

To begin with, the question arises whether citizenship is an inducement to, or a recognition of, assimilation and loyalty. In its usual interpretation, the term appears to signify the latter more than it does the former. Given a commonly accepted social and political context, citizenship, besides granting privileges and imposing duties, also assumes the role of a classifying agent: it 'places' a person according to where he belongs. If this is to be accepted as the general rule, citizenship can only be taken as a form of recognition since it is imperative that, for a person to be 'classified', he will first of all have to be identified, and identification must necessarily imply the recognition of certain qualities and attributes. The application of this principle (that is, of interpreting citizenship as a form of recognition) is fairly simple in relatively homogeneous societies where assimilation takes place almost as a matter of course, without the need for any inducements.[5]

In non-homogeneous societies with sizeable immigrant communities, it may be found that groups of people have to be induced to abandon their own ways of life and follow those of the country of their adoption. This is precisely the case in the Federation of Malaya. As mentioned a little earlier, it has been suggested that one of the most effective ways of solving the problem would be to cease treating these groups as alien and to accept them into a common fold through a generous grant of citizenship rights. It is possible that the Chinese in Malaya have for some time felt that they were not accepted as belonging to the country, and hence did not feel any obligation to adapt themselves to local conditions. But one can also understand the reluctance of the Malays to use citizenship as a means of inducing the others to become locally-oriented, since the numbers of non-Malays involved have been so large as to make the element of risk almost overwhelming.[6] The

5. In certain cases the principle can also be applied in the absence of social homogeneity, but only when the different cultures involved are mutually acceptable. Canada is a case in point.

6. Furthermore, the Malays have never believed—nor have they had any reason for believing—that the non-Malays would completely cease to be parochial if they were given the opportunity to become citizens.

Malays might have been persuaded to use citizenship as an inducement had the non-Malays formed only a small minority, for in that case not only would the consequences of failure have been small enough not to act as a deterrent, but the chances of success would also have been much greater.

The second question pertains to the principle of *jus soli*: should the policy of granting citizenship by birth be resolutely adhered to regardless of all considerations? As might be expected, the Malays and the non-Malays hold different views on this subject. While the former maintain that birth in a country is irrelevant as a citizenship qualification when it does not signify acceptance of a common society, the latter have tended to argue that it is indeed difficult for them to fit into a common fold as long as the fact of their not being Malays continues to be a basis for discriminatory treatment. To accusations of cultural parochialism the non-Malays answer that, in the first place, they have not been provided with the facilities to learn the Malay language and, in the second, that the sheer fact of physical separation has prevented them from establishing any appreciable social intercourse with the Malays. Thus they argue that their non-assimilation indicates neither an indifferent nor a defiant attitude towards the culture of the Malays.[7]

Finally, certain considerations arise as to the general nature of the relations between the majority and the minority or minorities in a country. In this respect, it will first of all have to be remembered that the Federation of Malaya is a somewhat unusual type of plural society in that no community is in an overall majority. The Malays are, however, the people of the country while the others are mostly recent settlers. Since they also constitute the most numerous group, the Malays have naturally come to assume a position of priority in political affairs. While due consideration will have to be given to the claims of the non-Malay communities (particularly in view of their economic and numerical strength and also because they now claim to have made Malaya their permanent home), it will also have to be realized that, in being preoccupied with the legitimacy of their own claims, the non-Malays might very well overlook some of the more justifiable

7. It should be explained that the word 'culture' as used here refers almost entirely to language, since the Malays do not expect others to change their religions or even most of their social customs.

claims of the Malay community. It is important that the Chinese and the Indians, in campaigning for their own rights, should continue to be aware of the obligations which they, as settlers, have towards the Malays.[8]

With these considerations in mind, an effort will now be made to analyse, in chronological order, the evolution of citizenship in the Federation of Malaya.

Prior to the Second World War there was no such thing as Malayan citizenship, simply because a Malayan State did not exist. As mentioned earlier, there was not even any administrative unity in the country, the Settlements of Singapore, Penang, and Malacca being the only territories where the British had direct jurisdiction. Those born in the Straits Settlements were thus automatically British subjects, while those born in the Malay States (which were only protected states and not colonies) did not acquire any common citizenship. Thus, apart from Europeans, the only British subjects in the States were either those who had been born in the Settlements and had later migrated to the Malay States, or immigrant Indians and Ceylonese. The Malays and locally-born Chinese were subjects of the Rulers.[9] It is thus clear that pre-war 'British Malaya' was little more than a geographical expression. The absence of a common national identity was emphasized by the presence not only of a 'mosaic of nationalities' but of a 'mosaic of governments' as well.[10] The only form of co-ordination was that

8. Of some relevance here are the words of E. Benes, who, in discussing the problem of majority-minority relations in their European context, observed: 'Before we begin to define the rights of minorities we must define the rights of majorities and the obligations of minorities.' ('The Organization of Postwar Europe', *Foreign Affairs*, Vol. XX, October 1941 to July 1942, p. 237.)

Although the problem in Malaya is not, strictly speaking, one of majority-minority relations, the spirit of the above remark is nevertheless very appropriate.

9. This local status of all Chinese born in the Malay States was recognized by a decision of the F.M.S. Supreme Court, and upheld by the Court of Appeal, in the case of *Ho Chik Kwan v. The British Resident, Selangor*, where it was maintained that a Chinese born and resident in a Malay State 'according to the general principle of international law became a natural born subject of the Ruler of that State'. It was by reason of this fact that local-born Chinese became classified as British protected persons together with the Malays.

Despite their local nationality, the Chinese continued to remain nationals of China since that country claimed them as its own nationals by *jus sanguinis*, and since the Malay States did not require their nationals to denounce any other national status. (F. G. Carnell, op. cit., p. 510.)

10. Ibid., p. 505.

signified by the office of the Governor of the Straits Settlements, who was also the High Commissioner of the Malay States.

The legal acceptance of locally-born non-Malays as State subjects did not carry with it any rights or privileges; nor did it confer any real political status. There was no such thing as representative government, and the principle of Malay paramountcy was formally declared by the British in 1927. The mass of the non-Malays, however, were quite satisfied to leave this principle unchallenged, and two reasons may be given for their acquiescence. In the first place, the executive power in the Malay States actually rested in the hands of the British and the professed principle of Malay dominance was really of little practical consequence. Secondly, as stated earlier, the non-Malay population was largely transient in character; citizenship privileges and participation in government were consequently not regarded as being of any urgent importance. The Malays, for their part, were quite content to remain subjects of their respective Rulers, and did not generally express any desire for the creation of a common nationality.

Briefly, this was the situation at the outbreak of the Second World War. The effects of the occupation on the political aspirations of the population have already been discussed, and so have the basic features of the Malayan Union scheme. Thus it is now possible to proceed directly to a detailed analysis of Malayan Union citizenship.

### *Malayan Union Citizenship*

The Malayan Union proposals conferred citizenship on the following:

(a) any person born in the Malayan Union or Singapore before the date when the Order came into force, who was ordinarily resident in either of the two areas on that date;

(b) any person, at least 18 years of age, who was ordinarily resident in the Malayan Union or Singapore on the date when the Order came into force, and who had resided in either territory for a minimum of 10 out of the 15 years preceding the 15th of February, 1942;[11]

11. Such persons had to take an oath of allegiance, stating that they would be faithful and loyal to the Union.

(c) any person born either in the Malayan Union or Singapore on or after the day when the Order came into force;

(d) any person born outside the Malayan Union or Singapore on or after the day when the Order came into force, whose father was a citizen of the Malayan Union at the time of that person's birth; and

(e) the minor children (children under 18 years of age) of persons classified under categories (a) and (b).[12]

In order to be naturalized as a citizen of the Malayan Union, a person

(i) had to have resided in the Malayan Union or Singapore during the year preceding the date of application, and for 4 out of the 8 years preceding that date;

(ii) had to give evidence of good character, and have an adequate knowledge of either Malay or English; and

(iii) had to take an oath of allegiance to the Malayan Union and indicate an intention to reside either in the Malayan Union or Singapore if the application were granted.[13]

The two most outstanding features of the new proposals were the absence of any distinction between Malays and non-Malays and the fact that citizenship qualifications were not in any way affected by the separation of Singapore from the mainland.

The best way of assessing the true significance of the above provisions would be to look at the relevant features of the country's population at the time.

In 1947, 62·5 per cent of the Chinese and 49·8 per cent of the Indian population in Malaya (including Singapore) were locally born.[14] This means that approximately the same percentages of these two communities were eligible to become citizens by operation of law under provision (a) mentioned above. At the same time, it was also found that 21·3 per cent of the Chinese community and 25·5 per cent of the Indian had arrived in Malaya either in 1930 or at some time previous to that date.[15] Assuming that almost all the persons in this category were at least eighteen years

12. Great Britain, Colonial Office, *Malayan Union and Singapore—Summary of Proposed Constitutional Arrangements*, 1946, Cmd. 6749, pp. 9–10.
13. Ibid., p. 9.
14. M. V. del Tufo, *A Report on the 1947 Census of Population*, pp. 84 and 85.
15. Ibid., p. 89.

of age in 1946,[16] this would mean that about 21 per cent of the Chinese and 25 per cent of the Indian community would have become citizens by operation of law under provision (b); thus roughly 83 per cent of the Chinese and 75 per cent of the Indians would have become citizens under provisions (a) and (b).[17] These are indeed large figures and, as stated by one writer, a vital outcome of the implementation of the new scheme would have been that: 'for the few thousands whose claims to greater political privileges could hardly be denied there were hundreds of thousands whose claim would have failed under the test of allegiance or even interest, and a similar number would not [have been] concerned to make any claim at all'.[18]

The roots of Malay apprehension now become clear: the non-Malays, having had little if any political authority before the War, were now to be made as much the masters of the country as the Malays themselves. Perhaps the only recognition given to Malay priority lay in the provisions governing citizenship by naturalization, where an 'adequate' knowledge of either Malay or English was required. This may well have appeared somewhat irrelevant and even farcical to the Malays since a large proportion of the non-Malays who were now entitled to become citizens by operation of law were not in fact adequately proficient in either language. Thus, to the Malay community, the new constitutional proposals represented a rejection of the hitherto accepted principle that Malaya was essentially a Malay country.

### *Citizenship under The Federation of Malaya Agreement, 1948*

The 1948 citizenship laws were largely based on the recommendations of the Working Committee. For this reason, it will be well worth considering the main features of these recommendations, the possible motives behind them, and the reactions which followed their publication.

The Working Committee recommended that two categories of persons be admitted to citizenship: those who would become citi-

16. After all, even a new-born child arriving as late as 1928 would have attained the right age.
17. It is possible that some of those who had arrived before 1930 might not have resided in Malaya for the required ten years prior to 1942; but since even some of those who had arrived between 1930 and 1932 might have qualified under provision (b), the figures given may be considered fairly accurate.
18. S. W. Jones, *Public Administration in Malaya*, p. 138.

zens by operation of law and those who could acquire citizenship by application. The following persons were to fall in the first category:

(a) any subject, whenever born, of His Highness the Ruler of any State;

(b) any British subject born in either of the Settlements (that is Penang and Malacca) and permanently resident in either of those territories;

(c) any British subject born in any of the territories to be comprised in the Federation whose father, either

(i) was himself born in any of these territories; or

(ii) had resided in any such territories for a continuous period of at least 15 years;

(d) any person, born in any of the territories to be comprised in the Federation, both of whose parents had been born in any of such territories and had resided therein for a continuous period of at least 15 years; and

(e) any person whose father was, at the time of that person's birth, himself a Federal citizen.[19]

A person was eligible to become a citizen by application if he satisfied the High Commissioner

(a) that either

(i) he was born in any of the territories to be comprised in the Federation and had been resident in any one or more of such territories for at least 10 out of the 15 years preceding the date of his application; or

(ii) he had been resident in any one or more of such territories for at least 15 out of the 20 years immediately preceding that date;

(b) that he was of good character;

(c) that he had an adequate knowledge of either Malay or English;[20]

19. Malayan Union, *Constitutional Proposals for Malaya: Report of the Working Committee Appointed by a Conference of His Excellency the Governor of the Malayan Union, Their Highnesses the Rulers of the Malay States and the representatives of the United Malays' National Organization*, 1946, p. 66 (Article 128 of 'Draft Federation Agreement').

20. 'Adequate knowledge' of the Malay language was to mean:

(i) 'in the case of a person who applies for Federal citizenship within a period of two years from the commencement of this Agreement, ability to speak that language with reasonable proficiency; and

(ii) in the case of any other person, ability to speak that language and, unless prevented by blindness or other physical cause, read and write it, in the Jawi or Rumi script, with reasonable proficiency'.

(d) that he had made a declaration of permanent settlement; and

(e) that he would be willing to take an oath of allegiance to the Federation if his application were approved.[21]

Four important features stand out in the Working Committee's recommendations. Foremost among these is the reversion to the pre-war policy of recognizing Malaya as primarily a Malay country. Saying that the Malays, who were the indigenous people, would steadily become submerged by the other communities unless the granting of citizenship was confined to those who regarded Malaya as their only homeland, the Committee declared:

The Malays live in a country in which they, owing to the influx of foreign immigrants, are already numerically inferior. It is important to emphasize that the Malays have no alternative homeland, whilst the remainder of the population, with few exceptions, retain in varying degrees a connection with their country of origin, and, in very many cases, regard that country and not Malaya as the primary object of their loyalty and affection. In these circumstances, the insistence by the Malay members of the Committee on a strict interpretation of the Secretary of State's statement that citizenship should be extended only to those who 'regard Malaya as their real home and as the object of their loyalty' was considered by the Committee as a whole to be justified.[22]

The second important feature lies in the meaning which was given to citizenship. The Report said:

Before proceeding to the detailed consideration of the various categories of persons who should be included as citizens, the Committee wished to have clearly before it the meaning of 'citizenship' and its implications. It was explained that it was not a nationality, neither could it develop into a nationality. It would not affect or impair, in any respect whatever, the status of British subjects in the Settlements or the status of subjects of Rulers in the Malay States. It is an addition to, and not a subtraction from, nationality and could be a qualification for electoral rights, for membership of Councils and for employment in Government service, and it could confer other privileges and impose obligations.[23]

By not creating a nationality, the proposed citizenship law partly ignored the desirability of encouraging a Malayan-consciousness. A Chinese, for example, could acquire Federal citizenship and at

21. Loc. cit. 22. Ibid., p. 23. 23. Loc. cit.

the same time continue to remain a national of China. The Malay was to continue being a subject of the Ruler of his State.

Although British subjects and subjects of Their Highnesses the Rulers were to retain their own status while acquiring the additional benefits of Federal citizenship, it was also provided that, in the case of the latter, only Malays would be given automatic Federal citizenship.[24] In other words, while a non-Malay could be a subject of the Ruler of his State under the Constitution of that State, he was not regarded as one for the purposes of Federal citizenship.

This introduces the third important feature of the Working Committee's recommendations, namely the definition of the subject of a Ruler. The expression 'subject of His Highness the Ruler of any State', as used in sub-clause (a) of the clause dealing with citizenship by operation of law, was to mean any person who

(i) belonged to an aboriginal tribe resident in that State;

(ii) was a Malay born in that State or born outside the Malay States of a father who, at the time of that person's birth, was a subject of the Ruler of that State; or

(iii) was naturalized as a subject of the Ruler of that State under any law for the time being in force.[25]

In the above context the word 'Malay' was to refer to a person who

(i) habitually spoke the Malay language;

(ii) professed the Muslim religion; and

(iii) conformed to Malay custom.[26]

Thus a 'subject of His Highness the Ruler of any State' and a 'Malay' were defined for purposes of citizenship, and the restrictive definition of the former (in that non-Malays were excluded) was to be valid only for purposes of Federal citizenship.

The definition of a 'Malay' for constitutional purposes deserves closer attention. Such a definition was made necessary once it was decided that only Malays could become Federal citizens automatically by virtue of being subjects of Their Highnesses the Rulers.[27]

24. This refers to sub-clause (a) mentioned on p. 76.

25. *Report of the Working Committee*, op. cit., p. 66, 'Draft Federation Agreement', Article 128, Clause (3) (a).

26. Ibid., p. 67, and ibid., Article 128, Clause (3) (b).

27. Thus the initial purpose of the definition was to disqualify the vast majority of the Chinese and Indians in the country.

By defining a 'Malay' in the terms mentioned above, all emphasis was placed on cultural rather than on ethnic or political attributes.[28] Broadly speaking, the definition arrived at might have been the result of two important considerations. First, by identifying a Malay purely by his cultural characteristics, it was possible to make automatic citizenship available to Indonesians (being culturally akin to the Malays) who were born in the country, without doing the same for the Chinese and the Indians. As already stated, it must be admitted that, from a purely legal standpoint, Indonesians are also 'aliens' like the Chinese and Indians. By defining a 'Malay' purely in cultural terms, however, a sieve was devised to separate the former from the two latter for purposes of Malayan citizenship. Thus the definition must have been partly aimed at increasing the Malaysian proportion of the citizenry; it was no doubt realized that the more Indonesians there were who became citizens of the Federation, the smaller would be the possibility of the Malays being politically swamped by the Chinese and Indians.

Secondly, the definition may be interpreted as being indicative of an outright assimilationist policy on the part of the Malays.[29] By using their 'voluntary' characteristics[30] as the basis of discrimination, the Malays may be considered to have entertained the hope that in the long run the non-Malays might be induced to become assimilated. In other words, by not accepting the principle of *jus soli* in the case of the non-Malays and by emphasizing the cultural attributes of the Malay community (and, at the same time, by making citizenship by application difficult), the draft proposals no doubt indicated the desire, on the part of the Working Committee, to ensure that the Malayan political community reflected a cultural homogeneity based on Malay characteristics.

The fourth important feature of the draft proposals is that birth and residence in Singapore were no longer accepted as being relevant as far as eligibility for citizenship on the mainland was

28. 'Political attributes' in the sense of differentiation between indigenous Malays and those with foreign roots, e.g. Indonesians.

29. Since, however, adherence to Islam was included as one of the qualifications, the possibility of assimilation (especially within any reasonable period of time) could not have been seriously contemplated.

30. 'Voluntary' in the sense that they can be acquired. 'Involuntary' characteristics (such as race, colour, and so on), on the other hand, cannot easily be used as a basis for assimilation since they prove to be far more enduring than the former.

concerned. This must have been intended to restrict the numerical strength of non-Malay citizens, both at that time as well as in the future.

The Report of the Working Committee was severely criticized by the non-Malay communities. The general line of complaint appeared to be that 'If the claims of the domiciled communities to citizenship are viewed in a way which would regard them as a nuisance and as interlopers, no useful purpose can be served by these attempts at constitution-making.'[31] In addition to criticizing the stringent regulations proposed in the Report, the non-Malays also failed to see why a Chinese (for example) born in either of the Settlements should be treated differently from another born in the States.[32] This complaint was made in many of the letters later submitted by Chinese to the Consultative Committee. Furthermore, while recognizing that there was nothing 'unholy' about the Malay insistence on 'real loyalty', they were of the opinion that the new proposals did not in any way encourage the emergence of such a loyalty among the non-Malays. The Secretary of the Pan-Malayan Council of Joint Action said:

> Nothing is to be gained by cold-shouldering of the non-Malay races; there is everything to be lost by it. The most important political task in Malaya is to create a real and valid sense of loyalty to Malaya among all races, by inspiring in the Malay a national loyalty over and above his natural loyalty to the Sultans as symbols of his racial history and traditions, and educating him to an adult understanding of his place as a Malayan; and by weaning the non-Malay races from their nostalgia for the homelands of their ancestors, by putting into their hands the real basis of an enduring loyalty.[33]

31. Federation of Malaya, *Constitutional Proposals for Malaya: Report of the Consultative Committee together with Proceedings of Six Public Meetings, Summary of Representations Made and Letters and Recommendations Considered by the Committee*, 1947, p. 114 (from the memorandum submitted by the Indian Association, Trengganu).
32. It will be remembered that any person born in either of the Settlements and permanently resident there was made a citizen by operation of law, while a Chinese born in one of the States could become a citizen only if both his parents had been born in any of such territories and had been resident therein for a continuous period of fifteen years. It is possible that the provision was included at the insistence of the British authorities who wanted to enhance the status of their own subjects. Malay acceptance of this provision must have been influenced by the consideration that only a limited number of Chinese would have been helped to qualify.
33. *Straits Budget*, 15 August 1946.

Another critic warned:

The Malayan Union . . . may be shortly replaced by the Malayan Federation plan sponsored by the Malay privileged classes and reactionary interests. Unless drastic changes are introduced into the latter plan, the effect will be to perpetuate the era of political tutelage which Malays and non-Malays alike have outgrown. The domiciled races will labour under a keen sense of injustice and frustration which augurs ill for their future co-operation in the development of Malaya.[34]

The Malays, for their part, were convinced that there was nothing unreasonable in their wanting to safeguard their own interests before meeting the demands of the others. They considered it foolhardy to treat the non-Malays as equals, if such treatment threatened to jeopardize their own position. Basically, it must be admitted that the Malays did, in fact, regard the Chinese and the Indians 'as a nuisance and as interlopers'. Indeed, one Malay organization went so far as to suggest that not only should 'Citizenship for the aliens except for the Indonesian Malays . . . be limited', but that 'The number of the aliens who may be granted citizenship in the Federation should be limited and should not be more than one quarter of the Malay population in the Federation. . . .'[35] The organization also suggested that, in the case of Malay immigrants, citizenship should be granted 'straightaway', regardless of their country of origin.[36]

The final proposals,[37] as embodied in the Federation of Malaya Agreement of 1948, contained two significant amendments to the recommendations of the Working Committee. First, it was decided that in the case of British subjects born in either of the two Settlements, permanent residence in any of the territories comprising the Federation was sufficient, instead of residence in the Settlements alone, as had been suggested by the Working

34. Tan Cheng Lock, *Malayan Problems*, p. iii (Foreword, by C. Q. Lee).

35. Report of the Consultative Committee, op. cit., p. 89 (from the memorandum submitted by the *Persatuan Melayu*, Ulu Trengganu).

36. Loc. cit.

37. While they were largely based on the draft submitted by the Working Committee, the final proposals also took into consideration the recommendations of the Consultative Committee, representing non-Malay opinion.

Although the majority view of the Consultative Committee accepted the Working Committee's proposals on citizenship by operation of law, its two Chinese members (The Honble. Col. H. S. Lee and Mr. Leong Yew Koh) maintained that all those who were either British subjects or were born in any of the Malay States should be made citizens automatically, if they were permanently resident in the Federation.

Committee. This provision no doubt helped to increase the number of non-Malays eligible to become citizens by operation of law. The 1947 census shows that, of a total of 184,114 Chinese who were born in Penang, 17,694 were enumerated outside the Straits Settlements. The figures in the case of Malacca were 6,358 out of 65,985.[38]

The second significant amendment involved the addition of a new sub-clause. It was now provided that automatic citizenship would also be conferred on 'any person born before, on or after the appointed day in any of the territories now to be comprised in the Federation who habitually [spoke] the Malay language and [conformed] to Malay custom'.[39] Since the definitions of a 'subject of His Highness the Ruler of any State' and a 'Malay', as recommended in the Working Committee's draft proposals, were left unchanged, it might be assumed that this new sub-clause was intended primarily for those non-Malays who, without becoming Muslims (in which case they would have been eligible to become classified as 'Malays'), had become assimilated into the Malay way of life. The number of non-Malays who would have been helped by this sub-clause (in other words, who would have qualified to become citizens only under this category) could not have been very substantial, since most of those affected would, in fact, have qualified under different sections. Most of the Straits Chinese, for example, would have qualified by virtue of being British subjects since they mostly belong to Penang and Malacca. However, the provision is significant in that it represents a definite inducement for the non-Malays to become assimilated into the Malay way of life.[40]

In so far as citizenship by application was concerned, the residence qualification was reduced to eight out of twelve years in the case of those born in the country;[41] for those born outside, it was decided not to alter the Working Committee's recommendation

38. Figures derived from information given in the *1947 Census Report*, pp. 88–89.

39. *Federation of Malaya Agreement*, 1948, Article 124, Clause (d).

40. Despite the motives which seem clear, this sub-clause is rather vague and its interpretation and application could not have been precise. The question is: what is Malay custom and how is one to prove that one conforms to it? The matter is further complicated by the fact that adherence to Islam would appear to be necessary if one is really to conform to 'Malay custom', since religion is a vital part of the Malay way of life.

41. It will be remembered that the Working Committee recommended ten out of fifteen years. The Consultative Committee, on the other hand, had recommended five out of ten.

of fifteen out of twenty years.[42] It was decided that the language test would be waived in the case of applicants who were over forty-five years of age and who had resided in the country for more than twenty years.[43]

The new scheme clearly preserved the pro-Malay tone set by the Working Committee. However, while non-Malays complained of being ignored and 'cold-shouldered', certain Malays still felt that the regulations governing the eligibility of non-Malays to become citizens were not sufficiently stringent.

Regardless of these complaints, and from a strictly non-partisan point of view, the new scheme may be criticized for one major shortcoming—the failure to create a nationality. The major problem in post-war Malaya (and this would be relevant in any plural society where there are immigrant communities) has been to convince the non-Malay communities that they have more in common with the Malays and with each other than with members of their own race either living in their motherlands, or coming in as immigrants. In this respect, it cannot be denied that the creation of a common local nationality could have been one of the ways in which the non-Malays might have been induced to weaken the links with their motherlands. Since Federal citizenship was not meant to be a nationality, non-Malay Federal citizens were not required to renounce any foreign nationality which they might have possessed. Admittedly, had a nationality indeed been created, the results might not have been obvious soon after its creation; but, in the long run, the presence of a local nationality might have acted as one of the most important factors in encouraging loyalty.

Since the new proposals were sanctioned by the leaders of the Malay community, the decision to admit non-Malays to a common citizenship revealed a certain change in political thinking. Although the numbers of non-Malays made eligible were by no means overwhelming, it should be remembered that, before the War, the Malays would probably have refused to entertain any possibility of such a concession. Even as it was, they were by no means fully sympathetic towards the new move; but an awareness of political necessities, coupled with enlightened leadership, made the new proposals possible. Their fears were mainly motivated by

42. The Consultative Committee had recommended a period of eight out of the fifteen years immediately preceding the date of application.

43. This had been proposed by the Consultative Committee.

the fact that they still remained largely uncertain of the loyalty and aspirations of the non-Malays. Thus while the non-Malays condemned the new scheme for being unreasonably stringent, the Malays could not but fear the element of uncertainty since the citizenship door was now opened equally 'to the minority who could truthfully affirm that Malaya was their real home and the object of their loyalty and to the many who could make no such claim'.[44] There was, however, some consolation in that those who fell under the latter category were now drastically reduced in number as compared to the earlier Malayan Union proposals.

The number of persons who became citizens under the new law indicates its practical implications. According to the *Annual Report for 1950*, it was estimated that approximately 3,120,000 persons had become Federal citizens by operation of law since 1 February 1948, the date when the Federation Agreement had come into force. Of this number, about 2,500,000 were Malaysians, 350,000 Chinese, and 225,000 Indians, Pakistanis, and Ceylonese.[45] After including the number of persons who had become citizens by application,[46] it was estimated that, in round figures, the total number of Federal citizens was about 3,275,000, of which 2,500,000 were Malays, 500,000 Chinese, and 230,000 Indians, Pakistanis, and Ceylonese.[47]

In 1951, largely as a result of the efforts of the Communities Liaison Committee,[48] an Ordinance was introduced in the Legis-

44. S. W. Jones, *Public Administration in Malaya*, p. 145.
The non-Malays, however, argued that the new proposals were so stringent that many who could truthfully affirm their loyalty to Malaya were denied the privilege of becoming the country's citizens. Despite this complaint, the Malay attitude was not wholly unreasonable since, had the persons referred to been allowed to become citizens, the concession would have had to be made at the further risk of increasing the numbers of those whose loyalty might have been clearly questionable. It was simply impossible to create an acceptable common denominator which, while enabling the deserving cases to become citizens, would successfully exclude the 'undesirables'.

45. Federation of Malaya, *Annual Report, 1950*, p. 24. The total population in 1950 was estimated at 5,226,549, of which 2,579,914 were Malaysians, 2,011,072 Chinese, and 564,454 Indians and Pakistanis.

46. The regulations under which registration was to be effected did not come into force until 1 February 1949.

47. *Annual Report, 1950*, op. cit., p. 24.

48. The Communities Liaison Committee was formed in 1948 with British encouragement (and especially at the inspiration of Mr. Malcolm MacDonald, then Commissioner-General for South East Asia) for the purpose of bringing together leaders of the various communities. The Committee also represented an effort to unite anti-Communist sentiment in the country.

lative Council embodying a set of new proposals concerning the citizenship issue. As originally worded, this Ordinance did not really lend itself to satisfying the desires of the non-Malays; it merely rephrased and reaffirmed the unquestioned priority which the Malays already had. The explanation appended to the new proposals made it quite clear that assimilation would be the basic prerequisite for the acquisition of citizenship: 'It is realized that the problem cannot be solved by legislation alone for legislation alone will not assimilate people and make them into a homogeneous and happy nation. A citizen if he is to be a good citizen must be a citizen in fact and not merely a foreigner, knowing neither the languages nor the customs of the country, on whom the law has conferred the privileges of citizenship because of some technical qualification.'[49]

It was thus decided that while the principle of 'citizenship by birth' should be applied in the case of Malays born in the Malay States ('because it is reasonably certain that these will be readily assimilated to the Federation's way of life'), its application should be delayed by one generation in the case of the non-Malays, 'because the probability is that a non-Malay of the first generation of local birth will not be assimilated to the Federation's way of life'.[50] However, those first-generation non-Malays who could show that they were 'in fact sufficiently assimilated' were to be given adequate facilities for acquiring citizenship. It was thought that the proposals were fair to the Malays as well as to the non-Malays:' . . . fair to the Malays because they plan to protect them from submergence by alien ways of life, and fair to the non-Malays because they admit them to citizenship if they have sufficiently assimilated themselves to this country's way of life.'[51]

At the second reading of the Bill, the *Mentri Besar* of Selangor summarized Malay opinion on this matter when he said: 'To this gift of citizenship no unusual strings are attached. Those who qualify will gain, those who do not qualify will lose nothing that they already have. No one is worse off; many will be better off. The conditions of obtaining State nationality are not onerous and are surely a fair and reasonable guarantee that the Malays

49. *Federation of Malaya Agreement (Amendment) Ordinance, 1951*, p. 15.
50. Loc. cit.
51. Ibid., p. 16.

retain their special position. . . . A certain courtesy is due to the ground landlord.'[52] To the non-Malays, however, this assurance that 'those who [did] not qualify [would] lose nothing that they already [had]' was indeed quite irrelevant. After all, their grievance stemmed mainly from the fact that they were not satisfied with what they already had; they were more interested in improving their status than in being assured that they would not be deprived of what they already possessed. A Chinese member of the Council, Mr. Koh Sin Hock, alleged that the Federation Agreement of 1948, though itself not democratic, was more acceptable than the amendment now proposed.[53] The Chinese-owned *Singapore Standard* expressed a similar view. In an editorial entitled 'Kill This Bill', it stated that while the 1948 provisions had given the non-Malays 'the privilege of entering the hallowed ground of citizenship through the tradesmen's entrance', the new Bill, 'instead of making a change for the better . . . [made] it even more obvious that the so-called aliens occupy an inferior position in Malaya'. There was now 'no question of non-Malays being able to walk through the tradesmen's entrance'; many who could have done so now had to stay out.[54]

Faced with strong opposition, the Bill was referred for further examination to a Select Committee, whose recommendations were embodied in the Federation of Malaya Agreement (Amendment) Ordinance of 1952.

Introduced in the form of a Federal Ordinance and nine State Nationality Enactments, the new proposals created two main avenues towards citizenship: state nationality and citizenship of the United Kingdom and Colonies. While the Federal Ordinance laid down the conditions of eligibility for citizens of the United Kingdom and Colonies, the State Nationality Enactments set out the qualifications necessary for one to become the subject of a Ruler, and hence a citizen of the Federation.

In addition to those who already were citizens under the existing Agreement, the Federal Ordinance allowed the following to become citizens by operation of law:

(a) any subject of His Highness the Ruler of any State;

52. Federation of Malaya, *Proceedings of the Legislative Council—11 and 12 July 1951*, p. 132.
53. Ibid., p. 135.
54. *Singapore Standard*, 11 July 1951.

(b) any citizen of the United Kingdom and Colonies born in either of the Settlements;

(c) any citizen of the United Kingdom and Colonies born in the Federation, one of whose parents was also locally-born;

(d) any citizen of the United Kingdom and Colonies who—

(i) if he was born before the day when the new legislation came into force, whose father was born in either of the Settlements and had, at the time of such person's birth, completed a period of 15 years' residence in the Federation;

and (ii) if he was born on or after the day the legislation came into force, whose father was himself a citizen;

(e) any person naturalized as a citizen of the United Kingdom and Colonies under the British Nationality Act of 1948, who had resided in the Settlements for periods amounting in the aggregate to not less than 10 out of the preceding 12 years, including continuous residence during the 2 years immediately preceding the date of application.[55]

Citizenship by application was open to any person of full capacity (meaning, any person who had attained the age of eighteen and was of sound mind) who, being a citizen of the United Kingdom and Colonies, was willing to take an oath of allegiance to the Federation, renouncing any nationality or citizenship other than citizenship of the United Kingdom and Colonies. A person who had absented himself from the Federation for a continuous period of five years during the ten years immediately preceding the date of his application was not entitled to be registered under this section unless he was certified by the High Commissioner to have maintained substantial connexion with the Federation during his absence.[56]

Citizenship by naturalization was to be available to any citizen of the United Kingdom and Colonies who

(a) had resided in the country for a total of 10 out of the 12 preceding years, including the two years immediately preceding the date of his application;

(b) was of good character;

(c) was 'not likely to become chargeable to the Federation';

(d) was reasonably proficient in Malay or English; and

55. *Federation of Malaya Agreement* (*Amendment*) *Ordinance, 1952*, Article 125.
56. Ibid., Article 126.

(e) intended to reside permanently in the Federation.[57]

Turning now to the State Nationality Enactments, the following were made eligible by law to become subjects of a Ruler and hence citizens of the Federation as provided by the Federal Ordinance:

(a) any person who belonged to any of the aboriginal tribes of the country, and who was resident in that State;

(b) any Malay born in that State;

(c) any person who, not being a Malay, was born in that State and one of whose parents was born in the Federation;

(d) any person not being a citizen of the U.K. and Colonies, who was born in the State and who was already a Federal citizen under the provisions of the Federation of Malaya Agreement, 1948; and

(e) any person, wherever born, whose father was a subject of the Ruler of that State.[58]

The definition of a 'Malay' as set out in the 1948 Agreement was left unchanged.

State nationality by registration was open to any person who, not being a minor, was born in the State of which he intended to become a national, provided:

(a) that he satisfied the Ruler that he could speak either Malay or English with reasonable proficiency;

(b) that he was of good character; and

(c) that he was willing to take an oath of allegiance to the Ruler, renouncing any other nationality or citizenship.[59]

With regard to the language requirement it was provided that, for a period of five years from the date when the new regulations came into force, the standard of proficiency prescribed in the Enactments[60] should be relaxed for any applicant who, in the opinion of the Language Board, had not had 'a reasonable opportunity of learning Malay or English and [was] otherwise a suitable person for registration as a subject of a Ruler'.[61]

57. Ibid., Article 131.

58. *State Nationality Enactments, 1952*, Article 4.

59. Ibid., Article 5.

60. As in the *Federal Ordinance*, it was stated:

'A person shall be deemed to be able to speak the Malay or English language with reasonable proficiency if in the opinion of a Language Board [to be appointed for the purpose of conducting language tests] he is able to say and understand what a person of his standing is likely to wish to say or understand in Malay or English in normal intercourse with a person of a different community.' (*Federal Ordinance*, Article 124 (Clause (k), and *State Enactments*, Article 2, Clause (5).)

61. *State Enactments*, Article 5, Clause (2).

The conditions governing naturalization were the same as those in the Federal Ordinance.[62]

The most outstanding feature of the new proposals was the fact that while the door to citizenship was opened considerably wider for the non-Malays, no progress was made in solving the more fundamental problems at hand, namely the creation of a Malayan nationality and the fostering of a common unity. The new scheme in effect created one citizenship and nine nationalities, and a person became a citizen of the Federation either by being a subject of a Ruler or by being a citizen of the United Kingdom and Colonies and possessing certain qualifications.

In explaining the inadequacies of the Ordinance, the general context in which it was introduced will first of all have to be understood. To begin with, by 1952 the need to give the non-Malay communities a permanent Malayan identity had become clear beyond question. This meant that a Malayan community had to be created, embracing Malays and non-Malays alike, and identifiable by a similarity and unity more deep-rooted than that provided by the mere presence of a common legal classification. Common citizenship is admittedly a vital prerequisite for the emergence of such a unity but, without the help of a common nationality, it might fail to go beyond creating a community identifiable only in legal terms.

Secondly, reference may be made to certain aspects of political advancement. Although self-government did not appear to be within easy reach in 1952, the broad features of post-war British colonial policy had become quite obvious. While in pre-war Malaya British rule was accepted almost instinctively, it was now possible to think in terms of the country being independent in the not too distant future. This consideration, like the former, should have led to the creation of a common nationality aimed at fostering a degree of national unity consonant with the need to establish adequate foundations for the building of an independent nation.

Finally, some recognition will have to be given to the war against the Communist insurgents which began in 1948 and which led to the declaration of a state of emergency during the same year.

62. One did not, of course, have to be a citizen of the United Kingdom and Colonies; and residence in any part of the Federation was substituted by residence in the State concerned.

Had a common nationality been created, the new citizenship proposals might have produced a greater sense of responsibility among the non-Malays (particularly the Chinese whose support was most vital and who in fact were shy of rallying to the Government's aid) by giving them a stronger feeling of local identity and interest.

These shortcomings did not go unnoticed or uncondemned. In speaking on the proposals a Chinese member of the Legislative Council observed:

Admittedly, the present proposals open the door wider to citizenship, but they do so at the expense of a return to that tragic parochialism which has always kept us divided. It seems to me to be a great psychological blunder of the first magnitude. How, I ask, can we become one nation with a Malayan nationality by creating at this stage in our history nine distinct State nationalities? If there is to be an effective Malayan national consciousness, we should do everything in our power to focus our loyalty on a single centre, and that is the Federation,[63]

adding later:

A Malayan nationality can only rise out of a sense of a social cohesion among our multi-racial communities, but how are we going to foster the growth of a Malayan consciousness by creating nine distinct State nationalities? If there is ultimately to be a Malayan nationality we should do everything in our power to promote loyalty to the Federation and not to individual member States and to promote racial harmony by ignoring racial differences.[64]

The parochialism referred to above affected the Malay and non-Malay communities differently. As mentioned in the last chapter, State loyalty had always constituted an integral part of the social and political life of the Malays. Thus in their case the new proposals in a way served to entrench such parochialism as already existed. In the case of the non-Malays, on the other hand, State loyalty was a new demand. They had never possessed a tradition of loyalty to the Sultans and, in all likelihood, it was not possible for them now suddenly to produce it on demand. To them State nationality was merely a requirement for Federal citizenship. Thus,

63. Federation of Malaya, *Legislative Council Debates* (7 and 8 May 1952), p. 168. The speaker was Mrs. B. H. Oon of Penang.
64. Ibid., p. 169.

while in the case of the Malays the new scheme failed to encourage the necessary transfer of loyalty from the State to the Federation, in the case of the non-Malays it did not even give scope for the emergence of any real loyalty.

Despite these criticisms, the 1952 Ordinance was by no means totally unimaginative. Apart from the Communist revolt, the political problems facing the country at that time were largely the outcome of the rejection by the Malays of the Malayan Union proposals. In 1946 the Malays had indicated beyond all doubt that they were not willing to give the non-Malay communities a political status equal to their own; they wanted to be certain that a non-Malay would be made eligible to become a citizen only if he could be identified as being Malayan in outlook. By 1952, however, certain sections of the non-Malay communities were insistent that they could pass a fair test of local identity. The problem was thus to define what a 'fair test' would be. Considering that the Federation was nothing more than a mere administrative unit,[65] the only reasonable test which could have been applied was one which could establish a legal tie with the Federation; and, as observed by one writer, 'this could not be achieved simply by transforming Federal citizenship into a Federation nationality': it would not have been possible to create the status of subject or national of the Federation because this would have implied 'that all the citizens would be subjects of all the Rulers taken collectively'.[66]

So it might be argued that, in the face of the various claims and counter-claims made by the Malays and the non-Malays, the new proposals were neither unrealistic nor out of tune with the need to proceed in the right direction: in the first place they did what could have been done to create a common status without unduly encroaching upon the rights of the Sultans and without completely disregarding the claims of the people, the non-Malays in particular; secondly, they required the Chinese and the Indians to choose between Malaya and their mother countries. Unlike the 1948 proposals, the new scheme not only conferred rights but imposed obligations as well.

65. In that it was a combination of nine protected Malay States and two Settlements where there were ten sovereigns—the nine Malay Rulers and the British Crown—and hence no single focus of national allegiance.
66. F. G. Carnell, 'Malayan Citizenship Legislation', op. cit., p. 514.

It is significant to note that while Malay quarters regarded the new Ordinance and State Enactments as constituting an unduly extravagant concession made to the non-Malays, the four Chinese members of the Select Committee which studied and reported on the original Bill accepted the new proposals only as a 'temporary measure';[67] they stated that they had not abandoned the principle of *jus soli* although this was not accepted in the new scheme. This brings out a very important feature of citizenship legislation in the Federation of Malaya, namely the ever present tendency for the Malays and the non-Malays equally to criticize every change effected in the name of compromise and expediency.

An inquiry into the actual effects of the new provisions proves most enlightening. It was estimated that, at 30 June 1953, 4,139,000 persons had become citizens/state nationals by operation of law.[68] Of this number, 2,727,000 were Malaysians, 1,157,000 Chinese, 222,000 Indians and Pakistanis, and 33,000 'Others'. It was also estimated that the number of persons who were granted certificates as state nationals (by registration under the State Nationality Enactments, 1952) between 15 September 1952 and 31 December 1953 amounted to 11,789.[69] During the same period, 26,545 persons were naturalized as state nationals.[70] These figures show that, by the end of 1953, approximately 4,177,350 persons had become citizens of the Federation of Malaya.

Of those who were not citizens/state nationals at this time, about 647,300 possessed the birth qualification necessary to acquire the status through registration. Taken by communal groups, this figure was made up of:[71]

67. Federation of Malaya, *Report of the Select Committee Appointed on the 11th day of July, 1951, to Examine and Report to the Legislative Council on the Bill, the Short Title of which is The Federation of Malaya Agreement (Amendment) Ordinance, 1951.* Paper to be laid before the Federal Legislative Council by Command of His Excellency the High Commissioner. No. 19 of 1952, p. 35.

68. No exact figures are available for this category of persons since there was no obligation for those qualifying for automatic citizenship to register themselves. Birth statistics are inadequate because birth alone in the Federation did not necessarily confer this status.

69. Of this number, 4,379 were Malaysians, 4,407 Chinese, 1,071 Indians, Pakistanis, and Ceylonese, and 1,932 'Others'. (*Annual Report, 1953*, p. 19.)

70. This comprised 14,216 Malaysians, 7,596 Chinese, 3,026 Indians, Pakistanis, and Ceylonese, and 1,707 'Others'. (Loc. cit.)

71. *Annual Report, 1953*, p. 17.

| | |
|---|---|
| Malaysians | — |
| Chinese | 433,000 |
| Indians and Pakistanis | 186,000 |
| Others | 28,300 |
| Total | 647,300 |

By adding these numbers to those who already were citizens/state nationals, it may be established that, at the end of 1953, approximately 4,424,650 persons had either already become citizens or possessed the birth qualification necessary to become registered as such. Since the total population of the country at this time was estimated at 5,705,952, this means that only about 1,281,300 persons were not included in any of the above categories and, significantly, 911,300 of them were in fact born outside the country.

One thing is now quite clear: apart from the language requirement, almost all persons born in the country were in one way or another eligible to become citizens of the country. When the language requirement is considered, it is worth noting that for a period of five years from the date when the new regulations came into force, the prescribed standard of proficiency was to be relaxed in the case of those who had not had a reasonable opportunity of learning Malay or English. Considering, in addition, that a good number of those who were not citizens and had been born outside the country must have possessed the necessary residential qualification to become naturalized as citizens/state nationals, the 1952 proposals did not fall far short of throwing the citizenship doors wide open.

The next important landmark in citizenship legislation came with the attainment of independence. Before analysing the provisions in the new Constitution, the views and recommendations of the Constitutional Commission (on whose proposals the final document was largely based) may briefly be discussed.

In submitting its recommendations on citizenship, the Commission explained that there were four main categories of persons who had to be considered: those who already were recognized as citizens; those born in the Federation on or after *Merdeka* Day; those born in the country before *Merdeka* Day and resident there on that day; and those resident in the country on *Merdeka* Day, but who were not born there. It was suggested that those who fell into the first category should continue to be citizens, and that those already entitled to become registered as citizens (under the provisions of the existing Federation of Malaya Agreement) should continue to be so entitled.[72] With regard to the second category of persons (those born in the country on or after *Merdeka* Day), it was proposed that these persons be also made citizens by operation of law.[73] Concerning suggestions from certain quarters that the principle of *jus soli* should be given retrospective effect, the Commission explained: 'We are not satisfied that it is entirely possible or desirable to provide that all those who were born in Malaya, whatever be the date of their birth, wherever they may be now and whatever be their present nationality should be retrospectively made citizens of the Federation by operation of law.'[74]

Concerning the third category (those born in the Federation before *Merdeka* Day and resident there on that day), it was recommended that these persons should be enabled to obtain citizenship 'without undue difficulty', provided they intended to reside permanently in the country and were prepared to take an oath of allegiance, while also declaring that they would not exercise any right or privilege which they might possess under the nationality laws of any foreign country.[75] The other conditions governing the eligibility of those belonging to this category were that they be over eighteen years of age and of good character, that they should have resided in the Federation for at least five out of the preceding seven years, and that they should have an elementary knowledge of the Malay language.[76]

As for those who came under the fourth category (resident in the Federation on *Merdeka* Day, but not born there), the Commission declared: 'Those to whom this recommendation applies are very numerous, and, in order that a sense of common nationality should develop, we think that it is important that those who have shown their loyalty to the Federation and have made it their

72. Great Britain, Colonial Office, *Report of the Federation of Malaya Constitutional Commission*, Colonial No. 330, 1957, Articles 14 and 15 (i) of Appendix II: 'Draft Constitution of the Federation of Malaya'.
73. 'Draft Constitution', op. cit., Article 14 (i) (a).
74. *Report of the Constitutional Commission*, p. 17.
75. 'Draft Constitution', op. cit., Articles 16 and 18 (i).
76. Ibid., Article 16. The language test was to be waived in the case of those who made their application within one year of *Merdeka* Day.

permanent home, should participate in the rights and duties of citizenship.'[77] On the question of eligibility, the only difference between this and the last category was that the period of residence enabling one to qualify was raised to eight out of the preceding twelve years.[78] It was also proposed that the language test should be waived (during the first year after independence) only in the case of those who, at the time of their application, had attained the age of forty-five[79]; even those under this age were required to have only an 'elementary' knowledge of the Malay language.[80]

Six main conditions governed a person's eligibility to become a citizen by naturalization: he had to be at least twenty-one years of age; he had to be of good character; he had to have resided in the Federation for at least ten out of the twelve years immediately preceding the date of his application; he had to give sufficient indication of an intention to reside permanently in the Federation; he had to take an oath of allegiance and promise not to exercise any rights or privileges which might have been granted to him by the nationality laws of a foreign country; and finally, he had to have an 'adequate' knowledge of the Malay language.[81]

One of the members of the Commission, Mr. Justice Abdul Hamid of Pakistan, was at variance with the majority view on one particular point relating to citizenship. As mentioned above, Article 15 (i) of the Draft Constitution provided that all those who had been entitled to become citizens before *Merdeka* Day should continue to be so entitled after that day. According to Article 126 of the Federation Agreement 1948, citizens of the United Kingdom and Colonies, born in the Federation, were as of right entitled to be registered as citizens of the Federation if they had resided in the country for five years or, if they had not so resided, were certified to have maintained a substantial connexion with the country. Mr. Justice Hamid was of the opinion that these persons

77. *Report of the Constitutional Commission*, p. 18.
78. 'Draft Constitution', op. cit., Article 17.
79. 'It might be unreasonable', it was explained, 'in some cases to expect persons over 45 years of age to learn Malay'. (*Report of the Constitutional Commission*, p. 18.)
80. The explanation for this was that '. . . it might also be unreasonable in some cases to expect younger people to have an extensive knowledge of Malay'. (Loc. cit.)
81. 'Adequate' as opposed to the 'elementary' knowledge required of persons in the third and fourth categories mentioned earlier. ('Draft Constitution', op. cit., Article 19.)

should not continue to be so entitled by reason of birth in and connexion with the Federation, since others who fell under the same category but were not citizens of the United Kingdom and Colonies had to satisfy additional requirements, namely those pertaining to character, residence, and language.[82]

Reactions to the Commission's Report followed the familiar pattern seen in the past. The Malays thought that they were giving too much and the non-Malays that they were being given too little. Dato' Onn, the president of Party Negara, stated that the Commission's proposals on citizenship were too lenient and had to be tightened if the Malays were to avoid being swamped in the future. He suggested three categories of future non-Malay citizens: those who already were subjects of any Ruler; those who already had become full citizens of the Federation; and those born in the Settlements (Penang and Malacca), provided they entirely relinquished all allegiance to the Queen.[83] Regarding the status of the others, Dato' Onn was of the opinion that 'the rest should be left for us [meaning, the Malays] to decide whether they can become Malayan citizens or not', adding, 'It should not be their right to be citizens'.[84] He felt that such a policy was necessary to create a preponderance of Malay citizens in the country.[85]

The *Utusan Melayu* (a Malay daily) was of the opinion that, in so far as the policy of nation-building in independent Malaya was concerned, one of the most important tasks was to distinguish effectively between citizens and non-citizens, and to ensure that all those who came within the former category had an undivided loyalty to the country. It was felt that 'In a country such as Malaya where hundreds of thousands of people [were] still hesitant on the citizenship issue and where a large number of people still [looked] towards Formosa, New Delhi or probably Peking, people with dual citizenship should not be allowed to be undecided in their stand.'[86] The newspaper maintained that the first duty of an independent country was to strengthen and protect its own

82. *Report of the Constitutional Commission*, pp. 95–96. (Note of Dissent by Mr. Justice Abdul Hamid.)
83. Federation of Malaya, Department of Information, *Daily Press Summary of Vernacular Papers*, 4 April 1957, p. 3 (from a news report in the *Utusan Melayu*—a Singapore Malay daily—4 April 1957).
84. Loc. cit.
85. Loc. cit.
86. Ibid., 30 May, 1957, p. 2 (from the editorial of the *Utusan Melayu*, 30 May 1957).

security; this security had to be assured if the nation-building programme were to be carried out peacefully. The implication was that this security could not be guaranteed as long as the loyalty of those selected to be citizens could not be established as being undivided. Yet another Malay view was that every person who was granted citizenship should accept that the Malays were the owners of the country.[87]

The non-Malays (the Chinese in particular), on the other hand, represented that a nation could not be built successfully on the assumption that one community had to be accorded special rights and privileges. To them equal citizenship rights and an easy access to citizenship were the real bases of nation-building, not an unduly strict and selective process of choosing citizens. They felt that their loyalty could not be questioned on the grounds of their cultural parochialism: after all, a majority of them had never had a reasonable opportunity to learn the Malay language. The *China Press* (a Kuala Lumpur Chinese daily) in an editorial entitled 'Citizenship regulations should be further relaxed' said: 'We feel that the most important thing in citizenship is the question of loyalty, and a knowledge of the Malay language is only of secondary importance.'[88]

Finding the recommendations of the Constitutional Commission inadequate, certain spokesmen of the Chinese community made four new demands: the retrospective application of the principle of *jus soli*; a five-year residence qualification for those not born in the country, together with the removal of the language test; equal rights and obligations for all citizens; and the acceptance of Chinese and Tamil as official languages. Judging from various reports and editorial comments made in Chinese newspapers, these claims appear to have been fairly widely supported by the Chinese community. However, the Malayan Chinese Association (the representative of the Chinese community in the ruling Alliance Party) refused to have anything to do with these claims having decided to stand firm by the Alliance recommendations. It was thus decided, by those supporting these claims, to ignore the M.C.A. attitude; and the campaign was carried on by various guilds and associations outside the M.C.A.'s influence and control.

87. Ibid., 18 April 1957, p. 3 (from the editorial of the *Warta Negara*—a Penang Malay daily—15 April 1957).
88. Ibid., 3 July 1957, p. 2 (from the editorial in the *China Press* of 3 July 1957).

A delegation was sent to London for the purpose of winning the support of British officialdom; but, because of the British Government's decision to place full faith in the Alliance as the only effective representative of the people, nothing significant resulted from this action.

The question of dual citizenship raised another point of conflict. The Constitutional Commission had recommended that persons born in Penang and Malacca should be given the opportunity of enjoying the rights of Malayan citizenship while continuing to remain citizens of the United Kingdom and Colonies.[89] The Alliance, however, took the view that there should only be a single nationality, and that subjects of the United Kingdom and Colonies should be given the alternative of either retaining their former status or giving it up in favour of Malayan citizenship. This view was also supported by the Rulers.[90] Saying that there was 'no question of compromise on this issue', Tengku Abdul Rahman explained the Alliance stand in these words: 'If Britain cedes Penang and Malacca to the Federation, all rights must go with this cession.'[91]

Certain sections of the Straits Chinese community found the Alliance's attitude over this issue rather disturbing. They did not, at the same time, find the Constitutional Commission's recommendation wholly acceptable, since this merely clarified the technicalities of their legal status without suggesting any real benefits. What they sought was an actual recognition of their distinctiveness, carrying with it the granting of a special status.[92] The Straits Chinese British Association, for example, demanded that ties be maintained between the Settlements and Britain, going to the extent of suggesting that consideration should be given to the Settlements' right to secede from the Federation.[93]

89. *Report of the Constitutional Commission*, p. 23. The Commission was careful to point out that the proposal was not intended to enhance the status of those affected while they were resident in Malaya.

90. *Straits Budget*, Singapore, 14 March 1957, p. 15.

91. Ibid., 11 April 1957, p. 11.

92. The Straits Chinese have always considered themselves to be a group apart from the rest of the Chinese population. One of them wrote in a letter to the *Straits Times* of 11 December 1948: 'The time has come for the Straits Chinese to assert themselves. If they don't they will be swamped by China-born Chinese.'

93. F. H. H. King, *The New Malayan Nation*, p. 13. The Secessionist movement was also strong (in Penang) in 1948 at the time of federation.

Four possible reasons may be given in explaining the demand for dual citizenship. To begin with, there is little doubt that there was some resentment about the continuation of the special position accorded to the Malays, especially since it was now suggested (by the U.M.N.O.) that this be extended to the Settlements as well.[94] It is quite likely that the Straits Chinese resented the prospect of being placed on the same level as all the other non-Malays in the country.

Secondly, it is possible to interpret the attitude of the Straits Chinese as reflecting the more general question of local Chinese confidence in the new Federation. It might have been thought that the federation of nine Malay States and two Settlements to form a single independent nation could not achieve lasting success, especially in the field of Malay/non-Malay relations. The Straits Chinese might have been of the opinion that, by maintaining certain ties with Britain, they could have established for themselves a status more desirable and permanent than that accorded to the other non-Malays.

Thirdly, it is possible that the desire for dual citizenship was influenced by considerations related to certain less vital but nevertheless alluring benefits to be derived from British status, such as the eligibility for British passports.

Finally, it should be recognized that a number of Straits Chinese were in fact proud of their British nationality. Added to this, no doubt, was the consideration that British protection might have been forthcoming if measures had been adopted locally which adversely affected the non-Malays.

The Malays, undoubtedly, had little sympathy with the idea of dual citizenship, and they had three main reasons for opposing it. To begin with, they regarded it as being contrary to the principle of undivided loyalty which they so urgently sought to establish: they did not agree that this loyalty could be created as long as some sections of the population enjoyed, or thought they enjoyed, the comforts and privileges of a non-local status. Secondly, considering the amount of political power in their own hands at the time of independence, the Malays could not but feel insulted at what appeared to be a lack of confidence in their own integrity and capacity for fair treatment; nobody need have sought continued

94. Up to this time, the Malays in Penang and Malacca had not enjoyed the same privileges as those in the Malay States.

British connexions had there been sufficient confidence in local affairs.[95] The Malays also realized that it was not possible effectively to establish a single loyalty on the assumption that those not having full confidence in local affairs should be consoled by the presence of a 'stand-by' status.

Finally, it was undoubtedly anomalous that, at a time when Malayan nationalism was reaching its moment of triumph, a section of the population should have sought continued identification with the colonial power. Satisfying the desires of this section, however small it might have been, would no doubt have tended to weaken the basis of nation-building, founded on the idea of a single identity.

### *The Final Proposals*

The proposals finally arrived at upheld most of the major recommendations made by the Constitutional Commission. It was agreed, for example, that all those who were citizens before *Merdeka* Day should continue to be citizens, and that all those born in the country on or after that day should be made citizens by operation of law.[96] The recommendations concerning citizenship by registration (both of persons born in the Federation before *Merdeka* Day and of those who were not born in the country but were resident there on that day) and naturalization were also accepted. There was, however, one significant change; it was related to the question of dual citizenship, and introduced a certain degree of strictness. As explained, the Constitutional Commission had recommended that certain citizens of the United Kingdom and Colonies who were born in the Federation before *Merdeka* Day and who were entitled, under clause 126 of the Federation of Malaya Agreement 1948, to be registered as citizens, should continue to be so entitled. It was now proposed that these persons should be accepted only on condition that they registered themselves within a period of one year from *Merdeka* Day. An Article to this effect (Article 170) was inserted among the temporary provisions in Part XIII of the Constitution.[97] This provision had

95. It should be noted that a considerable number of non-Malays were in agreement with these objections to dual citizenship. However, it is only the Malays who, as a community, had an undivided opinion on this matter.
96. Constitution of the Federation of Malaya, Article, 14, Clause (i) (a).
97. It was stated that those in this category who had absented themselves from the Federation for a continuous period of five years during the ten years

the effect of making Federal citizenship more distinct, in that non-local qualifications were not to constitute a permanent basis for eligibility.

The Constitution also provides that the Federal Government is entitled to deprive of his citizenship any person who either voluntarily obtains a foreign citizenship or exercises the rights of such citizenship, being rights accorded only to the citizens of that foreign country. For the purposes of this clause, Commonwealth countries are also classified as 'foreign' countries.[98]

immediately preceding the date of application would not be entitled to be registered unless it was certified by the Federation Government that they had maintained 'substantial connexion' with the Federation during the period in question. (Article 170, Clause (2).)

98. This means that a Federal citizen, while in another Commonwealth country, cannot exercise any right accorded only to citizens of that country and not to Commonwealth citizens generally.

# CHAPTER FOUR

# SPECIAL POSITION OF THE MALAYS; RELIGION; AND LANGUAGE

TOGETHER with citizenship, the issues now to be studied may be classified as the most outstanding of Malay/non-Malay disagreements within the general area of constitutional government. It may, however, be observed that while citizenship could be considered very much a matter of the past (meaning the period prior to the adoption of the present Constitution in 1957, when it dominated the scene more than any other single issue), the three issues under discussion derive most of their present significance by virtue of their crucial implications for the future.[1] In this respect one might very well suggest, without running any risk of oversimplification, that the future of communal relations in the Federation will hinge, to a very large extent, on the manner in which these issues are resolved, for on them are based most if not all the current ideas concerning what constitutes an 'equitable compromise'.

## THE SPECIAL POSITION OF THE MALAYS

Some of the basic problems and attitudes connected with this issue (such as Malay and non-Malay arguments concerning the legitimacy of their own claims, Malay fears of increased non-Malay power, and so on) have already been mentioned in the preceding chapters. Reference has also been made to the fact that the Malays, by virtue of being the indigenous people and also because

1. This, however, does not mean that citizenship has now become a completely closed subject. While some Malays complain that the present regulations are too lenient, sections of the non-Malay communities are still advocating the retrospective application of *jus soli*, which would confer automatic citizenship on everyone born in the Federation, whether before or after *Merdeka* Day. However, citizenship is only of secondary importance today when compared to some of the other issues, such as language and equal rights. After all, as already explained, conditions governing citizenship by application are now sufficiently relaxed to enable almost all the non-Malays in the country to become citizens without much difficulty.

of their comparative economic and social backwardness, have been given a 'special position' which makes them eligible for a certain amount of preferential treatment. Details of this 'special position', and the attitudes of the Malays and non-Malays towards it, will now be discussed.

At the very outset the following point must be understood: the very fact that the special position referred to above is a legal form of protection implies that, in its absence, the Malays might not enjoy the priorities which the Constitution now guarantees them.

It is also important, before proceeding with the general analysis, to place the issue of special Malay rights in its proper historical perspective.

As mentioned in Chapter Two, British authority was introduced into Malaya through treaties signed with the Sultans of the individual States. Thus, right from the beginning, the obligations of the British authorities were owed first and foremost to these Sultans and their Malay subjects. The full weight of this obligation was made manifest only with the arrival of vast numbers of Chinese and Indians, who supplied most of the manpower for the unprecedented economic development which soon followed. The British found it necessary to give the Sultans an assurance that the influx of non-Malays would not be allowed adversely to affect their positions or the position of their subjects. Politically, a policy of indirect rule was to guarantee this; economically, it was pointed out that the revenues resulting from the new leap in economic activity would be used to introduce better social services from which the Malays themselves would benefit.[2]

This policy of preserving Malay rights, and of effectively excluding the non-Malays from the country's political life, was fairly uncomplicated as long as the non-Malays constituted only a transient population which regarded Malaya as a foreign country ideal for a profitable sojourn. But, as already mentioned, the 1930s

2. Considerable progress was, in fact, made in the field of social services but, as the Malays came to realize later on, the benefits of this progress were largely confined to the more urban areas which they did not inhabit. This has become a sore point with the Malays in recent times, and rural development—aimed largely at benefiting the Malay community—has now become a very important aspect of Government policy. The introduction of elections has increased the political implications of this development, since a vast majority of the Malay voters—who constituted about 84 per cent of the total electorate in 1955 and 57 per cent in 1959—are in fact resident in rural areas.

and 1940s changed the basic character of these communities: they now became a part of the settled population, seeking local rights and a share in local politics. With this change, the question of special Malay rights ceased to be a matter of simple administrative policy, and became a very live political issue.

The old policy of strictly and effectively maintaining the special position of the Malays was now placed in direct conflict with the need to make concessions to the non-Malays. Thus was introduced the present era of changing definitions, regarding how special the special position of the Malays should be. Political advancement tended to make the situation yet more difficult in that the introduction of wide democratic measures (such as the liberalization of citizenship qualifications, the introduction of elections, and so on) made it progressively more difficult for special rights to be reserved for a single community; and yet the same political advancement made the Malays more dependent on guaranteed rights, because it made their position in the country less secure.

With this brief historical background, the actual constitutional steps taken with regard to special Malay rights may now be discussed.

As explained earlier, the Malayan Union scheme represented a complete abandonment of the pre-war policy of recognizing Malaya as a Malay country. Indirect rule was to be abandoned in the interests of a centralized and potentially democratic administration. Notwithstanding their success in causing the withdrawal of this scheme, the Malays found in these proposals a rude warning of what the future held in store for them; they could not any longer take their privileged position for granted, as they had done before the war.

The Federation of Malaya Agreement, which followed in 1948, made a half-hearted attempt to return to the pre-war policy. Although the special rights of the Malay community were once again given recognition, the claims of the non-Malays were not ignored. It was stated, for example, that the responsibilities of the High Commissioner were to include the safeguarding of the 'special position' of the Malays and the 'legitimate interests' of the other communities.[3] Together with the opening up of citizenship, this recognition that the non-Malays had 'legitimate interests' in

3. *Federation of Malaya Agreement, 1948*, Clause 19 (i) (d).

the country introduced a new phase in political thinking. The terms 'special position of the Malays' and 'legitimate interests of the other communities' have since become entrenched in the country's political vocabulary and, because it was inevitable that the former should conflict with the latter, much of the country's politics in recent years has revolved around efforts at definition, by the Malays on the one hand and the non-Malays on the other, aimed at benefiting their own interests.

As compared to the Federation Agreement, the State Agreements which complemented it showed a greater determination to safeguard Malay interests. For example, each of them provided 'that the Ruler desires, and His Majesty agrees, that it shall be a particular charge upon the Government of the State to provide for and encourage the education and training of the Malay inhabitants of the State so as to fit them to take a full share in the economic progress, social welfare, and Government of the State and of the Federation'.[4] While the Federation Agreement catered for a 'Malayan' community, the primary concern of the State Agreement lay in the restoration of the Malay character of each State.

Right up to 1952, the 'legitimate interests' of the non-Malays did not entitle them to enter the Malayan Civil Service. They had, however, for a long time been admitted to the other branches of the Public Service where they in fact outnumbered the Malays. As stated by General Sir Gerald Templer (High Commissioner from 1951 to 1954) in a speech to the Legislative Council in November 1952, the non-Malays outnumbered the Malays in the First Division of the other branches of the Public Service (excluding the Police) by 235 to 91.[5] It was in the course of the same speech that General Templer stated the policy which was to follow, of admitting qualified non-Malay Asians to the Civil Service in the proportion of one non-Malay to every four Malays, and of reserving a certain quota of licences (for certain business) and scholarships for the Malay community. In explaining the new policy, he observed:

4. Great Britain, Colonial Office, *Federation of Malaya: Summary of Revised Constitutional Proposals*, 1947, Cmd. 7171, p. 5. (This clause was included in each of the State Agreements.)
5. Federation of Malaya, *Report of the Proceedings of the Legislative Council*, 19–22 November 1952, p. 473.

> Members of the Council will, however, I feel sure agree that it is very necessary that the special position of the Malays should be retained in the Civil Service and imposed in the whole economic field. To this end, certain safeguards are necessary. I therefore propose that, as one of the safeguards, the number of non-Malay Federal citizens who are admitted into the Malayan Civil Service shall be limited to one for every four Malays admitted into that Service in the future. Other safeguards to secure and improve the position of the Malays are under consideration.[6]

Observing that there was a clear preponderance of non-Malays possessing the necessary educational qualifications for entry into the Civil Service, and explaining that this preponderance was likely to continue in view of the proportion of Malays to non-Malays who were then at the University of Malaya (73 Malays to 452 non-Malays),[7] the High Commissioner added:

> Their Highnesses and my Executive Council share with me the desire to redress this ill-balance as early as possible, and to equip a far larger number of Malays to take their place in the public service and also in professional positions outside that service. Action to this end has already been taken during recent months.[8] . . . Other proposals are under consideration.[9]

Regarding commerce and industry, General Templer thought it essential 'that the Malays should be encouraged and assisted to play a full part in the economic life of the country so that the present uneven economic balance may be redressed'.[10] Taken as a whole, the new proposals represented a compromise: the Malays were to lose their monopoly in the Civil Service, but were to get a certain amount of preferential treatment in the economic and educational fields.

The policy enunciated by General Templer remained in operation until 1957, when the attainment of independence necessitated a reconsideration of the entire issue of special Malay rights. Since the implementation of the new Constitution was now to be left entirely in the hands of the Malays and the non-Malays, the need for a workable compromise was more vital than ever before.

6. Loc. cit.
7. During the 1960/61 session the University had 2,295 students, of whom 1,563 were Chinese, 230 Malays, 428 Indians and Ceylonese, and 74 'Others'.
8. This refers to the erection of more hostels for Malay students near English schools, and the approval of scholarships for Malays.
9. *Legislative Council Debates*, 19–22 November 1952, pp. 473–4.
10. Ibid., p. 474.

The Constitutional Commission's terms of reference stated that provision should be made, in the Constitution, for the 'safeguarding of the special position of the Malays and the legitimate interests of the other communities'.[11] It was also required that steps should be taken to make possible the creation of a common nationality for the whole of the Federation, and to ensure a democratic form of government. The Commission considered the above requirements, and concluded that a common nationality was the basis upon which a unified Malayan nation was to be created, and that under a democratic form of government it was inherent that all the citizens of the Federation, regardless of race, creed, or culture, should have the benefits of certain fundamental rights including full equality before the law.[12] The Commission summarized the problem at hand by observing: 'We found it difficult, therefore, to reconcile the terms of our reference if the protection of the special position of the Malays signified the granting of special privileges, permanently, to one community and not to others.'[13] The Alliance, too, had been fully aware of the difficulty of giving the Malays a permanent advantage over the other communities, and its representatives, led by Tengku Abdul Rahman, had submitted that 'in an independent Malaya all nationals should be accorded equal rights, privileges and opportunities, and there must not be discrimination on grounds of race and creed . . .'[14] The Rulers had expressed the same sentiment in their memorandum to the Commission, in which they had stated that they looked forward 'to a time not too remote when it will become possible to eliminate Communalism as a force in the political and economic life of the country'.[15]

Despite these views, the Commission recognized that the Malays were in need of certain privileges if they were to compete favourably with the other communities; but it was decided that the privileges to be given should not be permanent.

In defining the field of special rights, the Commission was satisfied to accept the limits set by existing practice. Accordingly,

11. Great Britain, Colonial Office, *Report of the Federation of Malaya Constitutional Commission*, 1957, p. 70.
12. Ibid., pp. 70–71.
13. Ibid., p. 71.
14. Loc. cit.
15. Loc. cit.

the 'special position of the Malays' was to mean preferences in four different fields: reservation of land; quotas for admission to the Public Service; quotas in respect of the issuing of permits or licences for the operation of certain businesses; and preferences in connexion with scholarships, bursaries, and other forms of aid for educational purposes.[16] It remained to decide the precise extent to which preferences should continue to be given. In this connexion, the Commission found little opposition to the continuance of the existing system for a certain length of time,[17] but met with very strong opposition from sections of the non-Malay communities to any increase in the existing preferences, and also to their continuance for a prolonged period of time. The Commission decided that the existing preferences had to be maintained: 'The Malays would be at a serious and unfair disadvantage compared with the other communities if they [the preferences] were suddenly withdrawn.'[18] In the case of land (which was a State matter in which the Commission did not recommend giving any overriding powers to the Federation), it was added that there should be no extension of the Malay reservations,[19] and that each State should be left to bring about reductions in such reservations 'at the appropriate time'.[20] In view of varying conditions in the different States, it was decided that any specification with regard to the time when changes had to be introduced was unwise. In the other three fields, however, it was recommended that the entire matter be reviewed after fifteen years: the appropriate Government was to be responsible for presenting a report on the matter to the appropriate legislature; following this, the legislature was to determine whether to retain, reduce, or entirely discontinue any quota in existence.

The Commissioners were confident that, with the integration

16. The Commission's recommendations on this matter were included in two Articles: one dealing with land, and the other with the preferences and quotas mentioned.
17. *Report of the Constitutional Commission*, p. 72.
18. Loc. cit.
19. Two conditions were attached to this general rule: (a) that if a reserved area ceased to be so reserved, an equivalent area could be made available for reservation, provided that it was not occupied by a non-Malay; and (b) that in the event of an undeveloped area being opened up, part of it could be converted into a Malay reservation, provided that an equivalent area was made available to non-Malays. (*Report of the Constitutional Commission*, p. 72.)
20. Loc. cit., and Article 82 of the 'Draft Constitution'.

of the various communities into a common nationality, the necessity for the continuance of the preferences given to the Malays would automatically disappear. Their recommendations were made in the belief that the Malays needed to be assured that existing conditions would continue for a substantial period of time, but that the ultimate goal should be the gradual reduction of all preferences, culminating in their complete withdrawal.

As in the case of the proposals made by the Commission, the Constitution which finally emerged contained two Articles dealing with the special position of the Malays, one concerning land reservations (Article 89) and the other dealing with the reservation of quotas in respect of public service appointments, licences, and educational benefits (Article 153).

In the case of land reservations, four changes were made to the Commission's recommendations. The first of these concerned the amendment of existing laws: it was decided that an enactment of a State legislature for this purpose would not be valid merely by being passed by the majority of the total membership of the Legislative Assembly and by the votes of at least two-thirds of the members present and voting (as was proposed by the Commission), but that approval by resolution of both Houses of Parliament, passed in a similar manner, was also necessary.[21] This change was no doubt intended to safeguard the future of Malay reservations in those States where the non-Malays formed a majority of the population.[22]

Secondly, it was stated that land which had not been developed or cultivated could be declared as a Malay reservation, on condition that an equal area of similar land in the State concerned was made available for general alienation: further, the total area of such land in any State declared as a Malay reservation could not at any time exceed the total area of such land made available for general alienation.[23]

Thirdly, the Malay States were enabled to acquire by agreement developed or cultivated lands and to turn such lands into Malay reservations.[24]

21. Great Britain, Colonial Office, *Constitutional Proposals for the Federation of Malaya*, Cmnd. 210, 1957, p. 19; and *Constitution*, Article 89.

22. After all, the chances of non-Malay domination in these (non-Malay dominated) States are far from remote whereas Malay strength in Parliament is bound to be more enduring.

23. Cmnd. 210, op. cit., p. 19; and *Constitution*, Article 89.

24. Loc. cit.

Finally, it was now provided that the Government of any State should be entitled, in accordance with law, to acquire land for the settlement of Malays or other communities, and to establish trusts for that purpose.[25]

As mentioned earlier, the Constitutional Commission had recommended that there should be no extension of Malay reservations into undeveloped areas; this was clearly intended to preclude the possibility of any State Government attempting rapidly to consolidate and further the interests of the Malays at the expense of the other communities. The second, third, and fourth changes mentioned above, whilst going against this recommendation (in that it was now made possible for a State Government to declare undeveloped areas as Malay reservations, and also to acquire, for the same purpose, land which was already developed),[26] nevertheless retained the principle that the Malays should not be enabled to 'shut out' more and more land from the others without compensation, since it was made obligatory that Malay reservations could be extended only in direct proportion to the amount of land made available for general alienation. However, there is no denying that the final proposals weight the balance in favour of the Malays.

Regarding the reservation of quotas in respect of Public Service appointments, permits, and educational benefits, the recommendation of the Constitutional Commission, that the matter be left in the hands of the 'government of the day', was not accepted; instead it was provided that the *Yang di-Pertuan Agong* (Paramount Ruler) should be given responsibility in these matters;[27] he was now made responsible for safeguarding 'the special position of the Malays and the legitimate interests of the other communities'.[28] Clause (2) of Article 153 states:

. . . the Yang di-Pertuan Agong shall exercise his functions under this Constitution and federal law in such manner as may be necessary to safeguard the special position of the Malays and to ensure the reservation for Malays of such proportion as he may deem reasonable of positions in the public service (other than the public service of a State)

25. Cmnd. 210, op. cit., pp. 19–20.
26. The Commission had permitted extensions only in the case of undeveloped areas being opened up (see footnote 19, p. 108).
27. The Alliance had suggested this in its recommendations to the Commission. This view was supported by Mr. Justice Abdul Hamid, Pakistan's representative in the Commission, in his minority report.
28. Cmnd. 210, op. cit., p. 19, and *Constitution*, Article 153.

and of scholarships, exhibitions and other similar educational or training privileges or special facilities given or accorded by the Federal Government and, when any permit or licence for the operation of any trade or business is required by federal law, then, subject to the provisions of that law and this Article, of such permits and licences.

The Paramount Ruler was not by any means given the power to act arbitrarily in carrying out his duties with regard to the reservation of quotas in favour of the Malays. It was stipulated, for example, that no reservation could be made for a Malay at the expense of a person who already held an office, scholarship, permit, or licence. Clause (7) of Article 153 makes this quite clear when it states:

Nothing in this Article shall operate to deprive or authorise the deprivation of any person of any right, privilege, permit or licence accrued to or enjoyed or held by him or to authorise a refusal to renew to any person any such permit of licence or a refusal to grant to the heirs, successors or assigns of a person any permit or licence when the renewal or grant might reasonably be expected in the ordinary course of events.

It is further stated, in Clause (9), that 'Nothing in this Article shall empower Parliament to restrict business or trade solely for the purpose of reservations for Malays'.

With regard to the Commission's recommendation that the entire matter of special Malay rights be reviewed at the end of fifteen years, it was decided that it would be more desirable 'in the interests of the country as a whole as well as the Malays themselves' for the *Yang di-Pertuan Agong* to cause the matter to be reviewed from time to time.[29] This policy was no doubt aimed at introducing a certain amount of flexibility into the issue, and the Malays were no longer made to race against a time limit.

With this brief historical background, the issue of special Malay rights may now be studied from the point of view of public attitudes. For this purpose, the attitudes of the Malays and those of the non-Malays will be considered separately.

As a community, the Malays are naturally in favour of having special rights reserved for themselves. However, while some of them are more or less satisfied with the present policy, and are willing to accept the principle that their community needs to be

29. Cmnd. 210, op. cit., p. 19.

given special privileges only for so long as it finds itself unable to compete with the others on a basis of equality, there are others who completely disagree with the principle of special Malay rights as at present enunciated. Maintaining that the country belongs to the Malays and the Malays alone, the latter claim that what now constitute 'special rights' should in fact constitute 'natural rights'. They further argue that the privileges at present accorded to their community should be substantially increased and rendered more stable.

Those Malays who generally accept present policies with regard to 'special rights', may be said by and large to agree with the view that the Malays only constitute one of the major communities (although the most important) in the Malayan plural society; they accept that it takes Malays and non-Malays alike to make the Malayan nation. Even though most of them insist that their community should form the cultural and political backbone of the nation which is now being built, these Malays are generally willing to accept equally shared rights as the ultimate goal. As opposed to the views of the second group, they are also willing to recognize that the special rights at present accorded to the Malays do not constitute absolute rights, and that they are relevant only in a context of inequality. They see the special position of the Malays more as a form of protection than as an assertion of superior claims. For this reason, they also argue that it would be unwise to introduce wide democratic measures in the country while the different communities remain at different levels of economic well-being: the introduction of such measures might widen existing disparities by necessitating free competition when the Malays, as a community, are too weak to complete effectively.

In contrast to the first category, those belonging to the second take the attitude that, in Malaya, the Malays should not merely form one of the communities in a multi-racial society, but constitute the entire nation while the rest of the population is regarded as alien, enjoying only those rights which the Malays themselves think fit to give. As stated by *Warta Negara* (a Malay newspaper) in an editorial:

Once the national essence of the Malays has been lost any demand of the Malays is branded as a communal one, even their demand for special rights.

While the status of the Malays has fallen from that of a nation to that of a mere community, a demand has also come from the non-Malays for equality for all, which they regard as being democratic.

The editorial continued to assert that, under cover of democracy, the non-Malays were 'trying to trip the national struggle of the Malays for rights and privileges'.[30]

Those belonging to this category emphasize that the Malays are the rightful owners of the country, and insist that the non-Malays should be grateful for the rights which they have been given, instead of being jealous of the special privileges accorded to the Malay community.[31] Because of their preoccupation with the future of the 'Malay' as opposed to the 'Malayan' nation, these Malays have an entirely different conception of the type of national unity to be desired from those in the first category. They do not find it attractive to think in terms of a Malayan unity embracing all the communities, because this would imply a certain equality with the non-Malays. What they seek is a unity within the Malay community; a solidarity which will give them the strength to exert themselves in what they consider to be their country. Dr. Burhanuddin, the President of the Pan-Malayan Islamic Party (P.M.I.P.), for example, claimed that the object of his Association was to 'unite the Malays and the Muslims'.[32]

With the advent of independence, this latter category of Malays concentrated their efforts on establishing the political supremacy of their own community. They argued that since it was the Malays who had originally surrendered authority to British hands, they should also be the ones to inherit the power that was now being relinquished. Thus some were of the opinion that the post of Prime Minister in independent Malaya should be filled only by a Malay.[33] More recently, there have been demands that the post of *Mentri Besar* (Chief Minister) in the different States should also be reserved exclusively for Malays.[34] On the economic side, it was

30. Federation of Malaya, Department of Information, *Daily Press Summary of Vernacular Papers*, 18 April 1957, pp. 2–3 (from the editorial of *Warta Negara*, 15 April 1957).

31. This view was expressed in the editorial of the *Warta Negara* on 19 May 1957.

32. *Daily Press Summary of Vernacular Papers*, 29 May 1957, p. 4 (from the *Utusan Melayu*, 28 May 1957).

33. *Daily Press Summary of Vernacular Papers*, 16 April 1957, p. 3 (from *Kritik*—a Kuala Lumpur Malay weekly—16 April 1957).

34. This demand arises from the fear that, with the introduction of fully elected legislatures, the post of *Mentri Besar* in those States where the non-Malays constitute a majority of the population might very well go to a non-Malay.

felt by some that a fixed percentage of the country's industrial labour force should be made up of Malays. It was reported, for example, that the Penang and Province Wellesley branch of the United Malays National Organization (U.M.N.O.) had suggested that, after independence, a third of the employees in industries should be Malays; Klang U.M.N.O. had suggested that 51 per cent of the port workers at Port Swettenham should also be Malays.[35]

As a group, the Malays in this category may be said to represent the present trend in Malay nationalism. Their ranks appear to have swelled, especially in the predominantly Malay areas of the north-east where, aided by economic grievances, geographic isolation, and the simplicity of life in general, the Pan-Malayan Islamic Party has been successful in exaggerating and exploiting communal fears and jealousies.[36] The situation is made none the better by the fact that some of the most vital issues that have a direct bearing on communal relations (the education issue, for example) remain largely unresolved.

As in the case of the Malays, the non-Malay communities may also be divided into two groups. The more moderate of these is willing to agree that the Malays need to be given special privileges until such time as they are capable of competing without any help. The other tends to denounce the whole idea of special Malay rights as contrary to democratic principles. It may, however, be said that these two groups have one thing in common: they are both more concerned about the future of Malay rights (fearing that attempts may be made not only to extend them but also to make them more permanent) than the preferences which are at present given to the Malays and which, for all practical purposes, they can afford on a temporary basis.

In so far as those belonging to the first category are concerned, one may go so far as to suggest that some of them are even willing to regard the temporary grant of special privileges to the Malays more as a matter of right than as an unpleasant necessity. Typical of this attitude are the words of Mr. Tan Siew Sin (then the Minister for Commerce and Industry, and now the Minister for

35. *Daily Press Summary of Vernacular Papers*, 26 June 1957, pp. 1–2 (from the *China Press*—a Kuala Lumpur Chinese daily—editorial, 26 June 1957).

36. This is discussed in some detail in Chapter Five.

Finance) who, in defending the special position accorded to the Malays in the present Constitution, said:

In the first place, the principle of the special position of the Malays has already been embodied in the Federation of Malaya Agreement [the Agreement of 1948, which was in operation until 1957]. The Malays therefore cannot be expected to give up what they already have in the same way that they do not expect the other communities to give up their existing rights. Far more important, however, is the indisputable fact that as a race the Malays are economically backward and well behind the other races in this field. . . . An economically depressed Malay community in a prosperous Malaya will not mean a peaceful Malaya. An economically depressed Malay community will never be able to achieve the desired degree of co-operation with the substantially more prosperous non-Malay communities.[37]

As in the case of Malays falling under the first (that is, moderate) category, the non-Malays now under discussion have set their sights on a unity embracing all the communities; they want politics to be conducted more on a basis of partnership than communal bargaining. They believe that if the non-Malays tried to understand and respect some of the demands of the Malay community, the Malays would reciprocate by doing likewise. In this connexion Mr. Tan Siew Sin, in his speech referred to above, observed:

. . . there are extremist Malay political parties, but there are also extremist Chinese political parties and in my view we should not lose our sense of perspective and balance by paying undue regard to the lunatic fringe, which is to be found in every country and in every community in the world. I believe that there is an enormous fund of goodwill among both Malays and Chinese for one another and all that is required is leadership to harness that goodwill towards worthy objects.[38]

Among the non-Malays now being discussed, there are also those who, while approving the privileges temporarily given to the Malays, are nevertheless a little doubtful as to whether the matter of special Malay rights has been properly settled and its motives clearly understood. Notwithstanding their own desire to see the Malay community better equipped for free competition, they want to be sure that the Malays accept as being adequate—not just for

37. Federation of Malaya, *Legislative Council Debates*, October 1956–August 1957, p. 2870.
38. Ibid., pp. 2872–3.

the time being—the temporary and limited nature of the privileges which they now enjoy. Said the *China Press* in an editorial:

The question of special rights for a particular community may be excusable at the start of the building of the nation, but if the period of 'special rights' is not restricted, or the scope of special rights is not clearly defined, then endless disputes . . . will arise later on. For the granting of special rights, whether right or wrong, has in fact caused those with special rights and those without them to be in opposite positions, a cause which may breed mutual mistrust and aversion among the people.[39]

This uneasiness, quite widespread as the 1957 Constitution was being drawn up, has persisted to the present day, largely because the Malay community has itself continued to remain divided in its views.

The second category of non-Malays harp on the theme of equality, refusing to accept that historical and economic considerations may entitle the Malays to a certain amount of preferences, even if temporary. The basis of their argument is that, in an independent and democratic society, there is no place for a 'special rights group'. In view of this attitude, those belonging to this category tend (at present at least) to give first priority to a non-Malay unity aimed at stripping Malay privileges.[40] The root of the disagreement between this group and the first categories of Malays and non-Malays mentioned stems from differing interpretations of 'equality'. While these persons argue that there cannot be equality if a particular section of the population is given special rights, the others (that is, those in sympathy with the present policy) assert that the Malays need to be given certain privileges if there is to be any real equality between them and the non-Malays. A non-Malay member of the Legislative Assembly said, when the 1957 constitutional proposals were being debated:

We are not deliberating on a constitution for a united Malayan nation but on proposals designed to promote the growth of a united Malayan nation in the future. . . . But how can national unity be attained if half,

39. *Daily Press Summary of Vernacular Papers*, 24 May 1957, p. 2.
40. A common pattern may now be seen in the manner in which the Malays and the non-Malays are divided, within themselves, in their attitudes towards the question of special privileges. It is clear, for example, that the corresponding categories in both groups tend to have very similar views and aspirations, especially with regard to the type of unity to be desired.

or more than half, of the population of this country is suffering from a sense of frustration arising out of inequality of opportunity for advancement in the economic and educational fields? The special rights accorded the Malays in the Draft Constitution [are] calculated to remove this inequality of opportunity.[41]

The conflict between the second group of non-Malays and the second group of Malays (that is, the extremists in both cases) is much less complicated. While the former, as already mentioned, condemn Malay privileges as being contrary to the principle of equality, the latter do not believe that there should be equality at all: to them the non-Malays do not have the right to belong to the same class of citizens as the Malays. This leaves little hope for agreement, and much therefore depends on the degree to which the two moderate groups are able to increase their influence within their own communities. On this will rest the possibility of a suitable compromise between Malay and non-Malay points of view.

## RELIGION

Religion is a recent recruit into the field of Malay/non-Malay conflict. The establishment of Islam as the State religion in the present Constitution has created a certain scope for disagreement on what the practical implications of this new provision should be. More important, however, are the extra-constitutional forces which have caused religious issues to assume a political role: the rise of Malay nationalism and the emergence of religious political bodies may be considered the two most outstanding examples. Before proceeding to analyse more fully the role which religion now plays in determining certain political attitudes, it is necessary to give some account of the history of religious affairs.

A characteristic of all the Agreements signed between Britain and the Malay Sultans (beginning with the Pangkor Agreement of 1874), which enabled the former to assume political control in the Malay States, was the fact that no infringement was made on the fields of Mohammedan religion and Malay custom: the Sultans continued to be the supreme authorities in these matters. The Malays were pleased with this arrangement, and the non-Malays were not affected by it. Consequently, religion raised little controversy.

41. *Legislative Council Debates*, October 1956–August 1957, col. 2949. The speaker was Mr. S. Chelvasingam MacIntyre, a Ceylonese.

It was with the Malayan Union proposals that the Malays first became concerned about their religious rights. These proposals required the Sultans to surrender a great deal of their authority as the traditional leaders of their respective States. In each State, the main body of law ceased to require the assent of the Ruler; it was now to be the Governor who approved such legislation, and no exception was made in the case of the religion and custom of the Malays. As a compensation, it was proposed that the Ruler of each State should preside over a Malay Advisory Council, appointed by him but with the approval of the Governor.[42] Although the Rulers, acting with the help of their Councils, were given legislative powers within their States on matters pertaining to the Mohammedan religion,[43] it was also provided that all such legislation had to secure the Governor's approval.[44]

The Malays found these arrangements clearly unacceptable; to them it was quite ridiculous to have the Governor associated with legislation concerning matters primarily related to the Mohammedan religion. Although they were far more concerned with some of the other aspects of the new proposals (such as the abolition of their special privileges and the introduction of undifferentiated eligibility for citizenship), this particular grievance is important in that, for the first time, it enabled religion to find a place in the language of agitation.

The Federation of Malaya Agreement, which followed in 1948, restored the Sultans as the traditional and spiritual leaders of their respective States. Although no stipulation was made in the Agreement with regard to an official religion for the whole country, the Constitution of each Malay State provided that 'The Religion of the State shall be the Muslim religion, as heretofore professed and practised in the State.'

These Constitutions further stated that:

The Head of the Religion of the State shall be His Highness, and His Highness will, in due course, cause laws to be enacted for the purpose

42. Great Britain, Colonial Office, *Malayan Union and Singapore—Summary of Proposed Constitutional Arrangements*, 1946, p. 9.

43. This did not include the collection of tithes and taxes.

44. In this connexion, the Governor was to be assisted by a Central Advisory Council of the Malay Rulers under his chairmanship. This Council had the additional privilege of discussing matters not pertaining to the Mohammedan religion, either at the request of the Governor or at that of any Ruler acting with the consent of the Governor.

of regulating religious affairs and for the constitution of a *Majlis Ugama Islam dan Adat Isti' adat Melayu*, to be called in English *Council of Religion and Malay Custom*, to aid and advise him in all matters relating to the Religion of the State and Malay custom.

This recognition of Islam as the official religion of each Malay State went uncontested by the non-Malays. They obviously did not mind the Malay States preserving their Malay character, as long as they themselves were not adversely affected by it. Thus religion once again became an uncontroversial subject until 1957, when the attainment of independence and the drawing up of the new Constitution gave it fresh significance.

In the course of formulating the Draft Constitution, the Constitutional Commission received representations that Islam should be established as the official religion of the Federation. The memorandum submitted by the Alliance, for example, had stated:

> The religion of [Malaya] shall be Islam. The observance of this principle shall not impose any disability on non-Muslim nationals professing and practising their own religions and shall not imply that the State is not a secular State.[45]

Despite this recommendation, the Commission decided not to make any stipulation on the matter in question, pointing out that the Counsel for the Rulers had himself made a request to that effect when he had stated:

> It is Their Highnesses' considered view that it would not be desirable to insert some declaration as has been suggested that the Muslim Faith or Islamic Faith be the established religion of the Federation. Their Highnesses are not in favour of such a declaration being inserted and that is a matter of specified instruction in which I myself have played very little part.[46]

The reasons behind Their Highnesses' attitude on this matter are not difficult to understand. As explained later by the Keeper of the Rulers' Seal, Tuan Haji Mustapha Albakri, they were of the opinion that the establishment of Islam as the State religion would invariably have 'tended to prejudice' their own positions as Heads of the Faith in their respective States.[47] Such a move would further have constituted an encroachment upon the right of the

45. *Report of the Constitutional Commission*, 1957, p. 73.
46. Loc. cit. 47. *Straits Budget*, Singapore, 28 February 1957, p. 15.

States to have full control over matters pertaining to the Muslim faith. Another cause for apprehension was the fact that, with the establishment of Islam as the State religion, efforts might have been made to establish a Ministry of Religious Affairs; such a move would undoubtedly have undermined the Sultans' authority with regard to religious matters.[48]

The Constitutional Commission was not unanimous in making its recommendation on the matter of State religion. Mr. Justice Abdul Hamid dissented from the majority view, giving his support to the Alliance recommendation that Islam be established as the official religion of the Federation. He considered a provision to this effect 'innocuous', stating: 'In all the Constitutions of the Malay States a provision of this type already exists. All that is required to be done is to transplant it from the State constitutions and to embed it in the Federal.'[49]

The treatment of religion in the final Constitution was a victory for the Alliance: the Commission's recommendation that no stipulation be made on the matter was rejected, and recognition given to the suggestion (made by the Alliance and supported by Mr. Justice Abdul Hamid) that Islam be established as the State religion. Clause (1) of Article 3 reads: 'Islam is the religion of the Federation; but other religions may be practised in peace and harmony in any part of the Federation.' This provision, while setting up Islam in a special position, has not caused the Constitution to fall short of establishing the Federation as a secular state. All religions are given ample safeguards with regard to their future in the country. In this connexion it is stated in Article 11 that every person has the right to pursue his own religious convictions and, subject to Clause (4) of the same Article,[50] to propagate it. It is further provided (Clause (3) of the same Article) that every religious group has the right to manage its own affairs, cater for the establishment and maintenance of institutions either for religious or charitable ends and, in accordance with law, to acquire, own, and administer property.

48. Loc. cit.

49. *Report of the Constitutional Commission*, p. 99.

50. Clause (4) reads: 'State law may control or restrict the propagation of any religious doctrine or belief among persons professing the Muslim religion.' In view of Islam's establishment as the State religion this is understandable, the purpose being to reduce the vulnerability of Muslims to proselytization by other religions.

Despite its seemingly superficial implications, the establishment of Islam as the State religion is not totally void of practical consequences, and educational preferences may be cited as evidence of this fact. Clause (2) of Article 12 states:

Every religious group has the right to establish and maintain institutions for the education of children and provide therein instruction in its own religion, and there shall be no discrimination on the grounds only of religion in any law relating to such institutions or in the administration of any such law; but federal law may provide for special financial aid for the establishment or maintenance of Muslim institutions or the instruction in Muslim religion of persons professing that religion.

The effect of this provision on Muslim religious schools has now become clear. At a press conference in August 1959, Tengku Abdul Rahman revealed the Government's plan to bring the Muslim College and other Islamic religious schools throughout the country under the control and care of the Education Ministry; plans were also in progress to draw up a new curriculum for these schools so as to bring their status in line with that of the other schools under the Ministry. In this way, it was expected that the students in these schools would gradually become entitled to work in the Government services.[51]

As far as the Rulers are concerned, assurance has been given that the establishment of Islam as the State religion will not in any way violate their traditional leadership in the Malay States. This guarantee is given in Clause (2) of Article 3 where it is stated that, subject to the Constitution of each State, all rights, privileges, prerogatives, and powers enjoyed by each Ruler are left 'unaffected and unimpaired'.[52] Further, no Ministry of Religious Affairs has been established; in this connexion, the Prime Minister explained:

It has been suggested that there should be a Ministry for Religious Affairs. It has to be remembered that Their Highnesses are the Heads of the religion in their own States and although they have agreed to authorise the *Yang di-Pertuan Agong* to represent them in any acts, observances or ceremonies agreed by the Conference of Rulers as extending to the Federation as a whole, Their Highnesses felt that establishment of a Federal Ministry for Muslim Religious Affairs would

51. *Daily Press Summary of Vernacular Papers*, 28 August 1959, p. 6 (from a news report in the *Utusan Melayu* of the same date).

52. In Malacca and Penang, which have no Sultans, the *Yang di-Pertuan Agong* is given the position of Head of the Muslim Religion (Article 3, Clause (13)).

affect adversely their position as heads of Muslim religion in their own States. If necessary, a Muslim Department of Religious Affairs will be set up as part of the establishment of the Yang di-Pertuan Agong.[53]

Having briefly studied the constitutional aspects of the religious issue, one may now proceed to analyse the different attitudes and demands which have enabled religion to make what the national elections of 1959 have shown to be significant inroads into the field of political behaviour.

To begin with, what connexion there is between religion and politics is confined to the Malay community; as far as the others are concerned, the only relevance which religion has in political behaviour has nothing to do with particular faiths, but arises from the common fear of Malay religious nationalism. Thus the future of communal relations, in so far as it is dictated by religious considerations, will depend almost entirely on the extent to which religious considerations succeed in politically unifying the Malays.

If one is to divide the Malay community by its attitudes towards the position of Islam in the local context, a most convenient method would be initially to separate the moderate elements from the extremist.

The most important characteristic of those described as 'moderate' is that they are willing, and often anxious, to keep religion away from politics. They are prepared to accept the recognition of Islam as the State religion mainly as an instrument to help the Constitution preserve and display the outward features of a Malay State. They consider it neither fair nor necessary that this provision should be used to consolidate the interests of the Malays at the expense of the other communities. In emphasizing the need for an effective partnership with the other communities, these Malays condemn the efforts of the extremist quarters to introduce an Islamic system of rule into the country. Tengku Abdul Rahman, for example, stated in a public address: 'Our country has many races and unless we are prepared to drown every non-Malay, we can never think of an Islamic administration.'[54]

The actions and aspirations of the extremists can be best understood if viewed in terms of Malay nationalism. That the ultimate aim of these Malays is the establishment of Malay supremacy, cannot be questioned; the immediate task of the hard

53. *Legislative Council Debates*, October 1956–August 1957, cols. 2862–3.
54. *Straits Times*, Singapore, 1 May 1959.

core of this group, however, is to convert their own community to their way of thinking. In trying to achieve this intermediate goal, the tendency has been for them grossly to exaggerate, and on occasions even entirely misrepresent, the dictates of Islam to the simpler rural folk who constitute the vast majority of the Malay population. Some of the tactics and propaganda used during the two national elections (discussed in Chapters Five and Six) are clear examples of this fact. Further evidence of this may be seen in a memorandum submitted by the *Lembaga Kesatuan Melayu*, Johore, to the Consultative Committee in 1947 where, among other things, it was stated:

Let it be known that the handing over of Islamic Government to the non-Muslim is very much against Islamic regulation and the organization of our Government. By that deed we are forced to sin for not obeying God's orders in verse 38:42, verse 3:158 and verse 38:26 and Prophet Mohammed's message. . . .
An Islamic person will bear the heaviest burden when his belief is endangered. The greatest danger will come when this belief is not evaluated and we allow our motherland which has been given to us by God to slip away. . . .
When we look at the handing over of a Government of Islam to the Government of non-Islam we shall find that the action is against the wishes of Islam (Holy Quran 4:58, 2:38, 3:158) because there are many matters and rightful claims of Islamic people which will not be available when the country is under the Government of non-Islam.
According to Islam there is no separation between politics and religion. It is a great sin to all the Islamic people, including all those who take part or agree to transfer the Government of the Malay States to non-Islam. Those people, therefore, are not doing their duty to God and are therefore traitors to their country.[55]

The opinions expressed in this quotation, although expressed

55. Federation of Malaya, *Report of the Consultative Committee*, 1947, pp. 116–17. According to Abdullah Yusuf Ali's translation of the Koran, generally regarded as reliable, verse 2:38 says:

We said: 'Get ye down all together;
And if, as is sure, there come to you
Guidance from Me, whosoever
Follows My guidance, on them
Shall be no fear, nor shall they grieve.'

Says verse 3:158:

And if ye die, or are slain,
Lo! it is unto God
That ye are brought together.

And verse 38:26:

O David! We did indeed
Make thee a vicegerent
On earth: so judge thou
Between men in truth (and justice)
Nor follow thou the lusts
(Of thy heart), for they will
Mislead thee from the Path
Of God: for those who
Wander astray from the Path
of God, is a Penalty Grievous
For that they forget
The Day of Account.

These verses no doubt appear quite irrelevant to the sentiments expressed in the memorandum. It is, of course, possible that verse numbers get slightly changed in translation; I have myself come across three translations where the numbering has differed. But even when this is taken into account, there seems to be little of direct bearing on the claims made in the memorandum. In Abdullah Yusuf Ali's translation, the appropriate verses probably are 2:41 (for 2:38), 3:161 (for 3:158), and 38:28 (for 38:26). The texts of these verses are as follows:

*2:41:* And believe in what I reveal,
Confirming the revelation
Which is with you,
And be not the first to reject
Faith therein, nor sell My Signs
For a small price; and fear Me,
And Me alone.

*3:161:* No prophet could (ever)
Be false to his trust.
If any person is so false,
He shall, on the Day
Of Judgment, restore
What he misappropriated;
Then shall every soul
Receive its due,—
Whatever it earned,—
And none shall be
Dealt with unjustly.

*38:28:* Shall We treat those
Who believe and work deeds
Of righteousness, the same
As those who do mischief
On earth? Shall We treat
Those who guard against evil,
The same as those who
Turn aside from the right?

If these are indeed the appropriate verses, it is not difficult to see that their relevance to Malayan politics is at best tenuous.
(Translations from: Abdullah Yusuf Ali, *The Holy Qur-an: Text, Translation and Commentary.*)

in connexion with the Malayan Union proposals which sought to give complete control of the Malay States to Great Britain, have not by any means sunk into irrelevance today: it is the local non-Malays who are now represented as wearing the robes of the designing usurper. Protests have arisen that the mere establishment of Islam as the State religion is far from satisfactory, and that adherence to Islamic principles of administration should become an integral part of the country's political framework.[56]

Although the goals of those seeking to further the interests of Islam are largely political, certain purely religious motives may also be discerned. For example, it is felt that Islam should consolidate its position *vis-à-vis* the other religions, and that better facilities should be provided for Islamic education among the Malays. In an editorial, the *Utusan Melayu* suggested that the State Religious Departments should be provided with better equipment in the way of public address units, films, books, and magazines; it also proposed that the Malayan Film Unit should produce films of a religious character.[57] These suggestions are not harmful as long as the purpose is to enable Muslims to understand their own religion better rather than encourage them to think of it as being in conflict with its political surroundings.

Finally, there are those who show concern for the future of Islam and of Islamic education because they are convinced that there is a direct correlation between the future well-being of Islam and the future well-being of the country. The Committee set up to consider financial aids to non-Government Islamic religious schools, for example, stated in its Report published in 1957 that

> the religion of Islam in this country has preserved the moral peace and faithfulness of the Malays towards the country. It is on this account that the Malays have become the strong foundation in this country of resistance against threats to its peace. . . . We are of the opinion that it is highly important that the religion of Islam should be well and properly treated for the welfare and peace of this country.[58]

56. Although the P.M.I.P. makes frequent reference to this, no effort seems to have been made to specify what these 'Islamic principles of administration' really are.
57. *Daily Press Summary of Vernacular Papers*, 5 September 1959—from the editorial of the *Utusan Melayu*, 4 September 1959. (There are also those who carry these suggestions somewhat further, urging that Islam should be taught to non-Muslims as well, e.g. *Malaya Merdeka*, editorial, 25 July 1959.)
58. Federation of Malaya, *Report of the Committee to Consider Financial Aids to Non-Government Islamic Religious Schools*, 1957, p. 6.

While non-Muslims may find it difficult to accept this view, the importance of satisfying the Malays that Islamic education is not totally neglected by the Government should not be overlooked. The above Committee, for example, stated that, in the course of interviews, it had become clear that the Muslims attributed the success of Christian Missionary schools to Government aid. It was thought that Islamic schools had not advanced because such aid had been lacking; and, as pointed out by the Committee's Report, it would be bad for the country if the Muslims (meaning the Malays) thought in these terms.

Despite these arguments it should once again be emphasized that it is the political motive behind the religious issue which demands attention at the present moment. A close political unification of the Malay community based on religious sentiment cannot but isolate that community and render it ill-disposed to any effective partnership with the others simply because the unity in question, in addition to excluding the non-Malays, must of necessity narrow the outlook of the Malays and render them a more distinct compartment within the Malayan society.

## LANGUAGE

The language issue is inherently the most explosive of the three discussed in the present chapter. In purely constitutional terms the religious issue, for example, can indeed be 'innocuous': the establishment of Islam as the State religion has not been made to imply any curtailment of religious freedom. Furthermore, religious qualifications have not been made necessary in any respect, and one does not have to be a Muslim to become a citizen or to be eligible for Government appointment. The same cannot be said of the language issue. Malay cannot be established as the only official language without seriously affecting the non-Malay communities. In addition to the material advantages and disadvantages (for the Malays on the one hand and the non-Malays on the other) which are clearly implied, the situation is complicated by considerations pertaining to cultural values and pride.

The present educational policy of the Federation is the product of the recommendations made by the Education Committee led by Dato Abdul Razak, then the Minister for Education,[59] in 1956. While minor additions have been made to meet new demands, the

59. Dato Razak is now the Minister for Defence.

basic features of the policy accepted in 1956 still remain intact. For this reason, an attempt will now be made to present the general principles enunciated by the Razak Report (as the Report of the Education Committee, 1956, has come to be popularly known).

The Committee in question was appointed in September 1955, and the following was included in its terms of reference:

> To examine the present educational policy of the Federation of Malaya and to recommend any alterations or adaptations that are necessary with a view to establishing a national system of education acceptable to the people of the Federation as a whole which will satisfy their needs and promote their cultural, social, economic and political development as a nation, having regard to the intention to make Malay the national language of the country whilst preserving and sustaining the growth of the language and culture of other communities in the country.[60]

The terms of reference made it quite clear that education had a crucial political role to play in Malaya in that a proper policy could be vitally instrumental in promoting the social and political unification of the country's mixed population.[61] In recognizing this task, and in suggesting a solution, the Committee stated: 'One of the fundamental requirements of educational policy in the Federation of Malaya is to orientate all schools, primary and secondary, to a Malayan outlook. We consider that the way to do this is to ensure a common content in the syllabuses of all schools.'[62] A common content syllabus, it was felt, would ensure that all pupils followed the same curriculum, whatever their language of instruction may be.

As far as the teaching and use of the national language were concerned, the Committee was of the opinion 'that the ultimate objective of educational policy in this country must be to bring together the children of all races under a national educational system in which the national language is the main medium of instruction, though we recognize that progess towards this goal cannot be rushed and must be gradual.'[63] In order to give Malay

60. Federation of Malaya, *Report of the Education Committee, 1956*, p. 1, (hereinafter referred to as the *Razak Report*).
61. Here one encounters yet another problem peculiar to plural societies like Malaya. Political unification, allied very much to social unification, is seldom a primary feature of educational policy in relatively homogeneous (and democratic) societies.
62. *Razak Report*, p. 17.
63. Ibid., p. 3.

the status worthy of a national language, it was felt that it 'must be learnt in all schools, and . . . that the teaching of Malay to and the learning of Malay by all pupils shall be a condition of Government assistance in all schools.'[64] Concerning the script to be used in teaching the national language, the use of *Rumi* (Roman script) was recommended, provided that arrangements were made for the learning of *Jawi* (Pesso-Arabic script) by Muslim pupils.[65]

An important section of the recommendations concerning the national language was that which suggested possible incentives for its learning. Saying that incentives and rewards were necessary 'for reaching adequate standards in Malay', the Committee suggested the following examples:[66]

(a) Malay could be made a qualification for entry into the Government service;

(b) it could be made a factor to be taken into consideration in selection for secondary education, and could be made compulsory in all Government examinations;

(c) it could be made a requirement for those seeking scholarships from public funds;

(d) bonuses could be provided at various levels in Government service to encourage increased proficiency in Malay;

(e) grants-in-aid to schools could be made to depend in part on the successful learning of Malay as and when sufficient facilities were available; and

(f) Malay could be made a compulsory part of teacher training courses and examinations.

In making its recommendations on the policy to be adopted, the Committee gave separate treatment to the different levels of education. As regards primary education, it suggested that all Primary Schools should fall into two broad types:[67]

(a) Standard Primary schools, in which the medium of instruction would be the Malayan national language; and

64. Ibid., p. 4.
65. Ibid., p. 5.
66. Ibid., pp. 4–5.
67. Ibid., p. 9.

The Committee recognized, at the same time, that it would be necessary for a while to assist financially other primary schools in which the medium of instruction was Malay, Kuo Yu, Tamil, or English, but in which the teachers did not have the same qualification as those in the Standard and Standard-type primary schools. These schools were classified *non-standard schools*.

(b) Standard-type Primary schools, in which the medium of instruction could be Kuo Yu or Tamil or English.

It was recommended that English should be made a compulsory subject in all primary schools. As far as instruction in Tamil or Kuo Yu was concerned, it was proposed that such instruction should be made available at the request of the parents of fifteen children from any one school.[68]

Concerning secondary education, the Committee had this to say:

Recognizing that the aim of secondary education is to train employable and loyal Malayan citizens and that one of its primary functions is to foster and encourage the cultures and languages of the Malayan community, we recommend that the aim should be to establish one type of National Secondary School where the pupils work towards a common final examination, but where there is sufficient flexibility in the curriculum to allow schools or parts of schools to give particular attention to various languages and cultures.[69]

It was recommended that the study of Malay and English should be made compulsory in all secondary schools:

The reason for the study of Malay is the intention, referred to in our terms of reference, to make Malay the national language of our country. The reason for teaching English is that we desire that no secondary school pupil shall be at a disadvantage in the matter either of employment or of higher education in Malaya or overseas as long as it is necessary to use the English language for these purposes.[70]

Concerning the medium of instruction, the Committee saw no reason for altering the practice in Chinese secondary schools of using Kuo Yu as the general medium, provided that the other requirements mentioned above were satisfied.[71]

On the matter of religious instruction in schools, the Committee recommended that in any assisted school where not less than fifteen pupils professed the Muslim religion, religious instruction for them should be provided at public expense. Instruction in other religions to other pupils could be provided so long as no additional cost fell on public funds, and so long as no child was required to attend classes in religious instruction without the parents' consent.[72]

On the whole, the Committee's recommendations may be said to have fully satisfied the requirements expressed in the terms of

68. Ibid., p. 10. 69. Ibid., p. 12.
70. Loc. cit. 71. Ibid., p. 12. 72. Ibid., p. 18.

reference. Bearing in mind local conditions and needs, the methods proposed concerning the encouragement of a local orientation, the establishment of Malay as the national language, and the safeguarding of all other languages and cultures may indeed be said to constitute an ideal blueprint. While the main features of the policy which has followed have been commonly accepted as adequate, there has, however, been some disagreement over details. In particular, as will be seen later, disagreement has turned on whether or not a common language medium (Malay) is implied in the Committee's recommendation regarding a 'common final examination'.[73]

In 1960, an Education Review Committee was set up to look into the implementation of the 1956 proposals. This Committee's Report contains a very detailed account of the working of the 1956 policy, and of its suitability for the future; suffice it to say here that it found the 1956 scheme both feasible and popular. In its own recommendations, the 1960 Committee made a clear statement on the disputed question of the language medium for Government-sponsored examinations, the main point being that these examinations can be written only in one of the two official languages, i.e. Malay or English.

The treatment of 'Language' in the present Constitution may now be studied.

In its draft proposals, the Constitutional Commission proposed (Article 140) that Malay should be established as the national language; since a very substantial portion of the non-Malay population was not fluent in Malay, English was to continue as an official language for a period of at least ten years. At the end of that period, Parliament was to decide when any change with regard to this matter should be brought into effect. Concerning the other languages in the country, the Commission did not feel that any of them should be given an official status: this had not been found necessary in the past, and the establishment of any of them as an official language would have led to great inconvenience.[74] It was felt, however, that notices, announcements, and other documents which had been published in Chinese and Tamil (in addition to Malay and English) should continue to be so published.

Next, the Commission dealt with the question of multi-lingual-

73. See the Committee's statement on secondary education on p. 129 above.
74. *Report of the Constitutional Commission*, p. 74.

ism in the legislatures, and its recommendations on this issue proved to be extremely controversial, being strongly opposed by the Malays. Saying: 'We have been impressed by representations that the existing law may prevent the election to the legislatures of persons whom the electors may desire to elect,'[75] the Commission went on to make two proposals:

(a) that there should not be any language qualification for candidates wishing to contest elections; and

(b) that for a period of 10 years there should be a limited right for members of a legislature to speak in a Chinese or Indian language.[76]

Stating that they did not recommend the institution of a system of interpreters ('it would be cumbersome and expensive and might be difficult to operate'), the Commission made it quite clear that the proposal was meant only for those who could not speak fluently in either Malay or English, if it was also possible that a member who could speak the language used could take the chair and a record be kept of the speech. It was further stated that speeches in the Chinese and Indian languages should be exceptional, and that there was no intention of making these languages acceptable in ordinary debate.[77]

Concerning the future relationship between Malay and English, the Commission stated that there were some purposes ('such as the authoritative text of an Act of Parliament and proceedings in Courts of Justice other than taking of evidence') for which the use of the English language should be retained for a considerable number of years. It was, however, felt that for all ordinary purposes Malay should in due course become the only official language.[78]

By and large, the Constitution which finally emerged agreed with the first part of the Commission's recommendations, i.e. concerning the establishment of Malay as the national language and the continued use of English as an official language for a period of ten years from *Merdeka* Day and thereafter until otherwise provided by Parliament. In establishing Malay as the national language, Article 152 lays down two conditions:

(a) that no person should be prevented from using (other than for official purposes), teaching or learning any other language; and

(b) that the Federal and State Governments should not in any

75. Loc. cit. 76. Loc. cit.
77. Loc. cit. 78. Loc. cit.

way be discouraged from preserving and sustaining the use and study of the languages of the other communities in the country. In explaining the continued use of English as an official language, Clause (2) of the same Article states that the language may be used in both Houses of Parliament, in the legislative assemblies of the States, and for all other official purposes. Clause (3) stipulates that, for the period stated above, the authoritative texts of all Bills and amendments to be moved in either House of Parliament, and of Acts of Parliament together with all subsidiary legislation issued by the Federal Government, shall be in the English language. Clause (4) adds that, for the same period, all proceedings in the Supreme Court shall be in the English language as well.

As far as the question of multi-lingualism is concerned, however, the recommendations of the Constitutional Commission were rejected.

With this background, the 'language problem' will now be studied from the point of view of communal attitudes.

It is a common characteristic of nationalist movements that success in gaining political independence from the external power is followed by efforts to regenerate and glorify the local cultural heritage. In Malaya, however, it has not been possible for this course of events to be automatic: the attainment of political independence has left the Malays still facing the very basic problem of persuading the other communities to accept a cultural uniformity based on Malay characteristics. For reasons that will be given later, the non-Malays have shown a strong determination to resist all efforts at cultural unification, and this has left the Malays with the feeling that their own nationalism has yet to reach fruition. Herein lies the most vital feature of present Malay attitudes as regards the status of their language.

It was during the first overt expression of nationalist feeling in 1946 (following the introduction of the Malayan Union proposals) that the Malays began showing concern for the future of their language. Some of the Malay political organizations which sprang up during this period demanded, among other things, that Malay be established as the country's official language.[79] This demand was again frequently sounded when the Federation of Malaya

79. As an example, one may mention the demand to this effect made by the *Pusat Tenga Ra'ayat* (People's United Front), which was a coalition of several Malay organizations.

Agreement of 1948 was being drawn up, as may be seen in several memoranda submitted to the Consultative Committee. With the acceptance of the Agreement of 1948, the issue tended to lose its urgency although it was not completely forgotten. In the years that followed, the Government for its part showed concern by making efforts to understand the issues involved (both from the Malay as well as the non-Malay point of view) in the hope of formulating an acceptable educational policy, as indicated by the setting up of two Committees, one (the Barnes Committee) to study and report on Malay education and the other (the Fenn-Wu Mission) to do the same in respect of Chinese education, in 1951.

The introduction of national elections in 1955 gave new scope for propaganda on Malay and non-Malay rights, and the language issue consequently assumed fresh political significance. A few months before the elections a Malay member of the Legislative Council, a member of Party Negara, introduced a motion in the Assembly designed to clear all doubts regarding the recognition of Malay as the country's national language.[80] The opinions expressed in his speech are indeed typical of Malay cultural nationalism. He stated, for example: 'By adopting Malay as the national language of this country, the future Malaya as an independent nation and country will profit by her kinship with Indonesia and other islands of the Eastern Archipelago, and not pass into uneasy history as an island of foreign reaction in a sea of Malay culture enriched by Malay tradition and enlivened by the Malay language.'[81] It is interesting to note the extent to which the type of cultural nationalism represented by the above statement is, in fact, more cultural than national.

The language issue has retained its significance as a component of Malay nationalism to the present day. In this connexion, it is important to realize that, despite the attainment of independence, the Malays do not feel the uninhibited comfort of 'being in their own home'. They find that, despite the lip-service given to Malay as the national language of the country by everyone, a strong cultural barrier continues to separate them from the rest of the popu-

80. According to the Agreement of 1948, English and Malay had been established as official languages. The speaker now wanted to make sure that everybody accepted Malay as the only national language, although there were two official languages.

81. Federation of Malaya, *Report of the Proceedings of the Legislative Council*, 30 and 31 March 1955, col. 111. The speaker was Enche Mohammed Raschid.

lation. Even verbal intercourse is often impossible, let alone a common social life. As a Malay member of the Legislative Council put it, '. . . If a Malay went to Petaling Street[82] and he felt that he is somewhere in China, he is not far off. This is the fate of the Malays and the Malay language.'[83] It is easy to see why the Malays still continue to regard the others very much as strangers even if they have become Malayans politically. Other arguments aside, they consider it necessary for a non-Malay to become at least partially assimilated into Malay culture if he is to do justice to his Malayan status.

One now begins to understand the Malay desire for cultural integration; but cultural factors are by no means their only consideration. They are also alarmed by the extent to which cultural differences, and the desire to preserve them, are in fact responsible for the continuing division of the Malayan political society into communal compartments; after all, it is by being made a compartment that they themselves feel the full force of non-Malay numerical strength. They realize that, with cultural integration, some of the demands which are at present regarded as emanating from the Malay compartment, and hence treated with suspicion and even defiance by the others, will come to be commonly accepted as being part of normal Government policy. Of particular importance here is the sort of educational policy which the Malays want to see adopted.

While the general conveniences to be gained from cultural uniformity, and the increased currency which such a uniformity would give to the Malay language, may be considered as important motives in the case of those advocating a Malay-oriented educational system, of equal if not greater importance are the material advantages which such a system would bestow on the Malays. This introduces the question of the economic motives underlying the language issue.

Until recently, Malay education has been restricted almost entirely to the primary level.[84] Coupled with the scarcity of Eng-

82. Petaling Street is one of the centres of Chinese congestion in Kuala Lumpur.
83. *Legislative Council Debates*, 30 and 31 March 1955, col. 113.
84. In 1957, out of 2,172 Government-aided Malay schools only 81 provided secondary education. During the same year, only 6,134 boys and 2,391 girls were enrolled in Malay secondary schools, as compared to 233,662 boys and 161,494 girls who were in primary schools. (Federation of Malaya, *Annual Report on Education, 1957*, pp. 79–80.)

lish schools in the rural areas, this fact has effectively restricted the occupational horizons of the Malay community. Even those educated at the secondary level in Malay have been largely confined to becoming teachers, poorly paid and often provided with the minimum facilities. It was with these conditions in mind that the Barnes Committee on Malay Education recommended, in 1951, that one of the main aims behind Malay education should be 'to encourage and enable the Malay community to occupy its rightful place in relation to other communal groups in the mixed society of Malaya'.[85] In addition to these factors, it is also a sore point with the Malays that English and Chinese education go up to university level. By contrast their position is, needless to say, aggravating.

While one can understand Malay anxiety and impatience as regards the status of their language and the educational policy which will determine it, it is also important that due consideration be given to non-Malay attitudes on this matter. In demanding a Malay-oriented educational policy, the Malays will have to have some regard for simple realities; nothing will be gained by uncompromising parochialism of the type displayed by a member of the Malayan Muslim Association who maintained that, by accepting *Rumi* as adequate for educational purposes and by not insisting on *Jawi*, the Education Ministry was 'sacrificing the culture of the natives for the sake of the interests of non-Malays'.[86] No effort at cultural unification can pretend to be well-intentioned, in terms of providing benefits for all and being instrumental in reducing culturally inspired political tensions, if the basis of that unification is so rigid as to be completely unpalatable to the non-Malays, and if it is evidently designed to meet Malay tastes only.

In discussing non-Malay attitudes towards the language issue and education policy, it will first of all have to be realized that the strong sense of cultural separateness at present displayed by the Chinese and Indians—the former in particular—may largely be attributed to the *laissez-faire* policy adopted by the Colonial Government towards education in the 1920s and 1930s. During this period no effort was made to formulate and enforce a unified

85. Federation of Malaya, *Report of the Committee on Malay Education*, p. 9.

86. Federation of Malaya, Department of Information, *Daily Press Summary of Vernacular Papers*, 9 September 1957—from a news report in the *Utusan Melayu* of the same date. (The speaker, Enche Syed Mohamad Ali Alsagof made this remark in the course of an address on 'Islam in Independent Malaya'.)

policy aimed at ensuring a local orientation in education; both the content of teaching as well as the recruitment of teachers went unsupervised. In consequence, it became normal for Chinese schools to recruit their teachers from China and for the instruction given in these schools to be consonant with the mood of nationalism in that country. Since the schools were also not financially dependent on the Government, what resulted was a completely independent attitude which has persisted, in varying degrees, to the present day, and which has rendered the implementation of present policies difficult.

While accepting the desirability of a local orientation in education, the non-Malays continue to insist on cultural pluralism. They are willing to become Malayans politically; culturally, however, they are determined to remain Chinese and Indians. In advocating a policy of cultural pluralism, the non-Malays protest that it is meaningless to ask them to become absorbed into a common Malayan culture because that culture has yet to be identified. Consequently, they point out that what is in fact being required of them is not affiliation to a Malayan culture but a surrender to Malay culture; and this is automatically repugnant to them, since they consider their own cultures to be superior to that of the Malays. On the specific question of language, many non-Malays remain convinced of the inferiority of Malay, not only in comparison to their own languages but (and this is particularly true in the case of the English-educated), also in relation to English. Thus, while the Malays accuse the non-Malays of being culturally parochial, thereby frustrating efforts at unification, the non-Malays complain that it is the Malays who, by attempting to preserve and cultivate their own culture at the expense of the others, are responsible for any ill-feeling which may exist.

Despite their refusal to accept cultural homogeneity, the non-Malays have in recent years become increasingly aware of their local identity. While seeking to preserve their own cultures, they are aware that their educational policies should not distract the people from their sense of local allegiance or their tolerance and appreciation of other cultures. They also consider it desirable that a certain amount of Malay culture, particularly the language, should become familiar to all. This was exactly the attitude encouraged by the *Fenn-Wu Report on Chinese Education* in 1951, where it was stated: 'No group whose concern is completely the preservation of its own culture, or whose basic loyalty lies elsewhere, can render patriotic service to Malaya.'[87] The Report also advised the Chinese not to over-emphasize the 'Chineseness of Chinese schools',[88] pointing out that there was no real use in maintaining the forms, methods and contents of education in China. Concerning the political aspect of education, it stated: 'There is no place in Chinese schools, or indeed in the life of the Chinese in Malaya, for China-centered political loyalties or controls. The mixing of foreign politics with education has not contributed to academic quality and has created misunderstanding for which the Chinese are themselves largely to blame.'[89]

In presenting the case for cultural pluralism, the non-Malays argue that it would be best for the country if the emerging culture derives its strength and character from contributions made by all sections of the population, instead of being based on Malay culture alone. In this connexion the above Report stated:

> By virtue of its composite population it (that is, the Federation) should be a land where the developing culture draws its validity from acceptance of the high values of other cultures. The people of Malaya will have to learn to understand and appreciate their cultural differences. They should be proud of their spirit of mutual tolerance. . . . no deculturized group will have anything to offer. The resulting culture will be the weaker for the poverty of its contributing units.[90]

However laudable this view may be, it cannot be denied that, in the light of local realities, it is somewhat idealistic. To begin with, as admitted by the Report, the creation of a common culture out of the diverse units is bound to be a very gradual process. Political dispositions being more restless, it is inevitable that this form of cultural evolution will have difficulty keeping in step with the appetite for quick solutions. However well-intentioned and attractive the ultimate cultural goals of the non-Malays may be, it is the political factor which is dominant today. The Malays are more interested in securing their own superiority and in establishing their own language as the basis for a rapid cultural unification

87. Federation of Malaya, Report of a Mission Invited by the Federation Government to Study the Problem of the Education of Chinese in Malaya: *Chinese Schools and the Education of Chinese Malayans* (*Fenn-Wu Report*), 1951, p. 4.
88. Ibid., p. 13.
89. Loc. cit.
90. Ibid., p. 4.

than they are in the purely cultural benefits which may be gained from a process of gradual evolution. Here one may detect the root of a very serious political problem which cannot be solved by vague conceptions of 'cultural evolution'. Much as the non-Malays may resent it, cultural policies will have to be planned and properly disciplined and a certain amount of uniformity will have to be conceded. It is only by doing this that the more pressing political issues stand a chance of being settled.

While the need for a planned and well-defined educational policy may be presented in the above terms, it should not be overlooked that a policy of this kind has immense shortcomings as well. The difficulty of reaching agreement over details is a good example of this, and recent events have made this quite clear. In April 1959 there were signs of serious discontent in the Chinese community over certain aspects of the educational policy. Although protests were largely touched off by the question of the language to be used in examinations (the Chinese objected to the principle that Malay should be made the medium for Government-sponsored examinations for all students, even those educated in Chinese schools),[91] various other grievances were brought to light. At a meeting sponsored by three of the country's most influential Chinese educational groups (the MCA Central Committee on Education, the All-Malaya Chinese School Management Committee Association, and the United Chinese School Teachers Association), a call was made for a 'fair and equitable' deal for Chinese education. While encouraging the compulsory teaching of Malay as a subject in all vernacular schools, the policy statement which emerged from this meeting made the following demands:

(a) mother tongue to be the main medium of instruction in the vernacular schools;

(b) medium of examination to be the same as the medium of instruction;

(c) fair proportion to be maintained in budgeting for all educational expenditure;

(d) remuneration for all vernacular school teachers to be on an equal basis;

(e) fair and equitable basis to be maintained with respect to grants for school buildings and equipment;

(f) junior and advanced vernacular vocational schools to be

91. See p. 130.

established, with the main vernacular languages as the media of instruction;

(g) all encouragement to be given for people to start more schools and classes;

(h) advisory committee to be appointed by the Government to assist in solving Chinese educational problems; and

(i) grants made by the Government to Chinese schools to be increased by 100 per cent.[92]

The nature and significance of these demands were adequately summarized by the *Straits Times* in an editorial where it was stated:

. . . while the language of the Chinese guilds and educationalists may have softened, their attitude of protest has remained unchanged.
It is hard to accept this complaint at face value, bearing in mind the picture that Inche Khir Johari [the Minister for Education] presented to the Federal Legislature when speaking on the education budget last December.[93]
. . . the real issues which continue to divide the Government and the Chinese schools have little to do with the physical problems of education. These arise generally from different interpretations of accepted policy, and specifically disagreement turns on the question of the language to be used in examinations. Unless these differences are resolved sooner or later, the policy that was acclaimed on all sides when it was announced will stand in danger of collapse.[94]

The stand taken by the Chinese educational authorities is a clear indication of the absence of any permanent agreement between Malays and non-Malays on educational policy.

Having discussed the major characteristics of Malay and non-Malay attitudes towards the language issue, a few observations may now be made on the influence of English education and the role played by the English-educated.

92. *Straits Times*, Singapore, 27 April 1959, pp. 1–2.
93. During this speech, Inche Johari had pointed out that there had been a large saving on the item 'Grants to Chinese Secondary Schools', because many of these schools had not accepted the conditions for full Government assistance. (Up to the end of 1958, only 11 such schools had accepted the conditions and received full assistance.) The situation was, however, more encouraging in the case of Chinese-medium primary schools. Since 1955, 787 such schools (or 85 per cent of schools which had only been partially assisted in 1955) had accepted the conditions for full grant-in-aid, and thus become converted into standard-type primary schools. (Federation of Malaya, *Legislative Council Debates*, 3–13 December 1958, pp. 5930–2.)
94. *Straits Times*, Singapore, editorial, 29 April 1959.

English education has played, and continues to play, a very vital role in the political life of the country. In a sense, it may even be observed that the English-educated are the only group of people who, while belonging to different communities, have become identifiable as a single social and cultural unit. It should however, be added that they have not generally become assimilated into an entirely separate unit, but retain, in varying degrees, their own communal affiliations. While this retention of communal sympathies may appear unsatisfactory at face value, there is a positive side as well: it is only by preserving their communal ties that the English-educated (who, as already pointed out, are better equipped to conduct inter-communal relations today) can continue to be accepted as the political leaders of their respective communities. English, it must be remembered, is still the main vehicle of communal bargaining at the higher levels.

The attainment of independence, however, has tended to weaken the claim of the English-educated to political leadership. They have lost their value as agents of nationalism, in the sense that they are no longer required to represent the views and desires of the people to a colonial power. Today, while national considerations have not become totally absent, the need to represent communal interests has taken precedence over the importance of presenting national claims. English-educated leaders have thus been compelled to justify their leadership on grounds quite different from those which initially placed them in power.

In conclusion, some attention may be given to the future of the Malay language, particularly as regards its status *vis-à-vis* English.

As already pointed out, the present Constitution provides that Malay shall be made the only official language in 1967, unless otherwise provided by Parliament. The progress made since independence does not however suggest that Malay education will be sufficiently advanced and widespread by that time to enable the complete abandonment of English. The most outstanding shortcoming in this respect is the acute shortage of textbooks and qualified Malay teachers, a fact which non-Malays frequently point to in support of their argument that the time is yet to arrive when any compulsion can be employed in relation to the learning and use of the Malay language. There are also doubts as to whether Malay is (or will be) sufficiently developed to replace English not only as the language of administration but also as the medium of instruction in higher education. While this lack of confidence is more obvious in the case of the non-Malays, it appears that there are also some Malays who are similarly inclined.[95] Inche Syed Nasir bin Ismail, the director of *Dewan Bahasa dan Pustaka* (Language and Literary Agency),[96] for example, stated that one of the most serious disadvantages faced in propagating Malay was the absence of a 'right attitude and right spirit' among some Malay teachers who had too much 'belief in English'.[97]

While some may give preference to the continuation of English for administrative and educational purposes, hardly any argument is now presented in favour of that language once the question of cultural unification is raised. Although views may vary as regards the extent to which cultural unification should be carried, almost everyone is agreed that Malay should form the linguistic basis of that unification. The absence of any support for English is not just a result of continuing anti-colonial sentiment; the desire to cultivate local cultural traditions may be considered a strong motivating force. Of some significance is the fact that the use of English, as compared to that of Malay, is too restricted to make an English-oriented cultural unification realistic.

95. Generally, however, the Malay community has full faith in the national language. Many of them in fact insist that Malay must completely replace English by 1967 if the political independence already attained is to be 'real', and if the Malay character of the country is to be recognized not merely in name but also in fact.

96. The *Dewan Bahasa dan Pustaka* is an independent corporate body set up by law to develop and popularize the national language.

97. *Straits Times*, Singapore, editorial, 22 April 1959.

## CHAPTER FIVE

# PARTY POLITICS

THIS chapter does not include a separate study of all the political parties which either have been or are in existence in the Federation of Malaya. Such a study, if undertaken, would have to include far too many parties, and hence might prove unduly lengthy and detailed in terms of the goals set in the present study. What is of direct concern here is the manner in which party politics is bound up with the general framework of communal politics. Thus emphasis will be placed not on the organization and functioning of the parties discussed, but rather on the extent to which these parties reflect communal aspirations and typify communal trends.

Elections were first held in the Federation of Malaya in 1952.[1] For this reason, party politics in the country may be divided into two periods: the period prior to 1952 and the period after it.[2] During the first period political parties were, understandably, only pressure groups which dedicated themselves to influencing official policy without actually thinking in terms of participation in government. Since 1952, however, parties have found it necessary to compete more directly with each other with a view to winning elections. The need to compete has produced a profound effect on the goals and methods of political parties:[3] witness the founding of the Alliance (initially just an electoral alliance between the United Malays' National Organization and the Malayan Chinese Association) before the Kuala Lumpur Municipal elections of 1952.

In addition to the two mentioned, a third period might have been expected: that from 1957, the year of independence. Prior to that

1. Only municipal and town council elections were held between 1952 and 1955. The first national elections were not held until July 1955.
2. It should be pointed out that political parties, constituted on popular lines, are essentially a post-war phenomenon in the country. The few that existed before the War, such as the *Kesatuan Melayu Singapura* (Singapore Malay Union), the *Kesatuan Melayu Muda* (Malay Youth Movement), and the *Persaudaraan Sahabat Pena* (Brotherhood of Pen Friends), were restricted to limited circles.
3. These changes were not made fully manifest until the introduction of Federal elections in 1955.

date, it was only natural that all the political parties in the country should have sought popular support on the basis of their own ideas about the most suitable constitutional future for the country. With the attainment of independence and the drawing up of the new Constitution (which, after all, was the result of an attempt to compromise differing points of view), attempts to represent the constitutional demands of the different communities should have ceased,[4] giving way to a rivalry based on the policies to be adopted by the Government within the framework of the Constitution. As things have turned out, however, most parties continue to be preoccupied with changing the Constitution to the advantage of their own communities.[5]

Before proceeding with the analysis proper, it may be useful to recall certain observations made in earlier parts of this book, which have a strong bearing on the general trend of party politics in the country.

To begin with there is the division of the Malayan society, first into Malay and non-Malay compartments and then into different sections within each community. The basis of the first division is only too clear: the Malays want to safeguard their 'special position' and establish their dominance in the country's political and social life; the non-Malays want to extend the limits of their 'legitimate interests'. Generally speaking, the internal division of the different communities is between the extreme communalists on the one hand and those willing to compromise on the other. Together, these divisions have played a very strong role in determining the policies of most parties.

The second important factor is the emergence of Malay nationalism.[6] In this connexion it should be observed that sections of the Malay community are becoming increasingly dissatisfied with the benefits which independence has brought them. Despite the withdrawal of the colonial power, they find that there has been little

4. It must be realized that a two-thirds majority in Parliament is needed for constitutional amendments. This clearly proves the futility of any attempt to change the Constitution for purely communal ends.
5. The Alliance, naturally, does not fall into this category of parties. This is so not only because it comprises three communal organizations which have to accommodate each other, but also because the present Constitution is largely the product of the party's own recommendations. It is, however, possible that the party may disintegrate, resulting in the member organizations becoming purely communal bodies.
6. See footnote 59 on p. 23 for what is meant by 'Malay nationalism'.

appreciable improvement in their own status: they continue to be politically insecure and economically depressed. They also find it difficult to make the non-Malays accept a cultural uniformity based on Malay characteristics. It is within this context of Malay nationalism that the role played by the Pan-Malayan Islamic Party, for example, can best be understood.

Finally, certain basic national policies are still in the process of being formulated. Although agreement has been reached (between the different communities) on most points of principle, certain controversial details remain to be settled.[7] This means that the days of communal bargaining are far from over, particularly in terms of party politics.

## THE PRE-1952 PERIOD

The origins and functioning of most of the parties during this period can best be understood if examined against the background of Britain's attempt at political experimentation in the immediate post-war period. As mentioned earlier, the Malayan Union proposals, by seeking to obliterate the special position of the Malay community, resulted in the rise of Malay nationalism on an unprecedented scale, leading to an extensive political mobilization of that community. Although non-Malay interest and participation were not totally lacking, the Malays undoubtedly dominated politics during this time. With this in mind, the period's most outstanding parties may now be studied.

### *The United Malays' National Organization* (*U.M.N.O.*)

The U.M.N.O. was without a doubt the most powerful political organization to emerge out of this early period. Bearing in mind the party's present outlook as a partner in the Alliance (with the Malayan Chinese Association and the Malayan Indian Congress), it would be interesting to take a brief look at its origins and initial functioning.

The U.M.N.O. was founded as a communal body, designed to champion the claims of the Malay community. In order fully to understand its original communal character, one must be aware not only of the implications of the Malayan Union proposals which were adverse to the Malays, but also of the hardening of

7. Controversy over some of the details of educational policy (see pp. 137–9 above) is a good example of this.

communal tensions which took place during the Japanese régime. Viewed against this background it becomes clear that, during its initial stages, the U.M.N.O. merely strove to exert the traditional rights of the Malay community in that it sought a re-establishment of the old order. In rejecting the Malayan Union scheme, the party claimed that the new proposals were not introduced in the proper constitutional manner, and hence were not binding on the Sultans and their subjects. The party demanded that the British Government restore the *status quo* by withdrawing the proposals immediately.

Whatever explanations may be given for the U.M.N.O.'s success in causing the abandonment of the Malayan Union, the rights and wrongs of the issues at stake were not of any decisive importance. What in fact proved to be literally overwhelming was the party's success in uniting the entire Malay community into a determined and demonstrative political army. Indeed, so strong was its influence that it was able to 'persuade' the Sultans not to attend the ceremony when Sir Edward Gent was formally installed as the Governor of the Malayan Union on 1 April 1946; the message conveyed to the rulers had stated that it was 'the desire of the People' that they should not attend the installation, and that they should further 'desist from taking part in any function connected with the Union'.[8] The message had also warned the Rulers that they would be disowned by the people if they insisted on recognizing the Union.[9] A complete boycott was thought essential. Those Malays who had been invited to become members of the Malayan Union Advisory Committee (the central legislature) had not only refused to attend the installation, but had also declined their seats; they had found it 'impossible to attend the funeral rights' of their 'birthright and liberty'.[10]

U.M.N.O.'s preoccupation with Malay rights being clear, sections of the non-Malay communities naturally began to feel apprehensive of the party and its relentless efforts at Malay unification. In an attempt to allay non-Malay fears, Dato' Onn (the 'father' of the party and its president until 1951) observed:

There have been suggestions that the unity of the Malays will be a danger to the other communities. I can assure these other communities that there will be no danger. The Malays have always been looked

8. H. Miller, *Prince and Premier*, p. 78.
9. *Straits Times*, 3 April 1946, p. 3.
10. H. Miller, op. cit., p. 78.

upon as a simple and law-abiding people, and we propose to live as such, but at the same time, like every other nation, we hope we still claim a place in our country.[11]

Despite this assurance, it took more than five years before the non-Malays got proof that the U.M.N.O. was actually willing to follow an inter-communal programme. During the interim period, developments were far from encouraging. To some extent, the outbreak of Communist terrorism may be held responsible for this.

It was not an uncommon tendency for Malays to identify the Communist threat as a Chinese threat, and this no doubt tended to make the entire Chinese community suspect, especially since it was found that they were not coming forward to the Government's aid. As far as the local population was concerned, military assistance to the Government came almost entirely from the Malay community. The U.M.N.O., for its part, was quick to note how the willing assistance given by the Malays stood in direct contrast to the seeming indifference of the other communities, particularly the Chinese; and it was not long before demands were made for something in recognition of this fact. In the autumn of 1948 the president of the U.M.N.O. made a trip to London, where he made the following demands:

(a) increased Malay participation in Federal administration (this was to include the appointment of Malays as heads of some of the Departments, and of a Malay as the deputy High Commissioner);

(b) an increase in the number of Malay military units; and

(c) a grant of £10 million from the British Government, to be given over a period of five to ten years, for utilization in raising the economic status of the Malays, largely through grants and aid to the peasantry.

These demands quite clearly indicated an attempt to safeguard the political and economic future of the Malay community; and they could not but make an unfavourable impression upon the Chinese, who must have viewed them as an attempt by the Malays to drive home the advantages which they had gained from the withdrawal of the Malayan Union. In Penang and Province Wellesley, some advocated secession from the Federation in favour of colony status. The Chinese majorities in these territories thereby indicated their resentment of a constitution which, in their eyes, was clearly weighted in favour of the Malays.

11. Ibid., p. 77.

Although the U.M.N.O., during these early years of its existence, catered solely for the interests of the Malay community, it was not long before its communal exclusiveness was questioned. Dato' Onn, for one, began seriously to consider a broadening of the party's base so as to admit non-Malays as members. His efforts in this direction failed to win popular support within the party, and this led to the resignation of many of the old leaders, notably of Dato' Onn himself. Dato' Onn subsequently founded the Independence of Malaya Party.

It was only with the introduction of municipal elections in 1952 that the U.M.N.O. recognized the advantages of an inter-communal approach in party politics. Its fortunes since that date will be discussed in the second part of this chapter, when the Alliance party is analysed.

*The Malayan Democratic Union* (*M.D.U.*)

The M.D.U. was founded in December 1945. Having originated as a non-communal organization, it gradually became the foremost spokesman of the non-Malay communities domiciled in the country. When the U.M.N.O. was formed, for example, the M.D.U. came out in a determined effort to provide an opposition which it hoped would offset some of the effects of the rise of Malay nationalism. In December 1946, the party provided the incentive and leadership in forming a federation of all the parties which opposed the U.M.N.O. so as to divert some of the support which was going to the latter. In addition to the M.D.U., the federation in question comprised the Malay Nationalist Party (a left-wing Malay organization), the Pan-Malayan Federation of Trade Unions (which gradually fell under strong Communist influence), the Malayan Union Congress, the Malayan Peoples' Anti-Japanese Army Old Comrades Association, the Malayan New Democratic Youth, the *Angkatan Wanita Sedara* (Women's Party), and the *Angkatan Permuda Insaf* (Youth Party). The Federation called itself the All-Malaya Council of Joint Action (A.M.C.J.A.).

Prior to studying the A.M.C.J.A., it may be best if the main features of the Malay Nationalist Party were first understood.

*The Malay Nationalist Party* (*M.N.P.*)

While the U.M.N.O. was purely a communal organization, the M.N.P. had certain ideological aspirations as well. Thus while the former merely represented the traditional claims of the Malays,[12] the latter sought to swell and unite the leftist elements within that community. The rivalry between the two parties had little to do with the Malayan Union scheme, to which they were equally opposed; their contest was for the leadership of the Malay community.[13]

Despite its communal base (and because of its ideological orientation), the M.N.P. emphasized amity between the different communities. The party made some general demands, such as civil liberties, lower taxes, aid for the peasants, better conditions for labour, and the right of self-determination. However, the communal element was by no means totally lacking, making itself clear in demands such as that for solidarity with the Indonesian Republic.[14]

Bearing in mind that the Malays were at this time influenced more by communal than ideological considerations, the failure of the M.N.P. to win over the support of that community is understandable: the Malays were naturally suspicious of any party which openly wooed the affections of non-Malay organizations.[15]

### *The All-Malaya Council of Joint Action (A.M.C.J.A.)*

As indicated by its membership, the A.M.C.J.A. embraced a queer assortment of political beliefs and aspirations. While the M.D.U. and M.N.P. (though influenced by communal sentiments) made at least some effort to formulate general policies, there were also those parties which were not only strictly communal but also represented intra-communal divisions.[16]

12. The U.M.N.O. was 'traditional' not in the sense that it was preoccupied with re-establishing traditional forms of authority (such as the Sultanate) but in the sense that it wanted full recognition to be given to the privileged position of the Malay community.
13. In 1946, the M.N.P.'s support was said to have been 60,000 strong. ('Britain Faces a New Malaya', *Amerasia*, Vol. 11, no. 1, January 1947, p. 13.)
14. It must be realized that had solidarity with Indonesia (leading to political union) been successfully established, the non-Malays in Malaya would have been transformed from a majority (in Malaya) to a fairly small minority in the larger Indonesian-Malayan union.
15. This refers to the M.N.P.'s membership in the A.M.C.J.A.
16. Two Malay parties, the Malay Peoples' Party and the Pan-Malayan Congress, provide the best examples of this. While the former demanded a 'Malaya for the Malays', glorified the doctrines of Islam, sought a re-establishment of Sultanate authority, and condemned the 'radicalism of the Chinese', the latter, on the other hand, based its programme on loyalty to the British

The inter-communal composition of the A.M.C.J.A. led to the advocacy of certain common rights; for example, equal political rights were claimed for all those who considered Malaya to be their real home and the object of their loyalty. But the special claims of the Malay community were also recognized, as was only natural in view of the heavy Malay membership in the Federation. It was agreed, among other things, that the Sultans should be reinstated as fully sovereign constitutional rulers, and that matters pertaining to the religion and custom of the Malays should be left entirely in the hands of that community. It was also resolved that a policy of encouraging the social and economic progress of the Malay community should be sincerely adhered to.

Taken as a whole, the A.M.C.J.A. typified the proliferation of poorly organized and loosely knit political parties which is usually seen with the awakening of political interest in colonial territories. Naturally, the common desire to oppose the U.M.N.O. was not sufficient to overcome the diversity of interests which had to be catered for. Since the foremost political issue of the time was communal in content (as represented by Malay attempts to restore privileges and non-Malay attempts to establish 'legitimate interests'), it was inevitable that the first split should have been on Malay/non-Malay lines.

*The Pusat Tenga Ra'ayat (Putera)*

It was soon clear that the Malays in the A.M.C.J.A. were Malays first and leftist anti-U.M.N.O. elements only next. Accompanied by the *Angkatan Permuda Insaf*, the M.N.P. withdrew from the main body (the A.M.C.J.A.) to organize a Malay Council of Joint Action. This move was the prelude to the founding of yet another front, the *Pusat Tenga Ra'ayat* (People's United Front), which comprised the main strength of the M.N.P., the *Angkatan Permuda Insaf*, the *Angkatan Wanita Sedara*, and several other less significant bodies.[17]

Having broken away from the inter-communal framework of the A.M.C.J.A., the parties which formed the Putera now had a

Government, being no doubt apprehensive of the political and economic future of the Malay community in the event of Britain's withdrawal.

17. The fact that a non-Malay (Mr. Tan Cheng Lock) was president was probably another reason for the A.M.C.J.A.'s failure to have much appeal among the Malays.

free hand to concentrate on Malay interests alone. Thus three new points were added to the A.M.C.J.A.'s programme, namely:

(a) that the official language of the country should be Malay;

(b) that Malaya's national flag should incorporate the Malay national colours (that is, the Indonesian red and white); and

(c) that the term 'Melayu' (or 'Malay') should be applied to all citizens of Malaya.

### *The Putera–A.M.C.J.A.*

The Putera–A.M.C.J.A. was a coalition between the *Pusat Tenga Ra'ayat* and the All-Malaya Council of Joint Action.

It was clear that, apart from the U.M.N.O., political parties in the country had become grouped into two main camps: the A.M.C.J.A. (now a predominantly Chinese organization) and the Putera (based on anti-U.M.N.O. Malay sentiment). Soon after the withdrawal of the Malayan Union (the immediate political crisis thus being over) a coalition was effected between these two groups. A natural outgrowth of this was the renewal of Sino-Malay political bargaining at party level; and the 'People's Constitution for Malaya', presented by the coalition for the consideration of the British Government at the end of 1947, gives some indication of the compromises which were made. No distinction was made between Malays and non-Malays as regards eligibility for citizenship; and all citizens were to 'enjoy equal fundamental rights and opportunities in the political, economic, educational and cultural spheres, regardless of race, creed, colour or sex'.[18]

While these provisions were undoubtedly of benefit to the non-Malays, safeguards for the Malay community were not forgotten, and the proposals on representation in the Legislative Assembly provide a good example.[19] Although there were to be no 'communal electorates, candidatures, representatives or allocation of seats whatever', a minimum of 55 per cent of the seats was to be held by Malays for the first three Assemblies;[20] if it was found that less than 55 per cent of those elected were Malays, then those Malay candidates who had polled the largest number of votes among those who were not returned were to be given that number

18. 'People's Constitution for Malaya' (mimeographed), section 6.
19. Members of the Assembly were to be directly elected by the people.
20. The life of each Assembly was to be three years.

of seats which would be required to bring Malay strength in the Assembly to 55 per cent of the total.[21]

The proposals also provided for the constitution of a Council of Races, which was to decide whether or not each Bill passed by the Assembly was in any way discriminatory.[22]

While these efforts were made to protect the interests of all the communities, care was also taken to give recognition to the Malay character of the country: all citizens were to be referred to as 'Melayus'; and Malay was to be made the official language.

Though far from inactive, the Putera–A.M.C.J.A. coalition failed to win popular support. The Malays, as already mentioned, were more attracted by the traditional (Malay) nationalism of the U.M.N.O., and preferred to support a party which had identified itself with Malay interests alone. It is also possible that the Malays suspected the strong Communist element within the coalition.[23]

The coalition's failure to win popular non-Malay support may be attributed to the general disinclination of the Chinese and Indians actively to participate in local politics at that time. As far as the middle classes were concerned (particularly the English-educated, who had found their places in the professions and in the Government services), it may be said that they were very suspicious of extreme left-wing politics; neither were these people sufficiently nationalistic to be inspired by the coalition's anti-colonial slogans. There was also the fear, common to Malays as well, that the granting of independence within the immediate future (as was advocated by the Putera–A.M.C.J.A.) might easily result in deep and hopeless communal separation.

21. With the same details and procedure as set out in the case of the Federal Legislative Assembly, the proportion of Malay representatives in the State Assemblies was to be no less than the proportion of Malay citizens to the total number of citizens resident in each State. ('People's Constitution for Malaya', section 32.)

22. A 'discriminatory Bill' was defined as one which 'either as a whole, or in any particular provision, [was] discriminatory on racial or religious grounds'.
The Council of Races was to comprise two members from each of the following communities: Malays, Chinese, Indians, Eurasians, Ceylonese, Aborigines, Arabs, Europeans, Jews, and 'Others'. If the Council decided (by a majority vote) that a Bill was in fact discriminatory, it could prevent it from being promulgated as law during the life of the Assembly responsible for the Bill.

23. The A.M.C.J.A., for example, was largely based on the labour unions, which were then Communist-dominated and comprised mainly Chinese and Indian immigrant workers.

To sum up, the limited support received by the Putera–A.M.C.J.A. may largely be explained by the fact that it emphasized ideology and a common Malayan nationalism at a time when communal interests clearly dominated the political scene.

With the outbreak of Communist guerilla warfare, and the subsequent declaration of the Emergency, the coalition became defunct since most of its member organizations, because of their extreme left-wing politics, were outlawed. Some of the leading members of the M.N.P., however, have recently resumed active participation in local politics, particularly as members of the Pan-Malayan Islamic Party.

*The Malayan Chinese Association* (*M.C.A.*)

Despite the increasing pace in Malayan politics (as depicted, for example, by the rise of the U.M.N.O. and its efforts to bring about the termination of the Malayan Union, on the one hand, and the efforts of the left-wing organizations to win mass support, on the other) the Chinese in Malaya were still in a state of comparative political apathy at the time of the declaration of the Emergency in 1948. For example, although the community remained dissatisfied with the Constitution of the Federation, its opposition to the new scheme did not in any way represent a forceful and sustained effort when compared to the Malay effort which resulted in the repeal of the Malayan Union.[24] It is possible that this was partly due to the fact that no effort was made to organize the community along lines which would have inspired a strong sense of identity and purpose. Such an effort was made in 1949 when the Malayan Chinese Association was founded under the aegis of the Communities Liaison Committee, with Mr. Tan Cheng Lock as president.

The founding of the M.C.A. served a dual purpose: it gave the British a better chance of obtaining co-operation from the Chinese community with a view to ending the Emergency; and it gave the

24. The Associated Chinese Chambers of Commerce, for example, withdrew their official opposition to the Federation proposals, agreeing to see how things went for a while.

It must be realized, however, that the Malays had more at stake than any of the other communities: the Malayan Union sought to abolish rights which they had enjoyed for a long time, and without which their position in the country might have become precarious. In this sense it is only natural that the reactions of the Malays should have been more forceful and sustained than those of the other communities.

Chinese themselves greatly increased scope for promoting communal solidarity so as to enhance the chances of improving their status under the new Constitution. To the wealthier and middle-class Chinese, the founding of the M.C.A. had yet another significance: it gave them the opportunity and the means to compete more effectively with the Communists in wooing the allegiance of the poorer classes within their community, especially the squatters.[25] Sir Henry Gurney, the High Commissioner from 1948 to 1951, had himself stated that he wanted the M.C.A. 'to be stronger than the M.C.P.' (Malayan Communist Party) and to provide the Chinese with an 'alternative standard to communism'.[26]

Thus, although to the British the M.C.A. was primarily of short-term value (in that its main use to them was connected with ending the Emergency), to the Chinese, who had broader constitutional objectives, it was a body with a more permanent significance.

During the early years of its existence, the M.C.A. neither competed against nor allied itself with other parties; it was, however, considerably active as regards the constitutional objectives of the Chinese community, maintaining consistent opposition to the Federal Constitution.[27] The interests of the Chinese community at large, and the offering of material aid to the handicapped within that community, were the party's two foremost considerations. The leadership and financial aid given by the party in assisting the resettlement of squatters into the 'new villages' was particularly outstanding.[28] Today, this resettlement has assumed a significance which goes beyond the original motive connected with the Emergency. As a result of it, more than half a million Chinese who previously were scattered in remote areas have now been made readily accessible to party political campaigns, and the electoral process in general.

25. 'Squatters' refers to those Chinese (about half a million strong) who lived largely on the periphery of the jungle and were exposed to Communist intimidation and extortion. As part of the anti-Communist effort, these people were resettled into 'new villages' which were both fenced and guarded.

26. *Malayan Mirror* (the official organ of the M.C.A.), 14 June 1953, p. 3.

27. Unlike the A.M.C.J.A., the M.C.A. placed prime emphasis on uniting the 'Malayan' Chinese so that there could be more scope for understanding and co-operation between themselves and the Government.

28. The party ran a lottery to raise funds for this as well as other purposes. Once its active participation in politics became apparent, this lottery was terminated by the Government.

Another important point in the M.C.A.'s original programme was the establishment of better understanding between the Malay and Chinese communities. In his inaugural speech, Mr. Tan Cheng Lock stated: 'It is a matter of supreme significance and indisputable necessity that a basic purpose of this organization must be the attainment of inter-communal understanding and friendship, particularly between the Malays and Chinese.' He urged the members of the Association to 'Wake up and unite not only among yourselves, but also with the Malays and other communities, to make this land one country and one nation'.[29] As will be seen later, Sino-Malay unity still continues to be one of the M.C.A.'s main objectives.

As is still the case today, the M.C.A., during the early years of its existence, represented varying political opinions while support was obtained mainly from the 'Malayanized' sections of the Chinese community. But the party did not represent the Chinese to the same extent as the U.M.N.O. represented the Malays. This, too, is still the case today: although the M.C.A. is the organization which represents the Chinese in the Alliance Party (and hence in the present Government as well), there is no assurance that its views are necessarily an accurate reflection of those of the Chinese population at large. The implication of this limitation will be considered in greater detail when the Alliance Party is studied in the second part of this chapter.

*The Malayan Indian Congress (M.I.C.)*

The M.I.C. was founded, in August 1946, for the basic purpose of representing the interests of the Indian community and providing a medium for the expression of Indian opinion in Malaya. However, it was not long before the party became involved in the activities of the left-wing in Malayan politics, once it had joined the A.M.C.J.A. While the political leanings of the party's leaders may have been partly responsible for this, one suspects that the M.I.C.'s decision to join the A.M.C.J.A. was considerably influenced by its own feeling of ineffectiveness. This possibility is strongly borne out by the fact that when all the other members of the A.M.C.J.A. either dissolved themselves or were driven underground as a result of the Emergency, the M.I.C. continued to maintain its legal existence by cleverly (and completely) return-

29. *Straits Times*, 28 February 1949, p. 1.

ing to its original function of being a communal party pure and simple.

Despite its local activities, an important feature of the M.I.C.'s early life was the keen interest shown in Indian politics; the success of the independence movement there must have largely provided the inspiration for this.

It would be no exaggeration to suggest that the M.I.C.'s present importance in the Malayan political scene derives almost entirely from its membership of the Alliance.[30] The extent to which its inclusion has enhanced the real strength of the Alliance is dubious, but the latter has attained greater stature by including representatives of all the three major communities within its organization. Not only do Indians constitute no more than about 12 per cent of the country's total population, but they do not form a sizeable portion of any Federal constituency either. Moreover, the M.I.C. itself does not have a wide following within the Indian community.[31]

### *The Independence of Malaya Party* (*I.M.P.*)

As already mentioned, the I.M.P. emerged out of Dato' Onn's failure to broaden the base of the U.M.N.O. so as to admit members of all the communities. Based on a non-communal programme, the new party also represented a political crystallization of the co-operative aspirations of the Communities Liaison Committee.

Prior to founding the I.M.P., Dato' Onn assured himself of the support of leading figures in the Chinese and Indian communities, notably of Dato' Tan Cheng Lock and Mr. P. P. Narayanan (who led the trade union movement and thus indirectly represented a considerable number of Indians).[32] Dato' Onn was emphatic in stating that, while the U.M.N.O. continued to retain its communal

30. The party was incorporated into the original U.M.N.O.-M.C.A. Alliance just before the first Federal elections in 1955.

31. For example, the party has little influence over the Trade Unions, although they are largely Indian-dominated. After the 1955 elections, three Indian Associations in the country (the Malayan Indian Association of Kuala Lumpur, and the Malayan-born Indian Associations of Penang and Johore) petitioned the High Commissioner for a seat in the Legislative Council for Malayan-born and -domiciled Indians; they were of the opinion that the M.I.C. was not representative of their interests. (*Malay Mail*, 30 July 1955.)

32. Indian support was further ensured by the enthusiasm shown by people like Mr. G. V. Thaver (president of the M.I.C.) and Dr. Samuel (president of the Federation of Indian Organizations).

outlook, some basis had to be created for effective understanding between the different communities resident in the country. Through the I.M.P. he hoped to bring about the changes which he considered to be both urgent and desirable: a unity embracing the entire settled population; the lessening of Sultanate authority; common citizenship; and the admission of Chinese and Indians into the administrative service.

At the inaugural meeting held on 15 September 1951, Dato' Onn addressed a truly cosmopolitan audience. Thirty of the seventy-five members of the Federal Legislative Council were said subsequently to have joined the party.

Despite these encouraging beginnings, it was not long before it became evident that the I.M.P. did not have the popular support of either the Malay or the Chinese community. As one might have expected, the strongest opposition came from the U.M.N.O. which accused the I.M.P. of being a 'destructive move' and resolved to expel from its own ranks those who belonged to that party as well. Other Malays were equally hostile. The president of the Malay Graduates' Association, for example, was of the opinion that Dato' Onn's decision to form the new party was 'not only highly irregular and improper, but was a betrayal of the birthright of the Malays'.[33]

To get a fuller understanding of Malay (particularly U.M.N.O.) resentment of the I.M.P., some of the relevant political issues of the period must be considered.

With the founding of the Malayan Chinese Association (M.C.A.), some sections of the U.M.N.O. had begun to fear that the former might some day become stronger than their own organization. It was partly as a result of this fear that Dato' Onn's efforts to admit non-Malays into the U.M.N.O. had failed to win popular support. At a time when they resented the Chinese condemnation of the Federation Agreement and feared the M.C.A., the Malays had found Dato' Onn's non-communal ideals quite out of place.

It is thus not surprising that the Malays were alarmed at the rise of the I.M.P. and its efforts to provide wider rights and opportunities for the non-Malays. A Malay, in a letter to the *Straits Times*, wrote:

The I.M.P. issue is a sad conflict in the history of the awakening of the Malays. U.M.N.O.'s hope to grow up as a strong independent party is

33. *Singapore Standard*, 9 July 1951.

eclipsed by the shadow of the I.M.P. Dato' Onn has evidently embarked upon a certain folly to throw the Malays into confusion and utter helplessness in the face of the fierce competition for power. . . . The Malays are economically backward. The object of the I.M.P. is to have Malaya as a country of one nationality, all sharing equal rights and privileges. Those who know the capabilities of the Malays know that their chance of survival . . . is nil. They will be reduced to the status of the Red Indians striving to live in the waste lands of America. . . . In short, the Malays should first be put in a sound economic position before they are put to face a trial in which they are not prepared to compete.[34]

Typical perhaps of the Malay attitude was the statement:

We all want independence, but to share our rights with those of whose loyalty we have grave doubts is a rash policy. The Malays . . . feel that the idea of being independent, popular though it is with other races, is not void of dangers and risks. They are aware that prejudices now rife in this country cannot and will not vanish even before such magic words as 'Independence' or 'Malayan'. Petty though these prejudices are, they are deep-rooted. Only a few at the top may be free from them. . . . Dato' Onn's proposed formation of the I.M.P. has allowed the non-Malays to be confused about our [Malay] rights. At a time when more than ever we want unity to lay stress on our demands he has started a move which undermines all our efforts.[35]

Faced with the emergence of the M.C.A. and the I.M.P.'s move to extend the rights of the non-Malays, the Malay community, led by U.M.N.O., considered it far more urgent to unite within itself rather than dilute its identity in a non-communal organization; and one has only to look at the I.M.P.'s eight-point programme to see how non-communal its objectives were, the eight points being:

34. *Straits Times*, 7 July 1951.
35. Ibid., 14 July 1951.

Opinions of this kind could not but cause some resentment among non-Malays. One of them, in a letter to the *Straits Times* (7 July 1951), wrote:

'What is really deplorable is the obvious fact that the very mention of anything concerning an alliance of the Malays with the other communities of this country throws some of the Malays into an agony of ill-humour. It is a pity that some leaders of Malay political thought cannot realize that without united effort of all communities who have made this country their permanent home, real political freedom can exist only in their imagination. . . . Up to the present the domiciled races have been kept guessing about their role, and they cannot have been very happy about it. But Dato' Onn's proposed new alignment, which is based on a just and profound policy, cannot fail to produce more agreeable results and create a happier atmosphere.'

(a) self-government within ten years;

(b) democratic elections to local government by 1953 and to the Central Legislature, based on adult suffrage, by 1955;

(c) Malayanization of the Civil Service and the creation of a Malayan Service as opposed to a Colonial Service;

(d) free and compulsory elementary education for all children between the ages of 6 and 12, by 1955;

(e) improved social services, especially in rural areas;

(f) subsidies and guaranteed prices for cultivators;

(g) full fruits of their industry to workers;

(h) reform of the feudal system in the Malay states.[36]

Considering the striking differences between the policies of the I.M.P. and the attitudes of the Malay community during this period, it is not surprising that the party failed to win Malay support: Dato' Onn had been far too optimistic in anticipating popular Malay support for the idea of a united Malayan nation at the time.

The Chinese too soon began to lose interest in the I.M.P. They began to doubt the effective leadership, on an inter-communal level, of a man (Dato' Onn) who could not obtain the support of his own community, and of a party which did not have the backing of the most numerous group in the country. The result was that, by the latter half of 1952, Indians constituted the majority of I.M.P. members.[37]

With the introduction of municipal elections in 1952, Chinese leaders in the I.M.P. (notably Dato' Tan Cheng Lock) hastily returned to the M.C.A., their own communal organization. They could hardly have failed to realize that talk of non-communal politics was meaningful only at the higher levels, and that elections, at that time, would be fought and won on communal platforms, as was evident from the continuing strength of the U.M.N.O.[38]

Faced with diminishing support, the I.M.P. dissolved itself in 1953. Having failed in his attempt to stimulate non-communal politics, Dato' Onn soon began to champion Malay communal demands. He played a leading role in launching the Malayan National Conference, which changed its name to Party Negara in

36. Silcock and Aziz, 'Nationalism in Malaya', op. cit., p. 334.

37. V. Purcell, *Malaya: Communist or Free?*, p. 102.

38. As things turned out, the U.M.N.O. and the M.C.A. decided to form an electoral alliance (without attempting a non-communal platform) to fight against the I.M.P.

February 1954. Led by him, Party Negara has based its programme on establishing Malay supremacy.[39]

## THE POST-1952 PERIOD

As stated earlier, party politics in the post-1952 period has been considerably influenced by the introduction of elections. Parties have become more dependent on public opinion; and since public opinion has been very much influenced by the rival attractions of communalism and inter-communal politics, political parties have also become classifiable along the same lines. The general pattern of party rivalries has thus been determined by the conflict between communalism and inter-communalism on the one hand, and Malay and non-Malay communalism on the other.[40]

As also explained at the outset of the present chapter, attention is now focused only on those parties which typify political trends in the country. Broadly speaking, four types of parties may be discerned: inter-communal parties, Malay communal parties, non-Malay communal parties, and parties based more on ideological than communal inspiration. No doubt most parties show some features of more than one of the above categories, but it is nevertheless true that a dominant characteristic is clear in every case. The Alliance is thus chosen to represent the first type, the Pan-Malayan Islamic Party the second, the People's Progressive Party[41] the third, and the Socialist Front the fourth.

### *The Alliance*

The Alliance Party had its beginnings in the electoral alliance between the U.M.N.O. and the M.C.A. just before the Kuala Lumpur municipal elections of 1952. Mutual opposition to the I.M.P. played an important role in encouraging a united effort by

39. Party Negara has never succeeded in winning popular support. It is in the unhappy position of being sandwiched between the extreme communalism of the more dynamic Pan-Malayan Islamic Party and the inter-communal policies of the U.M.N.O.

40. Non-Malays who advocate complete Malay/non-Malay equality at the present moment are here regarded as being 'communal'. The reason for this somewhat unusual definition lies in the contention (reflected in official policy) that the Malays should, as a matter of right, be given certain priorities. Thus, at present, non-communal politics would imply the advocacy of equal rights and privileges for everyone, with 'equality' defined in such a manner as to assume a few (defined) priorities in favour of the Malay community.

41. The People's Progressive Party was originally called the Perak Progressive Party, under which name it contested the 1955 elections.

these two parties; and their decision to form the (electoral) alliance had little to do with any identity of purpose.[42] For this reason, there was considerable truth in the early accusation that the Alliance was nothing more than a 'marriage of convenience'.

In discussing the origins of the Alliance, it must be understood that the experiment at Kuala Lumpur (repeated at the other Municipal elections which followed in other parts of the country) was not in any sense an experiment to test the possibility of non-communal voting; neither was it an effort to prove the non-communal aspirations of the U.M.N.O. and the M.C.A. What actually happened was that, through a simple system of apportionment, U.M.N.O. candidates were put up in predominantly Malay wards and M.C.A. candidates in those with a Chinese majority. This system of agreeing to share the elected seats to their mutual advantage proved to be a windfall for both parties. In the face of the I.M.P.'s non-communal platform, the U.M.N.O. and the M.C.A. were successful because they were practical enough to realize that at least for the first few elections to be held in the country, voting would almost certainly be communal.

In achieving its immediate ends, the Alliance, at least for the time being, ignored the desirability of campaigning on a non-communal platform. By doing so and succeeding as a result, it proved to the I.M.P. and the Labour Party[43] the fact that, under the existing social order, the notion that 'given a non-communal political platform, a Malay can get elected in a Chinese district or *vice versa*' was purely Utopian.[44] The I.M.P. and the Labour Party had definitely campaigned on a non-communal platform. This was laudable, but they lost.

Success at the Kuala Lumpur (and other) elections[45] led the

42. However, both the U.M.N.O. and the M.C.A. had by this time begun to realize that some kind of inter-communal effort was necessary, not merely in terms of electoral success, but also to prepare the ground for constitutional progress. But the realization was probably of no relevance as far as the Kuala Lumpur experiment was concerned; this move was purely of an *ad hoc* nature, initiated solely by local figures without any suggestion from the top.
43. The Labour Party also contested the elections on a platform which did not follow any communal directives.
44. F. G. Carnell, 'Constitutional Reform and Elections in Malaya', *Pacific Affairs*, vol. 27 (1954), p. 222.
45. At the Kuala Lumpur elections the Alliance won nine seats and the I.M.P. only two, one seat going to an Independent. During 1952 and 1953, the Alliance won ninety-four out of 124 seats contested in various Municipal and Town Council elections.

U.M.N.O. and the M.C.A. to think more seriously about their temporary but increasingly fruitful alliance. A series of meetings took place between the leaders of the two parties (Tengku Abdul Rahman and Sir Cheng-lock Tan),[46] resulting in the establishment of liaison committees linking the local branches of the two parties throughout the Federation. Discussions continued all the time and finally, on 17 March 1953, the Alliance made an announcement that it had reached agreement on the question of general elections for the Federal Legislative Council, stating that the 'agreed principle' would be forwarded for the consideration of the U.M.N.O. and the M.C.A. The draft plan called for a Council of seventy-five members of whom forty-four were to be elected and the remaining thirty-one nominated. At a general assembly of the U.M.N.O. held in Malacca on 6 April, the plan was approved, accompanied by a unanimous resolution calling for Federal elections by 1954, and for the resignation of all U.M.N.O. and M.C.A. members from the nominated Federal Legislative Council should the proposal be rejected by the Government.[47]

It is interesting to note that the Alliance made proposals only on the general question of the proportion of elected members in the Legislative Council; issues pertaining to communal relations were significantly left unresolved. This is understandable and may be attributed to the fact that the leaders of the party did not, at such an early stage, wish to disrupt the possibility of harmonious relations by attempting to solve the more 'difficult' problems.

Just before the Federal elections of 1955, the original U.M.N.O.–M.C.A. Alliance admitted the Malayan Indian Congress (M.I.C.) into its fold. With this move the party embraced all the three major communities of the country within its organization.

Some comments may now be made on the present position of the party in the context of communal politics in the country.

Although the Alliance contests elections as a single body, its member organizations continue to function on communal lines, being responsible to their own members. The Alliance is thus an

46. After receiving his knighthood, Dato' Tan Cheng Lock came to be known as Sir Cheng-lock Tan.

47. After further developments (resulting in a Council of ninety-eight with fifty-two elected members which the Alliance condemned on the grounds that an elected majority of six was insufficient) the Alliance did in fact withdraw its fourteen members from the Legislative Council when the latter met to debate the Federal Elections Bill.

inter-communal organization, and not non-communal as is often claimed.

At the centre of Alliance policy is the effort to reconcile communal with broader interests. While this was a source of strength in the period prior to independence, it has since lost the party a considerable amount of support. To understand the reasons for this, it is necessary to consider the general nature of the difficulties which have recently faced the party. These may be classified under two categories: 'internal problems' and 'external criticisms'.

*Internal Problems*

The internal problems of the Alliance stem from the fact that the member bodies continue to be constituted on purely communal lines. In the absence of direct membership,[48] the leaders of each group continue to be too concerned with the interests of their own organizations. Consequently, at the higher (that is, Alliance) level, outright bargaining has all too often taken precedence over reason and good sense. The row which took place over the allocation of seats for the 1959 elections[49] provides a good example of this: the leaders appeared to be more intent on securing a large number of nominations for their own members than in ensuring maximum success for the Alliance. During the State elections (held a few months before the Federal elections), there were even accusations that M.C.A. members had supported Chinese candidates belonging to other parties in preference to Indians representing the Alliance.[50] It is behaviour of this kind which has prevented the Alliance from becoming non-communal, and at times even from remaining truly inter-communal.

While most of the Alliance's internal problems arise in this way, some are also caused by troubles within the member groups.

48. There is no such thing as Alliance membership. Only the organizations have individual members.

49. Of a total of 104 seats, the U.M.N.O. originally wanted seventy-four nominations for itself, with twenty-eight for the M.C.A. and two for the M.I.C. The M.C.A. insisted on forty for itself. After considerable argument, the compromise finally arrived at gave the U.M.N.O. sixty-nine nominations and the M.C.A. thirty-one, with four going to the M.I.C.

50. The Selangor branch of the M.I.C., for example, alleged that M.C.A. men in *Rawang* and *Sentul* had supported non-Alliance candidates against those from the M.I.C., representing the Alliance. A similar complaint was lodged against the *Cameron Highlands* branch of the M.C.A. (*Daily Press Summary of Vernacular Papers*, 3 and 30 June 1959, from news reports in the *Tamil Nesan* of the same dates.)

Organizational difficulties within the U.M.N.O.,[51] for example, have been found to weaken the Alliance machinery at election time. Added to this is the very serious problem created by the presence of different factions within each group. The M.C.A. is probably the best example here; as observed by the *Straits Times* in an editorial: 'The M.C.A. has for years been weakened by factionalism. Old guard, young blood, Kuomintang diehards—all these familiar terms in the vocabulary of M.C.A. politics have merely been expressions of a basic inability to find firm common ground in the area of aims and politics.'[52]

### *Outside Criticism*

Criticism of the Alliance has become both more effective and more frequent in recent times, and the party's inter-communal programme may largely be held responsible for this. While compromises (between the member organizations) have been necessary to preserve internal unity, the party has found itself most vulnerable to criticism from communal elements outside it. Thus, while sections of the Malay community accuse the U.M.N.O. of having 'sold out' the interests of the Malays, several Chinese find the M.C.A. more concerned with placating U.M.N.O. demands than with fighting for Chinese rights. Two quotations from newspaper editorials, one from a Chinese newspaper and the other from a Malay paper, give some indication of the nature of these criticisms.[53] Said the Chinese paper:

We feel that we can no longer rely on the M.C.A. to accomplish this task [of fighting for Chinese rights], because it is a political party and not an organization to represent public opinions. Moreover, because of its association with the Alliance, it has many difficulties in this matter. As a matter of fact, the M.C.A. Central Working Committee . . . has already expressed clearly its attitude as follows:

'. . . that the M.C.A. still support the Alliance memorandum submitted to the Reid Commission . . . and that its special political sub-committee

51. These organizational difficulties are best reflected by the open (and not infrequent) disagreements between the central authority of the U.M.N.O. and the branches, not only over the selection of candidates but over general policies as well.
52. *Straits Times*, 31 July 1959.
53. The criticisms quoted here were both made just before independence, in connexion with the drawing up of the new Constitution.

is authorised to work together with the U.M.N.O. and the M.I.C. in making the necessary amendments to the Reid Constitutional Report.'

This is to say the M.C.A. will support the common views of the Alliance and can do nothing else. Unfortunately, the views of the Alliance and the demands of the Chinese are still greatly divided.[54]

The Malay newspaper was equally bitter in attacking the 'compromise policy' followed by the U.M.N.O. since the founding of the Alliance. It accused the Alliance of steering the Malays 'not towards independence which the Malays have wished for but towards an independence which is meant for the non-Malays and which will eliminate the Malays in their own country.'[55]

The Alliance's defence against these criticisms has assumed two forms. In the first place, the party has continued to emphasize the need for inter-communal co-operation: it has tried to drive home the fact that no community is sufficiently strong to control the others. Secondly, efforts have been made to satisfy each community that its own interests are carefully being safeguarded. U.M.N.O. leaders, for example, have taken great care to reiterate that their own organization would resist any attempt to withdraw or reduce the privileges accorded to the Malays.

Despite its difficulties and inadequacies, the Alliance continues to be by far the most powerful political organization in the country. More than any other party, it has adapted itself to local realities: it has paid heed to the vital necessity for a political party to embrace and cater for all the communities if it aspires to form the Government.[56]

There have been suggestions that the Alliance should transform itself into a single party with direct membership, and that the member-bodies should cease to exist. While this may be advantageous from an organizational point of view, present circumstances do not favour such a development. Communalism is still a very strong force in the country's political life, and as long as

54. *Daily Press Summary of Vernacular Papers*, 10 April 1957, pp. 1–2 (from the editorial of the *China Press* of the same date).

55. Ibid., 16 April 1957, p. 1 (from the editorial of the *Kritik*, 10 April).

56. The Alliance also has a better party organization than any of its rivals. At the 1955 elections, its success may well have been influenced by the record of opposition which it had established for itself in the old Legislative Council, the momentum it had gained through repeated victories in local elections, and its emphasis on independence. It could also be suggested that the Alliance owes some of its success to the personality of Tengku Abdul Rahman.

there are communal demands there will have to be communal parties to champion them. It is thus necessary that the U.M.N.O., M.C.A., and M.I.C. should continue functioning, because they still remain the agents through which support is channelled towards the Alliance. Secondly, it may be assumed that, under present conditions, the Malay section of the Alliance (that is, the U.M.N.O.) will consider any move to form a single non-communal party as something very much to its own disadvantage. While no reliable figures are available, it is possible that the membership of the M.C.A. could outnumber that of the U.M.N.O. This means that the Chinese might very well have the strongest voice in determining party policy should a single body be formed. As it is, however, the U.M.N.O. is without a doubt the senior partner of the Alliance, having considerable control over party programme.

### *The Pan-Malayan Islamic Party*

The Pan-Malayan Islamic Party (P.M.I.P.) is the most extreme Malay communal organization in the political arena. Its support is mostly derived from Malay fears (of non-Malay power) on the one hand, and dissatisfaction with Alliance policies on the other.

At the root of the P.M.I.P.'s programme is the belief that Malay nationalism still has a very important task to perform in the country, despite the attainment of independence. Using this argument, the party's leaders have spared no efforts in trying to stir the Malay community into a heightened awareness of its own rights. The attainment of political independence has thus been dubbed as nothing more than an 'empty victory' for the Malays.[57] According to Dr. Burhanuddin, the party's president,[58] this independence merely introduced a new phase in the political struggle of the Malay community, and the P.M.I.P. was dedicated to carrying this struggle further, so as to 'realize the aspirations of Islam' and re-establish Malaya as a Malay country.[59]

While the Alliance emphasizes the need for common participation in the country's political life, the P.M.I.P. insists that,

57. This view was expressed by Dr. Burhanuddin (the Party's president) a few days before independence.

58. Dr. Burhanuddin, it will be remembered, was the president of the Malay Nationalist Party before its dissolution.

59. *Daily Press Summary of Vernacular Papers*, 7 September 1957 (from a news report in the *Utusan Melayu* of the same date).

according to Islam, there can be no separation between religion and politics: it claims that one of the cornerstones of its programme is the establishment of a theocratic state, although little specification has been given as to what this really implies. The extent of the party's communal approach may be judged from the fact that its leaders have accused the U.M.N.O. of being 'Malayan' instead of 'Malay'.[60]

Though often exaggerated, the religious appeal of the P.M.I.P. is significant. With the help of rural religious leaders and Malay school teachers (who played an active role in the 1959 electoral campaign), the party has had some success in its attempt to explain political objectives in terms of Islamic doctrine. Up to the present (as will be seen when the 1959 elections are studied in the following chapter), this support has largely been confined to the predominantly Malay States (Kelantan and Trengganu) in the north-east. In commenting on the implications of this support (at the State elections) the *Straits Times* observed:

. . . the party's strength rests mainly on the deep-rooted traditional way of life of the rural Malay, and leaders who have emerged as candidates in the State elections . . . come mainly from the *kampongs*. A predominantly theocratic leadership among the opposition in the State Councils, and perhaps in Parliament,[61] would introduce a new and certainly 'interesting' phase. The question would be whether such an opposition would confine itself to secular problems. P.M.I.P. leaders have not been very responsible in public pronouncements on matters in which restraint and goodwill are called for. The P.M.I.P. will try to ride into State Councils on the communal fears of the Malays. But the tolerance and intelligence of the rural voter are Malaya's ultimate bulwark against racialism, and it will be a sad day if this bulwark is sapped.[62]

60. This view was expressed both by Inche Zulkifli (the party's vice-president) and Che' Khadijah Sidek (leader of the women's section) at public addresses. (*Daily Press Summary of Vernacular Papers*, 1 May 1959, p. 6, and 6 May 1959, p. 5.)

61. At the Parliamentary elections, however, the P.M.I.P. won only thirteen out of the 104 seats, having contested fifty-eight. All thirteen were won in Kelantan and Trengganu, where there were only sixteen seats in all.

62. *Straits Times*, Singapore, editorial, 4 May 1959. The *Straits Echo* (a Penang daily), however, was less pessimistic of the P.M.I.P.'s success in Kelantan. Said its editorial on 26 June 1959:

'The current country-wide elections are in themselves an indication of the growing political consciousness among Malayans everywhere. Though still sectarian in outlook in some States, there is no doubt that democratic prin-

Its religious appeal reflects only one aspect of the P.M.I.P.'s role as an agent of Malay nationalism. The party owes a considerable amount of its success to the manner in which it has managed to stir the communal fears of the Malays by attributing the economic grievances of that community to the generous treatment accorded to the non-Malays. Efforts have also been made to exploit Malay hopes and ambitions, however remote some of them may be. It has been asserted, for example, that the country belongs to the Malays alone and that, as such, their 'special rights' should be made both more extensive and more permanent, and should also constitute the basic features of a Malay national state. As mentioned earlier,[63] sections of the Malay community have in the past objected to the creation of a Malayan society where the Malays would only constitute one of the major communities; they have wanted the Malay 'community' to be elevated to the position of a Malay 'nation', the implication being that all the others would be regarded as aliens, enjoying only those rights and privileges which the Malays themselves might see fit to give. The P.M.I.P. has unreservedly allied itself to this view. Its leaders have demanded, among other things,[64]

(a) that citizenship laws should be made more stringent in the case of non-Malays;[65]

(b) that the establishment of Islam as the State religion should be made to have more practical consequences favouring the Malays;

(c) that immigration laws should be made more restrictive as regards non-Malays;

(d) that the posts of *mentris besar* (chief ministers in the Malay States), ministers, governors, and heads of the armed forces, should be reserved for Malays;

ciples are gradually permeating the masses who now realize the power they wield by exercising their voting rights. With the P.M.I.P. now staking its claim for power, issues are being more clearly defined. These are healthy developments in a nascent democracy.'

63. See pp. 112–13.

64. This list of demands has been compiled from the Party's 1959 Election Manifesto, and from various public pronouncements made by its leaders.

65. In a party broadcast before the 1959 Federal elections, Dr. Burhanuddin expressed the opinion that the principle of *jus soli* was 'a sharp tool to destroy the ownership and absolute rights of the Malays'. (*Daily Press Summary of Vernacular Papers*, 4 August 1959, from the *Utusan Melayu* of 3 August.)

(e) that Malay should immediately be made the country's national and only official language, and that educational policies should be substantially changed so as to produce a far more pronounced Malay orientation; and

(f) that a 'Melayu' (Malay) nationality should be introduced.[66]

The P.M.I.P.'s threat to the U.M.N.O. (and hence the Alliance) derives not only from the support which its communal programme has received from sections of the Malay rural community, but also from the attractions which this programme holds for U.M.N.O. dissidents. Dissatisfied with the Alliance educational policy, a number of Malay school teachers for example, have transferred their allegiance from the U.M.N.O. to the P.M.I.P.

Recent developments, however, have shown that there are still gaps in the party's popularity within its strongholds. In the Kelantan Town Council elections of May 1961, for example, the party won only 14 seats out of a total of 66, 51 (including 9 which were unopposed) going to the Alliance and one to Party Negara. Of the 6 town councils contested in the State, the Alliance won 5 (including Kota Bahru) and the P.M.I.P. only one. The results in Trengganu were much worse. Not only did the Alliance gain overwhelming majorities in all four town councils contested there, but the P.M.I.P. managed to win only a single seat. In both States many of the party's candidates lost their deposits. Six of those defeated were in fact State assemblymen, one of them the chairman of Kelantan's Land Development Board.

In viewing these Town Council elections, it has however to be noted that only about one-seventh or one-eighth of the total electorate in the two States was involved. Thus it cannot easily be inferred that there is also dissatisfaction with the P.M.I.P. in the rural areas.

In speculating on the P.M.I.P.'s future, two possible developments may be anticipated. First, it is possible that, should national policies (such as those pertaining to education) continue to produce dissatisfaction and dispute, communal tensions may very well harden instead of being steadily erased. Should this happen, parties like the P.M.I.P. will gain strength as champions of com-

66. It will be remembered that this was earlier advocated by the leftist Putera-A.M.C.J.A. coalition, largely at the insistence of the Malay Nationalist Party, some of whose members are now in the P.M.I.P.

munal rights. This, however, will offer no solution in so far as party politics within a framework of parliamentary democracy is concerned: however united they may become, the Malays cannot win a parliamentary majority sufficiently strong to control the others.[67] Thus nothing but deadlock can result.

The two States (Kelantan and Trengganu) where the P.M.I.P. came to power are characterized by isolation, predominantly Malay populations, economic backwardness, and a general simplicity of life. They are also areas where Chinese middlemen and money-lenders are greatly resented.[68] These States further comprise traditional societies where the country's political problems are not sufficiently understood and where religious leaders continue to exert much influence in social and political life. It is only natural that these conditions should have favoured the P.M.I.P. However, with economic development and the spread of education, a change in outlook is quite possible. With development, not only will geographic isolation be gradually overcome, but the composition of the society itself could change in that considerable numbers of non-Malays might settle in these territories. As in the more developed and cosmopolitan areas of the country, this might very well result in a realization that Malaya is not, and cannot be, just a Malay country, and that some kind of partnership is necessary, even if the idea is distasteful.

Religious teachers have played an active part in conducting the P.M.I.P.'s campaign. This has been made possible by the fact that religious instruction in the *kampongs* has largely been conducted without Government assistance or control; and this has given the teachers a free hand to use their influence to political advantage. With the assumption of wider responsibilities by the Education Ministry, however, it is likely that more and more religious instruction will be given by Government teachers, and this, no doubt, will tend to weaken the P.M.I.P.'s propaganda apparatus.

Thus the second possibility is that, with these changes, the P.M.I.P. will find the 'ground' less and less suited for its present propaganda.

67. This, no doubt, assumes that the non-Malays will also be equally united. Since a hardening of communal tensions (resulting in communally oriented political demands) is being assumed, this is plausible.

68. The fishermen, who constitute an important section of the community in these States, are particularly controlled by Chinese financiers.

*The People's Progressive Party*

The People's Progressive Party (P.P.P.) is the best example of non-Malay communalism in Malayan party politics.[69] Although the party claims to be ideologically inclined towards Socialism, most of its support (which is largely confined to Ipoh, in Perak) derives from its exploitation of Chinese chauvinism. Of particular significance is the manner in which the party's leaders (notably Mr. D. R. Seenivasagam, its secretary-general, who is also its leading figure) have played up to Chinese dissatisfaction with the Government's education policy.[70]

The main points contained in the P.P.P.'s 1959 Election Manifesto (which called itself a 'blueprint for equality and progress') give some indication of the party's general outlook.[71] The four most outstanding items listed in it were:

(a) the acceptance of Chinese and Tamil as official languages (with Malay recognized as the national language);[72]

(b) equal citizenship laws for everyone, based on the full application of the principle of *jus soli*;[73]

(c) equal privileges for all Malayans;[74] and

(d) the amendment of immigration and education laws, so as to give equal treatment to all communities.

It will be noted that each of the above items is a direct contradiction of the demands made by the P.M.I.P. This gives some indication of how hopeless is the division between Malay and non-Malay communalism.

The Manifesto laid considerable emphasis on education; this is understandable, considering that disagreement over the Government's educational policy[75] had flared up only a few months before the elections. It was thus maintained:

69. See footnote 40 on p. 159 for a definition of 'non-Malay communalism'.
70. It is worth noting that Ipoh has been a centre of Chinese student demonstrations.
71. Only those items which have a bearing on the communal aspect are mentioned here.
72. In this connexion it was stated that 'Malay, Chinese, and Tamil should stand recognized side by side for practical purposes and for the protection of the cultures of the races'. (Quoted in *Straits Times*, 6 August 1959, p. 2.)
73. The party sought to amend citizenship laws so as 'to establish for all time in Malaya only one class of citizens, all enjoying the same rights, privileges, security, and owing the same obligations'. (Loc. cit.)
74. As regards equal rights, it was stated that 'any semblance of special treatment to any one race will inevitably lead to frustration, suspicion and disappointment of the other citizens'. (Loc. cit.)
75. See pp. 138–9 above.

(a) that the mother tongue should be the medium of instruction and examination in all vernacular schools (though Malay should be made a compulsory subject);

(b) that educational institutions of all the communities, and teachers of all schools (vernacular or otherwise) should be treated impartially;

(c) that students from all recognized schools (i.e. including students from Chinese schools as well) should be treated equally as regards employment; and

(d) that travel restrictions placed on students in the Federation should be removed.[76]

In fact, the P.P.P. is as strongly dedicated to abolishing Malay privileges as the P.M.I.P. is to increasing them. As stated by Mr. D. R. Seenivasagam in a party broadcast, it is insistent that 'there should be no discrimination on grounds of race or religion';[77] the constitutional grant of special privileges to the Malays is thus branded as 'communal'. Under cover of this seemingly just cry for nation-wide equality, the P.P.P. has concentrated its efforts on exploiting Chinese dissatisfaction; the *Straits Times* was not far from the truth when it accused the party of having 'twanged hard at the chord of Chinese sensibilities and emotions'.[78]

### *The Socialist Front*

The Socialist Front (S.F.) comprises the Party Ra'ayat and the Labour Party of Malaya. Since the former is a Malay party and the latter is largely non-Malay, the Front is in some respects an intercommunal alliance. It is thus not surprising that, in attempting to embrace all the communities within its fold, the S.F. has a number of problems in common with the Alliance.

Perhaps the most outstanding problem faced by the S.F. (and this will have to be faced by any party which seeks an imperial implementation of socialist policies) is the difficulty of uniting the peasantry (which is largely Malay) and the industrial working class (mainly non-Malay) under a common cause: the fact that the

76. These restrictions were placed by the Government for fear that closer links might be established between Chinese school students in the Federation and their counterparts in Singapore, who are accused of being chauvinistic and partly Communist-infiltrated.
77. *Straits Times*, 2 August 1959.
78. Ibid., editorial, 24 August 1959.

former suspects, and is jealous of, the latter, already constitutes one of the main reasons for the P.M.I.P.'s popularity.

It is thus clear that it will not be sufficient for the S.F. to have a programme based on economic policies alone, however popular these may be; some stand will have to be taken on purely communal issues, such as those pertaining to culture. The Front has, in fact, attempted to state its position on these issues[79] but, like the Alliance, has been attacked equally by Malays and non-Malays.

The inability to satisfy communal demands is also reflected in the Front's divided leadership. Malay and non-Malay officials have often disagreed on matters such as special Malay rights, religion, and language. In April 1961, two non-Malay Labour Party leaders in Malacca resigned from their party because a Socialist Front document[80] had stated: 'Islam is Socialism and Socialism is Islam'; they were of the opinion that it was wrong and undesirable for an inter-communal socialist organization to hold such sectional views.[81]

Disputes like this are not the only indication of a basic lack of unity within the Front. In May 1961, Inche Ahmad Boestamam decided not to stand for re-election as the Front's chairman. He explained that he needed more time to organize and strengthen 'his party', Party Ra'ayat. While it may be argued that, by strengthening Party Ra'ayat, Inche Boestamam in fact sought to strengthen the S.F., it cannot be overlooked that the Front's difficulties seem to stem not so much from organizational difficulties as from the

79. It has maintained, for example, that although prime emphasis should be placed on the propagation of Malay as the national language (a common language not only meant 'unity of the masses', but was also necessary for the development of a 'Malayan Personality'*), every consideration should be given to the preservation and development of non-Malay cultures. On economic matters, the party's leaders have pointed out that they would not allow 'racial separatism' to hamper the country's development; they have indicated their resentment of any land development scheme which might maintain this separatism by providing for separate schemes. (*Straits Times*, 19 August 1959.)

* From the Front's 1959 Election Manifesto.

80. The document, 'Towards a New Malaya', had been passed by the Central Committee of the Front before the 1959 general elections.

81. The secretary-general of the Front, Inche Ishak bin Haji Mohamed, later explained that this statement on Islam and socialism had been made to 'nullify the present very rife belief among the Malay people that Socialism is contrary to the teachings of Islam'. (*Malay Mail*, 11 April 1961.)

Inche Ahmad Boestamam, then the chairman of the Front, stated that, in his opinion, this was a 'progressive conception'. (*Straits Times*, 8 April 1961.)

lack of agreement and co-operation between the two member parties; and if this is true Inche Boestamam would have done better to remain the Front's chairman and concentrate on bringing about closer co-ordination. As it is, his decision may be interpreted in two ways. First, it could indicate an effort to boost the prestige and bargaining power of Party Ra'ayat within the Front. Secondly, it might reflect an attempt to render that party stronger and more self-sufficient, so that it could stand on its own in the event of a complete break with the Labour Party. It is very possible that Party Ra'ayat would prefer to stand on its own if it can do so without much sacrifice: after all, its pro-Malay leanings have so often been opposed by the Labour Party.

This lack of internal unity was exposed even more glaringly during the local council elections of May 1961. The Johore branch of Party Ra'ayat strongly protested that the Labour Party had not in any way helped its candidates (i.e. S.F. candidates who belonged to Party Ra'ayat), thereby causing them to lose their seats. Annoyed at this, it threatened to break away from the Front. The situation was saved only through the personal intervention of Inche Boestamam. Following this crisis, it was decided that an inquiry should be conducted into the relations between the two members of the Front on a country-wide scale.

April–June 1961, we can see, was a period of awkward reappraisal: the unity of the Front clearly seemed a matter of great doubt. Paradoxically, it was also during this period that the Front made some significant gains at the Alliance's expense in the country-wide local council elections. Its success was most marked in George Town (Penang) where its candidates won fourteen of the fifteen seats contested, only one going to the Alliance. While the other gains were in no way as dramatic as this, and although the Alliance continued to be very successful on the whole, the fact that the Front made any gains at all is significant. The gains were restricted to urban areas (especially George Town, Kuantan, and Malacca), and could indicate two things. The first is the possible decline in the M.C.A.'s following. At an earlier election in Seremban, a group of Independents, who had received the 'approval' of Dr. Lim Chong Yew (the M.C.A. president who had resigned following the 1959 crisis), had scored victories over the party's candidates. Although M.C.A. leaders continued to assure their supporters that things were 'well under control', the defeat of the party's candidates in George Town, Kuantan, and Malacca cannot easily be dismissed as being of no great significance. The fact is that this loss of support in urban areas is quite visible. The second indication is that, although the elections were for local councils, dissatisfaction over national policies, especially education, played an important role in influencing the people's choice.

The internal divisions of the S.F., one can see, are very similar to those of the Alliance; and it is precisely for this reason that, like the Alliance, attempts to form a single party with direct membership have failed. The S.F., in fact, has an additional obstacle to surmount in that not only are the working classes unwilling to abandon their communal demands, but they are also poorly organized.[82] For this reason, it has been difficult to recruit an extensive, well-integrated and influential group of party officials from the working community. The party also continues to have difficulty in establishing its legitimacy within the political process because many still associate left-wing politics of any kind with subversion, a connexion which some of the other parties are only too keen to exploit and perpetuate. There is also a great deal of official concern with the activities of the S.F., and some of its members have in fact been arrested on charges of subversion.

The Socialist Front reveals a crucial fact about party politics in the Federation of Malaya: no socialist party can succeed in stirring up popular support as long as communal affiliations override economic interest. And it may be some time before political behaviour in the country is determined by ideological rather than communal considerations. For the present, the important thing is whether recent successes will encourage a closer unity within the party. Success, after all, is one of the important factors which has kept the Alliance Party together for such a long time and saved it from collapse at times of acute crisis.

82. The stunted growth of the trade union movement has also been due, in no small measure, to the restrictions arising out of the Emergency.

CHAPTER SIX

# THE 1955 AND 1959 GENERAL ELECTIONS

IN discussing national elections in the Federation of Malaya, the same three factors mentioned at the beginning of the last chapter[1] will have to be borne in mind. Also of considerable significance here is the recent nature of political development in the country, a fact which renders difficult any attempt at analysing electoral behaviour.

## (I)

## THE BACKGROUND TO NATIONAL ELECTIONS[2]

Given the choice between communal rolls and a common roll of electors (there being, no doubt, the possibility of variations being introduced to both), the Federation of Malaya has opted in favour of the latter in its pure and simple form. In making its recommendations, the Committee appointed (in 1953) to consider the question of elections to the Federal Legislative Council explained:[3] 'We are mindful of the fact that constitutional development in the Federation of Malaya presents problems that in their entirety find little parallel in other countries. The uncritical application of patterns which have been evolved elsewhere would not necessarily be advantageous to this country.'[4] In deciding the nature of the country's initiation to national elections, the Committee rejected, without opposition, the idea of communal rolls,

1. See pp. 143–4.
2. Prior to the introduction of Federal elections in 1955, national government was run by a nominated Legislative Council which, in its composition, gave recognition to the need for communal representation. The different proposals made, as regards the composition of the Federal Council under the Constitution of 1948, are given in Appendix I, with brief comments.
3. Appointed on 15 July 1953, this was a 46-man committee of the Federal Council. On 17 August, this somewhat bulky body delegated all detailed investigation to a group of twenty, made up of ten Malays, three Chinese, three Europeans, two Indians, one Ceylonese, and one Eurasian.
4. Federation of Malaya, *Report of the Committee Appointed to Examine the Question of Elections to the Federal Legislative Council*, 1954, p. 2. (Hereinafter referred to as the *Report of the Election Committee*.)

explaining that such a system 'would not be in keeping with the agreed object of promoting national unity amongst the peoples of Malaya and might arrest the process of assimilation and co-operation which is so essential if the country is to have a single united people'.[5]

Under some conditions of plurality, the introduction of communal rolls is admittedly one of the ways in which a certain brand of multi-communal government can be established and maintained. This being the case, it might be helpful at this point briefly to examine the choice between an electoral system based on communal rolls and one based on a common roll of electors. In this way the decision of the Election Committee may be more fully appreciated.

The problem of having to choose between communal rolls and a common roll is one that is inherent in plural societies. The question: 'How can one design an electoral system which recognizes the brute facts of the situation and yet avoids the full weight of the argument against separate rolls?'[6] is not one for which an answer, if found in one country, can be transferred to all. It is an oversimplification to suggest that all plural societies have the same problem, or set of problems; the truth is that the problems are almost invariably different, but stem from the common fact of plurality.

Communal rolls are in use when members of an electorate choose from a list of candidates, all of whom belong to their respective communities. Voters are thus linked together not by territory but by certain other characteristics. It might be argued that communal rolls are desirable in that they serve to 'mark time' until mutual fears and suspicions are sufficiently reduced to permit the introduction of a common roll, that they provide a constitutional stop-gap designed to accommodate non-constitutional change. It might further be added that, by preventing minorities from being 'swamped', such a system has the additional virtue of giving all sections of the population the opportunity to put their electoral rights to effective use.

This argument, however, overlooks the fact that what a system of communal rolls actually does is to retain communal differences

5. Ibid., p. 13.
6. W. J. M. Mackenzie, 'Representation in Plural Societies', *Political Studies*, Vol. 11 (1954), p. 63.

by offering neither the scope nor the inducements necessary for a gradual breaking-down of some of the original divisions. Thus in the final analysis it would seem that the system actually constitutes a standstill policy in that, while allowing for the participation in government of representatives of all communities, it does little to facilitate and encourage inter-communal co-operation. There is, in addition, the problem of 'who is to receive how many seats'. There will invariably have to be some measure of weightage,[7] and weightage can seldom be expected to gain popular acceptance. In the case of dependent territories, the greatest complication arises once the idea of independence begins to dominate the political scene. A full transfer of power seldom (if ever) takes place without being accompanied by grave doubts as to whether the power that is to be received will in fact be properly shared.

A system calling for a common roll, on the other hand, tends partially to ignore the existence of communal differences. For this reason it may be accused of running the risk of leaving important sections of the population unrepresented, thereby exerting a harmful influence on communal relations. This accusation, however, fails to hold as a generalization since degrees of political plurality are not the same in all localities; neither does the degree of plurality in any particular context have to remain static. A common roll system is imaginative in that, where complete inter-communal co-operation does not exist (but where at least some semblance of it is present), it indicates faith in the immediate scope for its development and thereby stands the chance of creating the goodwill so vital for its own survival. But at least some measure of co-operation (or even a willingness to co-operate) must exist for a common roll system to be feasible. Otherwise the functioning of political parties, the nature of electoral campaigns, and the behaviour of the electorate might all be out of tune with the electoral system, leaving important sections of the electorate without effective political influence.[8]

7. The need for weightage is, after all, one of the causes which make for communal rolls.

8. In other words, while the electoral system takes non-communal voting for granted, political parties may be constituted on communal lines, and voting may be based on communal motives.

Of course there are other methods besides the introduction of communal rolls which can be used to ensure the representation of all sections of the population. These will be mentioned later.

The Election Committee's decision not to introduce communal rolls should also be viewed in relation to the fact that a majority of its members were either M.N.C. (Malayan National Conference)[9] or Alliance members, and both groups had good reasons for not wanting a system based on communal rolls: the former, led largely by prominent Malays and hoping to establish itself as a more popular successor to the I.M.P., would naturally have found any electoral segregation of the population very much to the disadvantage of its own ambition of becoming a leading inter-communal organization; the latter, having found the precedent set by Municipal elections (which had no communal directives) to its definite advantage, similarly had little use for any experiment which stood against its own chances of success. Universal adult suffrage, on a non-communal basis, was the resultant agreement.

Despite the Committee's avowed bias against any institutionalization of communal divisions, its Report was not totally lacking in any communal gesture; it recommended that three nominated seats be reserved for the lesser minorities.[10] In explaining this provision, the Committee stated:

> Separate nomination would be undesirable in so far as it might delay the realization of a united Malayan nation where the separate racial groups would be integrated and would find their political voice through bodies organized on non-racial lines. Such provision [meaning, provision for the representation of minorities] should be contemplated therefore only in cases where there is, at present, no real prospect of adequate representation by other means.[11]

It was thus agreed that the provision in question was nothing more than a temporary measure, for otherwise it would have constituted a negation of the ultimate goal of a united Malayan nation. Representatives of minorities who sat on the Committee were in full agreement with this view.

9. The Malayan National Conference was formed on 27 July 1953, after it had become evident that the I.M.P. had failed to win popular support. Its inaugural meeting was called by a group of *mentris besar* under the leadership of Dato' Panglima Bukit Gantang, the *Mentri Besar* of Perak. All parties in the country were invited to participate in the Conference, but the Alliance and the Labour Party declined the invitation.

Failing to win non-Malay support, the M.N.C. changed itself into a more Malay organization, under the name of Party Negara. Dato' Onn, who had played a prominent role in the M.N.C., became the leader of the latter body.

10. These seats were to be filled by members appointed by the High Commissioner.

11. *Report of the Election Committee*, p. 5.

In deciding which of the minorities in the country were entitled to such treatment, the test to be applied was

> whether the community in question was of sufficient size and importance to the life of the country as a whole to merit some representation in Council, but not so numerous, widely spread and politically active as to ensure that its voting power must be taken into account by all political parties.[12]

The minorities which met these requirements were the Ceylonese, the Eurasians, and the Aborigines. The two former needed representation by nomination just because of the presence of 'a powerful element of communalism in the country'. The Aborigines were a special consideration because, although amounting to about 100,000, the degree to which they could have been expected to participate in the franchise was very limited.[13] Unlike the Ceylonese and Eurasian members, the member nominated to represent the Aborigines did not necessarily have to belong to the community he represented.

Also to be appointed were twenty members to represent 'scheduled interests', comprising six members for Commerce, six for Planting, four for Mining, two for Agriculture, and two for Trade Unions. Concerning the six members who were to represent Commerce, it was stated that election by a single comprehensive and non-racial body would normally have been preferred, but that the organization of the Chambers of Commerce in the Federation, and the complications which were understood to deter their amalgamation, 'left little alternative other than the proposed solution if comprehensive commercial representation [was] to be achieved'.[14] The result was that two of the members were to be chosen by the F.M.S. Chamber of Commerce in association with the Penang Chamber of Commerce; two by the Associated Chinese Chambers of Commerce; one by the Associated Indian Chambers of Commerce; and one by the High Commissioner, to represent Malay commercial interests. The six members for Planting were all to be chosen by the Rubber Producers' Council. Of the four members appointed to represent Mining interests, two were to be chosen by the F.M.S. Chamber of Mines and two by the High

12. Ibid., p. 6.
13. Ibid., pp. 6–7.
14. Ibid., p. 15.

Commissioner. Both members for Agriculture and Husbandry were to be appointed by the High Commissioner.

With regard to the two members who were to represent Trade Unions, the Committee stated that it fully recognized the importance 'of ensuring that the voice of labour be clearly and frequently heard in the Legislature'.[15] Agreeing that popular elections would normally be sufficient to enable this, it added:

In view of the recently declared policy of the M.T.U.C. [Malayan Trade Union Council] of refraining from participation in the political field, it will be necessary to make some limited provision during the first period of transition to an entirely elected Legislature for the M.T.U.C. and the vital interests for which it stands to be represented in the Legislative Council through nominated members.[16]

Thus Labour was in a way given the same treatment as racial minorities, a fact which suggests the decisive role which communal considerations were expected to play in the elections.

Taken as a whole, the Committee's recommendations called for a Council of ninety-two members, of whom forty-four were to be elected. The remaining forty-eight were to comprise the Speaker, three *ex officio* members, eleven members to represent the nine States and two Settlements,[17] twenty to represent 'scheduled interests', three to represent racial minorities, and ten 'Nominated Reserve'.

These recommendations, however, were far from being the product of unanimous agreement in the Committee. The full significance of the differences which existed among the members can be understood only if it is recalled once again that the Committee was largely composed of M.N.C. and Alliance members, representing the two foremost political organizations of the time.

So as to broaden the possibilities of success, the Committee had seen fit to invite suggestions both from individuals and organizations; this meant that M.N.C. and Alliance members in the Committee were in the curious position of having to review their own proposals, a factor which no doubt intensified the

15. Ibid., p. 5.
16. Loc. cit.
17. These members were specified to be the *Mentris Besar* in the case of the nine States, and a member from each of the Settlement Councils (to be appointed by the High Commissioner) in the case of Penang and Malacca.

element of rivalry. The Alliance-led minority group (which included the Labour leaders) proposed a Council of 100, of whom three-fifths (sixty) were to be elected; since the possibility of any party winning all the elected seats could not easily be entertained, they sought to increase the opportunity for the party holding a majority of seats to have a more effective voice in the running of the Government.[18] With regard to the date for holding Federal elections, this minority group maintained that it was possible for a constituency delimitation commission to complete its work in time to enable the holding of elections by November 1954. The majority group, however, considered this estimate to be over-optimistic and, deploring any haste in the matter, was satisfied to assert that the proper date would be fixed at the appropriate time.[19]

Concerning the method of the election, it was agreed that a system calling for electoral colleges should not be accepted, because 'the development of a healthy and vigorous democracy with an effective and popularly supported legislature will be more readily achieved by direct elections'.[20]

The Alliance refused to accept the situation as it was, and conducted a campaign aimed at preventing the implementation of the Committee's proposals. Led by Tengku Abdul Rahman and Sir Cheng-lock Tan, the party expressed, in no uncertain terms, that it would not be satisfied with tame compromises. Its stand was given full support by the Pan-Malayan Labour Party.

It was now for the High Commissioner and the Rulers to meet

18. Ibid., p. 8.
19. Ibid., p. 23.

This had been the view held in the plan submitted by the M.N.C. to the Committee, where it had been maintained that the Federation was not ready for an elected legislature, and that any move to force an election immediately would make 'a mockery of democracy'. This plan had been heartily condemned by the Alliance and the Labour Party. The former called the scheme 'a retrograde step' and a 'brazen effort to postpone the day when the Federation would have a popular Government' (*Straits Times*, 31 August 1953); the latter branded it as being nothing more than 'a job-preserving blue-print'. (*Malay Mail*, 14 September 1953.) The *Singapore Standard* warned that the acceptance of such 'stoogeocracy' would reduce Malaya to a position where it would be made 'the laughing stock of Asia and Africa', suggesting rather boldly that the M.N.C.'s plan was 'the product of men who [were] in a blue funk as to what their fate would be in a self-governing and democratic Malaya'. (*Singapore Standard*, 24 August 1953.)

From Carnell, 'Constitutional Reform and Elections in Malaya', *Pacific Affairs*, Vol. 27 (1954), pp. 225–6.

20. *Report of the Election Committee*, p. 12.

and consider the Committee's Report. The first meeting came and went without a decision being reached, since the Rulers were not united over the election issue. Fearing that the majority proposal calling for an elected minority might be accepted should they relax their own pressure, the Alliance petitioned the Rulers and the High Commissioner, while at the same time making demands for talks with the Colonial Secretary, Mr. Oliver Lyttelton, in London. Mr. Lyttelton, however, declined to receive the delegation and the Alliance's retort to this was an abandonment of its original demand for an elected majority of three-fifths, the new demand being for a fully elected Council. Despite the Colonial Secretary's refusal to see them, the Alliance delegation, headed by Tengku Abdul Rahman, left for London where, after successfully lobbying for British support, it was eventually received by Mr. Lyttelton.

As far as British colonial policy was concerned, submission to the Alliance's demands (even the original one calling for a three-fifths elected majority) would have constituted a marked deviation from established practice. No colony had up to that time advanced in one step from having a wholly nominated legislative council to having one with an elected majority. Despite this, the Colonial Office made a compromise in the Alliance's favour. This was made known when the Election Committee's recommendation advocating an elected minority was rejected, and provision made for a Council of ninety-eight with fifty-two elected seats—a majority of six.

This concession should not be mistaken for a 'surprise gift' from the British Government; it was very largely the product of the sustained pressure applied by the Alliance Party both on the Colonial Office and on influential circles in Malaya. For the first time ever, the Federation now beheld a united Sino-Malay political movement which not only claimed that it was undaunted and persistent, but was able to put weight behind its words.

The Alliance appeared to be far from satisfied with the concession. Claiming that an elected majority of six was too small to enable any single party in the Federal Council to obtain sufficient support to direct successfully the policies of the Executive Council, its leaders called for an immediate reappraisal of the election issue by a Royal Commission, failing which they threatened to boycott the Federal elections. In an effort to show that it 'meant business', the party withdrew its fourteen members from the Council as it met to debate the Federal Elections Bill. Although the move failed to alter the fate of the Bill, the Alliance succeeded in adding to its reputation of being the country's most dynamic political party.

The next major step came in April 1954, with the appointment of a three-man Constituency Delineation Commission 'for the purpose of dividing the country into constituencies in preparation for the holding of elections to the Federal Legislative Council'.[21] The terms of reference were not very precise: the Commission was merely asked to divide the country into constituencies which would provide for the election of fifty-two members to the Legislative Council, drawn in such a manner as to coincide so far as possible with the country's administrative districts, while at the same time embracing approximately equal portions of the population.[22] Although the Commission was empowered to recommend multiple-member constituencies 'for urban districts together with their contiguous areas', it decided against the creation of such constituencies, stating that 'a single member [can] represent the views and aspirations of a limited number of people in a comparatively small constituency more clearly and accurately than can two or more members in a correspondingly larger constituency', adding later: 'The necessity for simplicity and uniformity of procedure at the start of these new democratic processes in the Federation is a further argument against multiple-member constituencies.'[23] The result was the creation of fifty-two single-member constituencies.

The terms of reference were silent as to whether or not the Commission should give due consideration to the preponderance of any one community in particular localities. Interpreting this as being indicative of the commonly recognized hope that the future would bring the different groups into a single community, the Commission declared: 'In pursuance of this policy we have, in delineating constituencies, wholly ignored racial considerations; but we have taken into account community of interest where it

21. Federation of Malaya, *Report of the Constituency Delineation Commission*, 1954, p. 1.
22. Despite their efforts to adhere as closely as possible to the terms of reference, the Commission succeeded in satisfying this directive in only four States and Settlements. (Ibid., p. 8.)
23. Ibid., p. 9.

exists, for example in coastal as opposed to inland population groups; or where it depends upon occupation and industry.'[24]

Such was Malaya's experiment. Its real significance, in so far as representative government in plural societies is concerned, probably lies in the manner in which those responsible for it were willing to 'hope for the best' instead of falling back on established models. Taken by themselves, the facts of the communal distribution of population would probably have demanded either a certain degree of gerrymandering or a certain distortion of the franchise. With regard to the former, the most relevant example is perhaps the Ceylonese experiment in 'honest gerrymandering' (called 'honest swindling' by some), aimed at ensuring the representation of minorities by delimiting constituencies in such a manner as to limit communal antagonisms. This method has the virtue of giving recognition to communal divisions without making communalism a major issue but, like communal rolls, it does not encourage the emergence of non-communal voting.

As far as distortions of the franchise are concerned, examples are only too abundant, and it will suffice to mention just a few in order to present the general features of the policy. In Northern Rhodesia, for example, there was until 1958 a 'common roll' franchise limited to British subjects, which had the effect of excluding practically all the Africans in the territory because they were 'British protected persons', and not 'British subjects'.[25] Similarly, the African franchise law of 1956 in Kenya prevented the registration of a member of the Kikuyu, Embu, or Meru tribes until he had proved to the satisfaction of the District Commissioner that he had in some definite measure aided the administration in its battle against the Mau Mau. In so far as the adoption of plural votes is concerned, the best example is perhaps the 'Coutts' franchise introduced in 1956 (under the African elections law of that year) for Africans in Kenya. Special qualifications were listed under seven headings. Those qualifying under one heading were given one vote; those qualifying under two headings were given two votes; and those qualifying under three or more headings were given three votes.

24. Ibid., p. 4.

25. Helped by the property and income qualifications (one had to possess a house or building worth £250 within the territory; or a mining claim; or receive an annual income of £200, to be registered as a voter), this restriction resulted in only seven Africans being included in the 1957 voters' roll.

In some ways, the recommendations of the Election Committee and the Constituency Delineation Commission in the Federation of Malaya smoothed over the importance of communalism as a factor to be taken into consideration in determining the nature of the electoral process: no effort was made to ensure minority representation, and the idea of multiple-member constituencies with 'fancy franchises', such as 'plumping', and the limited vote, was discarded, and with it the assurance of minority representation—particularly the representation of the Indian community in large urban areas like Penang, Kuala Lumpur and Ipoh. Neither report made any reference to the strength which each community might have been expected to gain in the legislature.

At the time of the Constituency Delineation Commission's Report, it was indeed difficult to estimate whether or not the experiment would be successful and, if so, to what extent. Of the fifty-two constituencies which were created, fifty had a Malay majority and two a Chinese majority, while there was not a single one where the Indians accounted for even as much as 15 per cent of the electorate. Was the Federation indeed making a mockery of representative government? One critic referred to the Commission's report as 'a rather pedestrian and unimaginative document', the result of a 'growing ostrich-like belief in Malaya that communalism can best be scotched by refusing to recognize its existence. . . .'[26] If the Malayan situation was fundamentally the same as that found in India, Ceylon, Palestine, and some of the African plural societies, there was indeed good cause for alarm. The actual course of political development in the Federation, however, did not provide grounds for such a view.

Up to 27 July 1955 (the date of the first Federal elections) only some 25 per cent of the registered electorate had had the opportunity to vote in any previous election, and even those who had voted had not given any clear indication (assuming, for a while, that such a minority could) as to what the voting behaviour of the country would be were elections to be conducted on a non-communal basis. This was because the Alliance (which had won most of the seats in these early elections) had, during the first few years, merely followed a policy of apportionment, whereby Chinese candidates had been put up in Chinese areas and Malay

26. F. G. Carnell, 'Constitutional Reform and Elections in Malaya', *Pacific Affairs*, Vol. 27 (1954), p. 230.

candidates in Malay areas—a policy which had in no way tested the electorate's response to a national and supra-communal platform. These elections, furthermore, had mainly been held in urban areas; the votes of the mass of the electorate living in rural areas had never been tested.

What justification there was for criticism of the Commission's refusal to let the electoral pattern be dictated at least in part by communal considerations rested on the fact that, as only two constituencies had a Chinese majority, the assigning of a sufficient number of seats to Chinese candidates was invariably made difficult. This difficulty, however, was quite adequately overcome by the Alliance: after all, it was only to be expected that the U.M.N.O., in its efforts further to consolidate its partnership with the M.C.A., would make significant concessions to the latter in the choosing of candidates. Regarding fears that the policy of apportionment followed by the Alliance up to that time had not in any way indicated the possibility of non-communal voting, should the party have chosen to present a non-communal platform suffice it to say that since all previous elections had been for local councils, little reliable indication had been given as to whether or not the electorate (or at least that part of it which had voted in previous elections) would have reacted differently in the face of national issues—particularly at a time when independence appeared to be within reach.

(II)

In the interests of clarity, the following study of the 1955 and 1959 General Elections will give separate treatment to the following: the electorates; the candidates; the results; and the interpretation of the results.[27]

*The 1955 Elections*

The most outstanding feature of the Malayan electorate in 1955 was its uneven communal composition: of a total of just over 1,280,000 who ultimately were registered as electors,[28] approximately 84·2 per cent were Malays, 11·2 per cent Chinese, and the remaining 4·6 per cent mainly Indians.

27. It would be superfluous to analyse the reasons for the Alliance's success at the two elections (or, for that matter, to explain party performances generally); these have already been discussed in the chapter on *Party Politics*.

28. Registration was voluntary.

TABLE 8

*1955 Elections: communal breakdown of the electorate*

| *Communal group* | *Voters* | *(per cent)* |
|---|---|---|
| Malays | 1,078,000 | 84·2 |
| Chinese | 143,000 | 11·2 |
| Indians | 50,000 | 3·9 |
| Others | 9,000 | ·7 |
| Total | 1,280,000 | 100·0 |

Viewing the communal distribution of the electorate on a constituency basis, one finds an even greater absence of proportion; there were only two constituencies where the Malays accounted for less than 50 per cent of the electorate, and there were thirty-seven (out of the fifty-two) where they amounted to more than 75 per cent.[29] The main reason for this overwhelming preponderance of Malay electors is perhaps only too obvious: the Malays formed a good majority of Federal citizens. This advantage, however, would not have given the Malay community an electoral majority nearly as powerful as the one it in fact enjoyed but for the fact that about 75 per cent of Chinese and Indian Federal citizens were under twenty-one years of age and hence ineligible to register as electors.[30]

It was estimated that the number of Chinese who were eligible to vote amounted to 600,000, or about half the community's adult population.[31] Of this number, those who registered amounted only to 143,000, roughly one in every four, the result being that only one adult Chinese in approximately every eight actually cast a vote. While a lack of interest and insufficient confidence in the electoral process may be given as possible reasons for the low rate of Chinese participation in the elections, there could also be some truth in the observation that one of the main causes of this was 'the feeling of ineffectiveness which a minority group so often feels'.[32]

Turning to the Indian community one finds that, of a total of about 650,000 (in population), those who registered as electors

29. T. E. Smith, *Report on the First Election of Members to the Legislative Council of the Federation of Malaya*, p. 10.
30. T. E. Smith, op. cit., p. 11.
31. F. G. Carnell, 'The Malayan Elections', *Pacific Affairs*, Vol. 28 (1955), p. 316.
32. I. Tinker, 'Malayan Elections: Electoral Pattern for Plural Societies?', *Western Political Quarterly*, Vol. 9 (1956), p. 260.

amounted only to about 50,000. If the Indian adult population were estimated at half the total figure, approximately one Indian in every seven cast a vote at the Federal elections. This is indeed surprising in contrast to the disproportionately high degree of political consciousness and participation earlier displayed by the community in Singapore.

The net result of this severely restricted number of Chinese and Indian voters was that, particularly in the urban constituencies, the electorates were, in effect, somewhat unrepresentative minorities. The two Kuala Lumpur constituencies (*Kuala Lumpur Barat* and *Kuala Lumpur Timor*) perhaps provide the best examples of this. Here, out of a total population of 255,000, only 22,000 were ultimately registered as voters. Even more significant is the fact that, of those who registered, 64 per cent were Malays; and the Malays, as a community, are heavily outnumbered by the non-Malays in Kuala Lumpur. Thus the non-Malay vote in these urban areas was left largely untested at the elections.

On paper (and viewed as the beginning of an electoral experiment in a plural society), things perhaps could not have looked worse. The British had, up to this time, created an artificial democracy—a democracy based on an acquiescence that was more taken for granted than freely expressed—whereby members of all communities were made unofficial members of the Legislative Council. In a sense the introduction of elections, while furthering the definitive requirements of democracy, now somewhat threateningly implied a retrogression in its functioning: how democratic would the elections be to the non-Malays who outnumbered the Malays in population figures? But the most important fact was that everyone, whether Malay or non-Malay, who possessed the necessary qualifications, was given the right to vote. Despite the pro-Malay implications which the distribution of the electorate had at the time, this augured well for the future.

To turn from the communal characteristics of the electorate to those of the candidates themselves, it may perhaps be best to begin by discussing the manner in which communal allocation was conducted by the respective parties. The full significance of this allocation can be grasped only if reference is once again made to the extremely uneven communal distribution of the electorate; the implication being that, through a decision to effect a more equitable distribution in the line-up of their candidates, it was possible for the bigger parties (the Alliance in particular) to make representation in fact more democratic than the electoral framework (and the resultant distribution of the electorate) had made it.

Had there been any specific indication of purely communal voting, the Alliance would have had the alternative either of running more Chinese candidates than the electorates in the different constituencies would have permitted, thereby standing the risk of losing seats (to Party Negara and the Pan-Malayan Islamic Party in particular) in the interests of intra-party goodwill, or of doing exactly the reverse and putting up fifty Malay and only two Chinese candidates, thereby sacrificing the said goodwill in the interests of winning the elections. But, as earlier mentioned, there existed little indication of communal voting on any large scale, and the M.C.A. was given fifteen nominations.

This decision, however, was not effected without opposition. The M.C.A. had originally been assigned only twelve nominations but, following certain changes made in the whole line-up (to avoid a threatened rift), the figure was raised to fifteen. While some Malays questioned this decision on the grounds that there had not been any absolute necessity to be unduly liberal towards the M.C.A.,[33] the Chinese, on the other hand, criticized the leaders of their party for having been too submissive in their dealings with the U.M.N.O. In defending the number as being adequate, Mr. Leong Yew Koh, secretary-general of the M.C.A., explained that the Chinese expected to provide ten nominated members in the new Council: the representatives for Penang and Malacca, two of the six representatives for Commerce, two of the four representatives for Mining, one of the six for Planting, and three of the seven 'Nominated Reserve'.[34] As this would have given them twenty-five out of ninety-eight seats in the Council (assuming, of course, that all their candidates were elected)[35] it seemed a fair compromise,

33. It should be noted that significant sections of the politically active Malays view politics as a field meant to be dominated by their community, and in which their existing position of superiority must be jealously guarded.

34. Tinker, op. cit., p. 267.

As things turned out, the Chinese actually received eleven nominated seats (twenty-six including the elected members), since they were given two of the six Planting seats.

35. One would not have been wrong to make this assumption, which takes for granted non-communal voting by the Malays at the election, because, had communal voting in fact been expected, it would have been quite pointless to increase the number of Chinese candidates.

for on this basis the Chinese would have got 25·5 per cent of the seats in the Council while they constituted about 11 per cent of the electorate and about 40 per cent of the country's population.

This argument failed fully to satisfy the Chinese: they considered it a far cry from what they assumed to be their worth, or perhaps from what was necessary in order to safeguard their own interests. Some, including the *Singapore Standard*, were convinced that there would be several constituencies where the Chinese would vote against the Alliance candidates; and dissension went to a point where a member of the M.C.A. considered opposing Mr. Leong Yew Koh in Ipoh. The situation worsened when, three days before Nomination Day, Col. H. S. Lee, the man later referred to as the 'brains behind the almost frighteningly efficient machine that carried the Alliance into political power,[36] decided to withdraw from contesting the elections. His decision was severely criticized in an editorial of the *Singapore Standard* where it was observed: 'The public would like all self-styled leaders to have the courage to put their qualities of leadership to the public test by standing for election.'[37]

With two elected seats assigned to the M.I.C., the fifty-two Alliance candidates eventually comprised thirty-five Malays, fifteen Chinese, and two Indians (one of them in fact a Ceylonese),[38] a distribution which no community could seriously condemn. Party Negara, on the other hand, put up thirty candidates of whom twenty-nine were Malays and one Chinese; since the party did not contest in the two constituencies which had a Chinese majority, its lone Chinese candidate stood in a constituency with a Malay majority (Seremban), but was in fact opposed by another Chinese representing the Alliance.

The eleven candidates who represented the Pan-Malayan Islamic Party were all Malays. This needs no elaboration. All the candidates belonging to the National Association of Perak (eight Malays and one Chinese), the Perak Malay League (three Malays), and the Perak Progressive Party (one Malay and one Indian), only contested seats in Perak. There is nothing unusual in this since the parties in question were all only provincially organized.

36. *Straits Times*, 29 July 1955, p. 1.
37. Tinker, op. cit., p. 268 (from the *Singapore Standard*, 12 June 1955).
38. Throughout this chapter, Ceylonese candidates will be classified under the general category of 'Indians'.

In all, there were 129 candidates contesting the fifty-two seats. The following table classifies them by party and by community:

TABLE 9

1955 *Elections: classification of candidates by party and by community*

| *Party* | *Malays* | *Chinese* | *Indians* | *Total* |
|---|---|---|---|---|
| Alliance | 35 | 15 | 2 | 52 |
| Party Negara | 29 | 1 | — | 30 |
| Pan-Malayan Islamic Party | 11 | — | — | 11 |
| Labour Party | — | 2 | 2 | 4 |
| National Assoc. of Perak | 8 | 1 | — | 9 |
| Perak Malay League | 3 | — | — | 3 |
| Perak Progressive Party | 1 | — | 1 | 2 |
| Independent Candidates | 16 | 1 | 1 | 18 |
| Total | 103 | 20 | 6 | 129 |

Only three constituencies were uncontested by Malays: George Town (which had a clear majority of Chinese voters and where all three candidates were Chinese), Ipoh-Menglembu (the other constituency with a Chinese majority, where there were two Chinese (Alliance and National Association of Perak), and two Indians (one Independent and the other belonging to the P.P.P.), and finally Seremban, where there was a straight fight between two Chinese.

While there was little definite evidence to suggest communal voting, there was nothing much to indicate the contrary either. If communal voting had in fact been widespread, Party Negara might have stood some chance of beating the Alliance since U.M.N.O.'s communal appeal might very well have been diminished as a result of its partnership with the M.C.A. and M.I.C. Even if U.M.N.O.'s popularity had in fact ensured success for all the Malay candidates representing the Alliance, the party that would have stood to gain the most from communal voting would still have been Negara: of the twenty Malay candidates who opposed the Alliance's non-Malay candidates in constituencies with a Malay majority, eight belonged to Party Negara, three to the Pan-Malayan Islamic Party, three to the National Association of Perak, two to the Perak Malay League, and one to the Perak

Progressive Party, while three were Independents. Six of the eight Negara candidates mentioned were moreover the only Malay candidates running against the Alliance's non-Malays.

These were not unimportant considerations; and it is not surprising that the electoral campaign should have included issues which were undoubtedly communal. Perhaps assuming that voting would most probably be communal (or that it could be induced to become so), Party Negara lost no time in launching a pro-Malay campaign. As early as March (1955), its representatives made the question of national language a major topic for discussion at the Legislative Council.[39] Since it was evident that the U.M.N.O. would be 'cramped' in any strongly pro-Malay campaign because it could not afford to alienate the sympathies of its Chinese and Indian partners in the Alliance, Negara members in the Council had a field day in playing up to Malay sentiment. Enche Mohammed Raschid, who moved a motion to confirm that Malay was the only national (as different from 'official') language, took care to observe: 'It is fitting in my view that the National Council of my Party should have raised this matter at this time. As a national body, pledged to work for the national interests of Malaya, it is fitting and indeed right that it should have set its sights on a matter of national interest and importance, now embodied in the motion before the House.'[40] At one stage in the debate, Enche Mohammed Raschid made an interjection (in the course of a speech by Tengku Abdul Rahman) to express the view that the U.M.N.O.'s partnership with the M.C.A. amounted to nothing less than a betrayal of the Malay community.

In keeping with his position of leadership, Dato' Onn featured very prominently in Party Negara's election campaign. In a speech made over Radio Malaya on 5 July, he stated that his party would not accept a 'Babel of languages'; Malay had to be the only national language, with English as a second official language. He warned the Malays that, in the face of the increasing birth rate among the Chinese and Indian communities, a quota immigration system encouraging Malaysian immigration would have to be introduced if the Malays were to avoid the fate of being made a racial minority in their own country.[41] In its editorial, the *Straits Times* of 7 July

39. See pp. 133–4 for a brief discussion of this.

40. Federation of Malaya, *Report of the Proceedings of the Legislative Council*, 30–31 March 1955, col. 111.

41. *Straits Times*, 6 July 1955, p. 7.

commented: 'His approach [Dato' Onn's] is disturbingly communal. It seems to involve some sort of racial arithmetic.'[42] Stronger reactions came from a 'Federal citizen' who, in writing to the *Straits Times*, observed: 'Such ideas coming from the secretary of a party pledged to support the national and moral progress of the minorities is very disappointing to say the least. . . . If he considers Sumatrans are better citizens than those born here and have made this country the object of their allegiance, then I say Dato' Onn is a communalist. Once again religion is confused with nationalism.'[43]

Despite the fact that his party was based broadly on conservative foundations,[44] Dato' Onn was found making overtures to the former leaders of the banned left-wing Malay Nationalist Party. In this he was probably motivated by the possibility of winning over the support of Malay youth, both in the U.M.N.O. and in the newly organized Malay Nationalist Front, many of whom found great inspiration in the idea of 'Malaya for the Malays'.[45] Success at the elections might very well have left Dato' Onn facing serious differences within his own ranks.

With regard to the Alliance's proposal to establish a State Bank, Dato' Onn claimed that there was skulduggery afoot, interpreting the move to be a scheme designed to benefit the M.C.A. Chinese. Tengku Abdul Rahman was quick to react. Claiming that 'stooges were being used to spread false propaganda against the Alliance to the effect that he was selling 'the U.M.N.O. to the M.C.A. and the Malays to the Chinese', he declared: 'I want to tell you that no amount of money can buy the Malay race—the Malays can only be bought with my life.'[46]

Of the communally oriented campaigns, the most potent was the one conducted by the Pan-Malayan Islamic Party. Having the support of several rural religious leaders (whose measure of influ-

42. In a public speech made in June, Dato' Onn had made an even bolder statement on the question of immigration: 'If we do not want the Chinese to outnumber the Malays in this country, we must encourage more Indonesians to come here. The Indonesians—our history tells us—are our blood-brothers.' (*Straits Times*, editorial, 7 July 1955.)
43. Ibid., 20 July 1955, p. 6.
44. With regard to independence, for example, Party Negara sought its achievement within ten years, while the Alliance thought in terms of four.
45. F. G. Carnell, 'The Malayan Elections', *Pacific Affairs*, Vol. 28 (1955), p. 319.
46. Quoted in Tinker, op. cit., p. 274.

ence in the *kampongs* has already been mentioned), the party made an effort to exploit the religious sentiments of the Malay population. Just before the elections, there was a somewhat disturbing 'whisper campaign', attributed to the P.M.I.P., which warned voters that it was *haram* (forbidden) for a Muslim to cast his vote for a non-Muslim. In refuting the validity of this warning, Inche Nasaruddin Zakaria, a Kuala Lumpur religious leader (who was also an U.M.N.O. official), explained that there was nothing in the Koran to prove such a notion.[47]

In the face of communal attacks of this nature, the Alliance's campaign simply centred around the call for *Merdeka*. Over the question of citizenship, the party soon modified its original stand: having earlier promised to agitate for equal citizenship rights for all communities, it now began to call for the setting up of a neutral commission to conduct investigations into the problem. A very striking feature of the party's Manifesto was the fact that the more controversial issues, such as those pertaining to education and language, remained conspicuously vague.

In refusing to be perturbed by the somewhat alarming possibilities contained in the communal campaigns of Party Negara and the Pan-Malayan Islamic Party, the Alliance almost seemed to take it for granted that the non-communal voting implied in some of the local elections held earlier would continue at the national level. The Johore State elections, for example, had provided ample grounds for optimism in this respect: despite bitter opposition from Party Negara (and the electorate, it should be borne in mind, was predominantly Malay), the Alliance had won all sixteen seats contested, gathering 64 per cent of the total vote as against a mere 9·4 per cent obtained by Negara. Particularly significant was the fact that an Indian candidate, contesting the election on an Alliance ticket, had been elected with the day's greatest majority—8,018 votes over his closest rival. Indian votes had constituted an extremely small percentage of the total, and the overwhelming support given to the candidate in question by the Malay and Chinese voters had indeed given a valuable boost to the Alliance's morale.

It seems clear that the Labour Party did not contemplate much success at the elections; the very limited support received by the

47. Tinker, op. cit., p. 277.

party was well known in Malayan political circles. In fact, even the (Indian-dominated) leadership of the Malayan Trade Union Council decided not to give it their support, probably motivated by doubts as to whether affiliation to it would be in the interests of the satisfactory development of trade unionism.

Condemning the elections as nothing more than a 'farce', the Labour Party put up its four candidates mainly as a gesture against the 'reactionary aims' of the opposing parties.[48]

For a short time during the pre-election period, there was a possibility of an anti-Alliance electoral front, embracing all the parties with the exception of the P.M.I.P. Although moves of this kind are not exceptional as symptoms of pre-election panic, this attempt to include so many parties in a common front suggests the comparatively insignificant role played by ideology in party politics at the time. However, as is quite often the case with such attempts, the different parties could not come to full agreement, and contested the elections separately.

On 27 July, 84·86 per cent of the registered electorate cast their votes in the country's first national elections. In winning fifty-one out of the fifty-two elected seats, the Alliance got a total of 818,013 votes, four times the combined total of all its opponents put together and ten times the total obtained by Negara, a fact which clearly overrules the possibility that Negara lost because Malay votes had been split between the different Malay parties.

The only seat lost by the Alliance was in Krian (Perak), where a Malay candidate (Haji Ahmad bin Haji Hussain) belonging to the P.M.I.P. beat the Alliance candidate (also a Malay) by a mere 450 votes.[49] Of a total of seventy-seven candidates who opposed the Alliance, forty-three lost their deposits, having polled less than an eighth of the total number of valid votes cast in their respective constituencies. The smallest margin gained by an Alliance candidate amounted to more than 3,000. Inche Johari, the general secretary of the U.M.N.O.,[50] had the greatest majority of the day—29,646 votes over his closest rival.

48. F. G. Carnell, 'Malayan Elections', op. cit., p. 320. (From the *Malay Mail*, 27 July 1955.)

49. The number of votes declared invalid in this particular constituency amounted to 1,071. Whether or not the outcome of the election was affected by this is a matter purely for speculation.

50. Inche Johari later became the Minister for Education. He is now the Minister for Commerce and Industry.

TABLE 10

1955 *Elections: party performances*

| *Party* | *No. of candidates* | *Seats won* | *Votes polled* | *Percentage of total votes (spoilt votes excluded)* |
|---|---|---|---|---|
| Alliance | 52 | 51 | 818,013 | 79·6 |
| Negara | 30 | — | 78,909 | 7·6 |
| Pan-Malayan Islamic Party | 11 | 1 | 40,667 | 3·9 |
| National Assoc. of Perak | 9 | — | 20,996 | 2·0 |
| Perak Malay League | 3 | — | 5,433 | 0·5 |
| Labour Party | 4 | — | 4,786 | 0·4 |
| Perak Progressive Party | 2 | — | 1,081 | 0·1 |
| Independents | 18 | — | 31,642 | 3·0 |

It seems evident that the electorate gave national issues and the Alliance platform a definite priority over communal issues and individual candidates. The significance of this to the general theme of the present study accrues from the fact that, had communalism indeed dominated the political scene, votes would have gone either to the party with the greatest communal appeal or to individual candidates most acceptable to particular constituencies, the choice depending on the nature of communal sentiments in each locality.[51]

The above observation regarding the triumph of national issues over communal ones can be best substantiated if reference is once again made to the fourteen Malay-dominated constituencies where non-Malay Alliance candidates had fought against Malay candidates belonging to other parties. Out of a total of 247,069 valid votes cast in these constituencies, 205,004 went to the fourteen Alliance candidates and only 39,929 to the twenty non-Alliance Malay candidates, while 2,136 were cast in favour of other non-Malays (that is, non-Malays who did not belong to the Alliance).

51. The term 'nature of communal sentiments' should perhaps be explained. Had communal voting been vital to the political existence of the different groups in the country, the ballot would have tended to favour parties with categorically presented communal programmes; if on the other hand communalism had been nothing more than a matter of loose preferences and prejudices, it is quite likely that votes might have been cast in favour of individual candidates who had nothing but their own popularity to depend on.

Perhaps no example can do greater justice to the point in question than that of Mr. S. Chelvasingam MacIntyre, the M.I.C. candidate representing the Alliance, who contested the election in Batu Pahat. Of the 27,323 registered electors in this constituency, there were only 530 Indians and 5,679 Chinese. And yet, of a total of 21,685 valid votes that were cast in this constituency, Mr. MacIntyre collected 18,968, while his sole opponent, a Malay representing Party Negara, was able to get only 2,717.

The results in the fourteen constituencies in question are given in Appendix II (i). They indicate the extent to which non-communal voting was evident in these constituencies.

The Alliance had assumed that it would win the elections, confident that communal issues could tactfully be made subservient to certain national issues, particularly the call for independence. Said the elated Tengku Abdul Rahman when the results were all announced: 'The result today is the first step towards racial harmony in this plural society country. . . . It is one thing I am damned proud of.'[52]

Earlier elections in Singapore had revealed poor participation by the Chinese community; but the April (1955) elections there had been different in that a large Chinese vote had been recorded. Consequently, there was considerable speculation regarding the extent to which the community would participate in the Federal elections.

As the results were analysed it was found that, in the twenty-three constituencies where the Chinese electorate had accounted for at least 10 per cent of the total, the percentage vote was slightly lower than for the Federation as a whole: 79·92 per cent as compared to 84·86 per cent. This does not, however, necessarily indicate anything of particular significance, since the tendency in the earlier local elections had been for the rural voters to participate more actively than their urban counterparts—and most Chinese areas in the Federation are urban in character. At the same time, the lowest percentage poll recorded in the elections (52·6 per cent) was in George Town, one of the two constituencies with a Chinese majority and a constituency where all three candidates contesting were Chinese. In the other constituency with a Chinese majority (Ipoh-Menglembu), however, the vote turnout amounted to 82·7

52. *Straits Times*, 29 July 1955, p. 1.

per cent, and here (perhaps significantly) there were also two Indian candidates in addition to the two Chinese.

The results in these two constituencies may perhaps indicate communal voting by the Chinese community. It may be argued that the vote turnout in George Town was low because, in view of the fact that all three candidates contesting were Chinese, the electorate had assumed that a Chinese would be returned in any event; conversely, the high turnout in Ipoh-Menglembu could have been caused by the desire of the electorate to ensure a Chinese victory, the field being occupied by two non-Chinese as well. But there are other factors which need to be considered.

As explained in the *Report on the First Election of Members to the Legislative Council of the Federation of Malaya* (p. 26), Penang (where George Town is situated) was 'one of the few areas which experienced heavy showers on Polling Day'. To this may be added the already-mentioned fact that polling in urban districts was not expected to be as heavy as in the more rural areas. Penang Island, one of the two constituencies with a one-third Chinese electorate, was the only other constituency where the votes fell below 70 per cent. Here both candidates contesting were Malays, and this may lead to the suggestion that the low percentage was due to the fact that the Chinese, expecting a Malay candidate to win regardless of how they voted, had not seen much point in casting their votes. While this remains a possibility, the two factors which might call in question the validity of the assumption in the case of George Town are also applicable to Penang Island. In any event, there is nothing in the election results which conclusively proves that the Chinese sections of the electorate had in any way been less 'Malayan' in their outlook than their Malay counterparts.

Spared a sceptical post-mortem, the results in general would appear more than gratifying in almost every respect; to those who had earlier been suspicious, they were indeed startling.[53] Those

53. Mr. Carnell might be cited as an example. His condemnations of the Constituency Delineation Commission and his grave doubts regarding the outcome of the elections have already been briefly mentioned. In analysing the final results, he states: 'The results . . . have confounded some of the political prophets. . . . The most surprising thing about the election for the new Malayan Legislative Council was not the triumph of the triple Alliance of the United Malays National Organization, the Malayan Chinese Association, and the Malayan Indian Congress—this was generally expected—but that this party should have so completely annihilated its opponents.' ('The Malayan Elections', op. cit., p. 315.)

who expected to find fifty Malays and two Chinese elected, saw thirty-five Malays, fifteen Chinese, one Indian and one Ceylonese emerge as the day's victors—all but one Malay on an Alliance ticket.

However, although the voting appears to show a completely non-communal approach on the part of the electorate, there is one outstanding factor which should not be overlooked. On 27 July, the Malayan electorate was put to a test—a test which was to indicate its ability (or inability) to place national issues over the more emotional demands made by communalism.[54] On the surface the results of the elections would appear to indicate, with hardly a reservation, that the electorate had emerged fully triumphant, that it had proved its political maturity beyond all doubt. This may well be true, but with one vital limitation: the triumph of the electorate was in actual fact little more than a Malay triumph; the test had only proved the ability of the Malays to surmount the more extreme communal appeals. In both constituencies where the Chinese had formed a majority of the electorate, Chinese candidates were elected, and this means that the Chinese did not effectively exhibit their ability to vote non-communally. The Indians, on the other hand, had not even approached a majority in any of the constituencies; and this means that their votes were not tested either. It was only the Malays who returned candidates not of their own community.

It might be argued that, like the Malays, the Chinese had also voted along party and not communal lines: in both instances they had returned candidates belonging to the Alliance. Here was the rallying point for optimists; but the Ipoh By-election of 1956 gave rise to grave doubts about the future of non-communal voting. The 'Malayan' outlook once again appeared somewhat ephemeral.

In Ipoh, the general elections had seen Mr. Leong Yew Koh, the Alliance candidate (who was also the secretary-general of the M.C.A.), elected with a most convincing majority, all three of his opponents losing their deposits. The General Elections, however, had been held at a time when the Alliance stood as the symbol of the struggle for independence, and when the policies of the party, as the Government, had not been exposed to dispute. By the time

54. It is of course possible that it was the emotional appeal of *Merdeka* which proved to be more successful than that of communalism. If so, it might be suggested that the results indicate the triumph, not of political considerations over emotion, but of one form of emotion over another.

of the by-election, however, conditions had changed. The Alliance could no longer present an attractive dish to the electorate in the form of a general programme of peace, prosperity, and co-operation, since communal issues had increasingly undermined the roots of this co-operation. Perhaps more than anything else, the language issue, and educational policies in general, were now the salt and the pepper—they had to be in everything; and it took a communalist to make an attractive dish also taste good. Paradoxical though it may seem, it was an Indian, Mr. D. R. Seenivasagam, who best exploited the growing Chinese dissatisfaction in Ipoh. Allying himself closely with the sentiments of the Chinese community (and being a very vocal opponent of Government policies), he now emerged victorious in the very same constituency where he had lost his deposit not so long ago.

## THE 1959 ELECTIONS[55]

As compared to the electorate in 1955, the most outstanding feature of the 1959 electorate was its vastly increased proportion of non-Malay voters; while in 1955 the preponderance of Malays had been quite overwhelming, communal distribution of voters was now much more in proportion to the general distribution of population. Of the increased electorate of 2,144,829, it was estimated that about 1,217,000 were Malays, 764,000 Chinese, 159,000 Indians, and 4,000 'Others'.[56]

TABLE 11

1959 *Elections: communal breakdown of the electorate*

| *Communal group* | *Voters (approx.)* | *(per cent)* |
|---|---|---|
| Malays | 1,217,000 | 56·8 |
| Chinese | 764,000 | 35·6 |
| Indians | 159,000 | 7·4 |
| Others | 4,000 | 0·2 |
| Total | 2,144,000 | 100·0 |

55. In view of what has already been said in the chapter on *Party Politics* and in the analysis of the 1955 elections, just completed, it is unnecessary to give an account of party campaigns for the 1959 elections.

56. No official breakdown of the electorate by communities has been made available. Figures quoted here are obtained from the *Straits Times* of 19 August 1959.

Two reasons may be given for this substantial increase in the strength of the non-Malay vote. First, it will be remembered that about 75 per cent of Chinese and Indian Federal citizens in 1955 had been under twenty-one years of age. Since the 1959 elections were conducted on the registers of electors revised in the second half of 1958, those who had been between eighteen and twenty-one in 1955 had by this time qualified to register as electors.[57] Secondly, the Constitution of 1957 had made it easier for non-Malays to become citizens by registration and naturalization.[58]

The most important outcome of the swelling of the non-Malay vote was that, particularly in urban areas, the electorate became far more representative of the general population than it had been in 1955. Furthermore, while in that year the Malays had dominated fifty of the fifty-two constituencies, they now formed the most numerous group in only sixty-six out of the 104 constituencies, the total number of constituencies having been doubled.[59]

For the non-Malays, the situation was no doubt a great deal more satisfactory than it had been in 1955; now they did not have to regard themselves as ineffective participants in the electoral process, depending on Malay votes for seats in Parliament. For the Malays, on the other hand, the increased proportion of non-Malay voters must have weakened the argument for non-communal voting: the Chinese, in particular, were now in a position substantially to influence the outcome of the elections; and there was no reason why they had to be further helped.

Considering that the electorate in 1959 became much more representative of the general population, the communal distribution of candidates is very interesting: it indicates the extent to which nominations were determined by the prospect of communal support.

In all, there were 259 candidates contesting the 104 seats. Of them, 157 were Malays, seventy-nine Chinese, and twenty-three Indians. The following table classifies them by party and by community:

57. Registration was still voluntary.

58. In addition, special concessions were made for those who applied for citizenship within twelve months of Independence Day.

59. This and most of the other figures which follow (on the 1959 elections) were derived from the information given in a series of reports which appeared in the *Straits Times* between 21 July and 14 August, and which were based on a survey conducted by the newspaper.

TABLE 12

1959 *Elections: candidates—by party and by community*

| | *Malays* | *Chinese* | *Indians* | *Total* |
|---|---|---|---|---|
| Alliance | 69 | 31 | 4 | 104 |
| P.M.I.P. | 58 | — | — | 58 |
| Socialist Front | 11 | 20 | 7 | 38 |
| P.P.P. | 1 | 9 | 9 | 19 |
| Negara | 10 | — | — | 10 |
| Malayan Party | — | 1 | 1 | 2 |
| Semangat Permuda Melayu | 1 | — | — | 1 |
| Province Wellesley Labour | — | 1 | — | 1 |
| Independents | 7 | 17 | 2 | 26 |
| Total | 157 | 79 | 23 | 259 |

Of the 150 candidates who contested constituencies in which the Malays were the most numerous section of the electorate, 136 were Malays and only fourteen either Chinese or Indian.[60] Similarly, in those constituencies where Chinese voters were the most numerous group, there were sixty-nine Chinese and seventeen Indian candidates, with only twenty-two Malays.

Within the Alliance, the allocation of seats favoured the U.M.N.O.: while the Malays constituted 57 per cent of the electorate and were the most numerous group in 63·4 per cent of the constituencies, the U.M.N.O. was given 66·5 per cent (sixty-nine out of 104) of the total Alliance nominations. The M.C.A., on the other hand, was given only 29·8 per cent of the nominations (thirty-one out of 104), and the Chinese constituted 36 per cent of the electorate and were the most numerous group in 36·5 per cent of the constituencies.[61]

Of the fifty-eight candidates put up by the P.M.I.P., fifty-two contested constituencies in which Malay votes were the most numerous. Twenty of the party's candidates were or had been

60. Furthermore, of the total of 157 Malay candidates who contested the elections, 116 contested against each other, that is without any non-Malay opposition.

61. See footnote 49 on p. 162 for the original claims made by the U.M.N.O. and the M.C.A.

religious teachers; another seven were teachers in Malay or Arabic schools.

As may be seen in Table 12 above, the P.P.P.'s nominations, too, contained an interesting feature: while functioning mainly as a representative of Chinese communal interests, the party's nineteen candidates had only nine Chinese, with nine Indians and one Malay. All except the single Malay and one of the Indians contested constituencies where the Chinese were the most numerous section of the electorate.

On polling day, 73·3 per cent of the registered electorate cast their votes. In winning seventy-four of the 104 seats, the Alliance achieved a success which, though not quite as dramatic as the one in 1955, nevertheless provided an easy working majority in Parliament.[62]

TABLE 13

1959 *Elections: number of seats won by each party*

| | |
|---|---|
| Alliance | 74 |
| P.M.I.P. | 13 |
| S.F. | 8 |
| P.P.P. | 4 |
| Negara | 1 |
| Malayan Party | 1 |
| Independents | 3 |
| Total | 104 |

Despite the Alliance's continuing success in terms of seats, the percentage drop in popular support which it suffered was fairly substantial: the 1959 results did not have the same character of a stampede that one associates with the victory of 1955. The most disturbing factor, however, was not the mere decline in popular support, but the fact that votes were largely lost to communal parties: the P.M.I.P. and the P.P.P. In 1955 the Alliance had won 79·6 per cent of the valid votes cast; in 1959 this was reduced to 51·5 per cent. The P.M.I.P. and the P.P.P., having won 3·9 per

62. Three of the Alliance's candidates, two Malays and one Indian, were returned unopposed.

cent and 0·1 per cent respectively in 1955, now obtained 21·2 per cent and 6·4 per cent of the total vote.[63]

TABLE 14

*1959 Elections: percentage of valid votes by parties*[64]

| *Party* | *Overall* | *In constituencies contested* |
|---|---|---|
| Alliance | 51·5 | 51·5 |
| P.M.I.P. | 21·2 | 36·2 |
| S.F. | 13·0 | 34·8 |
| Negara | 2·2 | 22·2 |
| P.P.P. | 6·4 | 32·2 |
| Malayan Party | 0·9 | 41·5 |
| Independents | 4·8 | 20·4 |
| Total | 100·0 | |

A breakdown of the results on a State basis gives clear indication of how party support is, to a very striking extent, regionalized. The Alliance won all twelve seats in Kedah, both the seats in Perlis, all six seats in Pahang, and all sixteen seats in Johore, but lost fourteen of the sixteen seats in Kelantan and Trengganu; it was generally very successful in all the other States. The P.M.I.P. won all its thirteen seats in Kelantan and Trengganu; the P.P.P. won all four seats in Perak; and the Socialist Front won its eight seats in Selangor and Penang. These results bear out some of the observations made in the last chapter, as regards party support.

Although it has been pointed out that nominations were very strongly influenced by communal considerations, the results of the elections did not lack evidence of non-communal voting.

63. It has, of course, to be recognized that both the P.M.I.P. and the P.P.P. contested more seats in 1959 than they had in 1955. P.M.I.P. nominations increased from eleven to fifty-eight; the P.P.P.'s from two to nineteen. (The fact that there were twice as many constituencies in 1959 does not lessen the implications of this increase in the number of nominations because the electorate, too, had very nearly doubled.)

64. These figures were obtained from Mr. T. E. Smith, the secretary of the Institute of Commonwealth Studies, University of London. Mr. Smith was the supervisor of elections in the Federation for the 1955 General Elections.

There were fifteen constituencies in which the candidates returned did not belong to the community which formed the largest section of the electorate. In four of these constituencies, however, this was inevitable: in one, an Indian was returned unopposed; in the other three, where the Chinese comprised the most numerous section of the electorate, no Chinese candidates stood. Thus there are only eleven constituencies which need to be considered as significant in this connexion. Details of the voting in these constituencies are given in Appendix II (ii).[65]

Considering that the education issue had flared up just before the elections, another encouraging feature was that the Alliance won in twenty-four of the forty constituencies where the Chinese vote was either dominant or very nearly equal to that of the Malays; of the seats it lost, half went to the Socialist Front, which is also an inter-communal organization. Commenting on this, the *Straits Times* of 21 August 1959 observed:

> Altogether, the outlook is healthier than appeared at an earlier stage of events: Communalism, if far from extinct or even quiescent, at least has not spread. If a section of the more numerous and livelier opposition may feel disposed to resort to it, the Government is strong enough to resist pressure, and to pursue policies that would break down barriers that now divide us.

The general outcome of the elections, and the ministerial appointments which followed, give an interesting indication of how political power is concentrated in the hands of the Malay community. If the general distribution of population (by communities) is taken to be the broadest index of political power, it can be noticed that, at each remove from this broad base, a higher and higher proportion of political power is held in Malay hands. Conversely, the Chinese are less and less favourably represented at all but one of the levels away from the base. Table 16 illustrates this feature in detail.

65. In studying the details given in Appendix II (ii) it must be borne in mind that, in those Chinese-dominated constituencies where Indian candidates belonging to the P.P.P. were successful, non-communal voting did not actually reflect non-communal or inter-communal politics, since the P.P.P. is in fact an anti-Malay (and largely pro-Chinese) party. For this reason, the very substantial majorities won by Mr. D. R. Seenivasagam (the leader of the P.P.P.) and his brother Mr. S. P. Seenivasagam in Ipoh and Menglembu are essentially misleading in terms of inter-communal politics. They were in fact returned on a communal vote.

TABLE 15

1959 *Elections: seats won by parties—on a State basis*
(*percentage of valid votes won, in parenthesis*)[66]

| *State* | *Alliance* | *P.M.I.P.* | *S.F.* | *P.P.P.* | *Negara* | *Mal. P.* | *Ind.* | *Total* |
|---|---|---|---|---|---|---|---|---|
| Kedah | 12<br>(65·1) | —<br>(26·8) | —<br>(7·2) | —<br>(—) | —<br>(—) | —<br>(—) | —<br>(0·9) | 12 |
| Perlis | 2<br>(59·6) | —<br>(40·4) | —<br>(—) | —<br>(—) | —<br>(—) | —<br>(—) | —<br>(—) | 2 |
| Penang | 5<br>(44·0) | —<br>(10·8) | 3<br>(38·2) | —<br>(2·9) | —<br>(—) | —<br>(—) | —<br>(4·1) | 8 |
| Perak | 15<br>(49·6) | —<br>(15·4) | —<br>(2·9) | 4<br>(26·9) | —<br>(—) | —<br>(—) | 1<br>(5·2) | 20 |
| Selangor | 9<br>(44·3) | —<br>(7·9) | 5<br>(30·4) | —<br>(4·0) | —<br>(—) | —<br>(2·0) | —<br>(11·4) | 14 |
| Malacca | 3<br>(58·9) | —<br>(16·1) | —<br>(11·5) | —<br>(—) | —<br>(—) | 1<br>(12·8) | —<br>(0·7) | 4 |
| Negri Sembilan | 4<br>(51·9) | —<br>(16·7) | —<br>(10·9) | —<br>(—) | —<br>(6·0) | —<br>(—) | 2<br>(14·5) | 6 |
| Johore | 16<br>(65·7) | —<br>(2·3) | —<br>(14·2) | —<br>(1·0) | —<br>(9·4) | —<br>(—) | —<br>(7·4) | 16 |
| Trengganu | 1<br>(37·4) | 4<br>(47·6) | —<br>(0·9) | —<br>(—) | 1<br>(11·9) | —<br>(—) | —<br>(2·2) | 6 |
| Kelantan | 1<br>(31·4) | 9<br>(68·3) | —<br>(—) | —<br>(—) | —<br>(0·3) | —<br>(—) | —<br>(—) | 10 |
| Pahang | 6<br>(66·9) | —<br>(11·7) | —<br>(21·4) | —<br>(—) | —<br>(—) | —<br>(—) | —<br>(—) | 6 |

66. Figures obtained from Mr. T. E. Smith.

TABLE 16

*Communal distribution of political power at various levels*

| *Communal group* | Percentage | | | | |
|---|---|---|---|---|---|
| | *of population* | *of electorate* | *of constituencies* | *of seats* | *of cabinet appointments* |
| Malays | 49 | 57 | 63·5 | 64 | 67 |
| Chinese | 38 | 36 | 36·5 | 27 | 25 |
| Indians | 12 | 7 | — | 9 | 8 |

While the success of the two national elections held so far cannot be denied, it would be unwise to use their outcome either to perceive voting trends or to forecast the future pattern of representative government. In this connexion, it is particularly important to emphasize the 'special' conditions which governed the 1955 General Election: first, it was held during the pre-independence period, and hence its outcome might have been influenced by certain distinct considerations; secondly, as already mentioned, the electorate in 1955 was rather unrepresentative of the general population. This makes the election of that year different from that of 1959 and those which are to follow.

If, however, the mere fact of success is taken to be all-important, it may be possible to find some significance. It could, for example, be observed that by not resorting to any electoral device aimed at ensuring some degree of communal representation, and by succeeding despite the communal divisions within its society, the Federation of Malaya has contributed towards the solving of electoral problems in plural societies. Precedents, ranging from the communal rolls attempted in India to the 'honest gerrymandering' of Ceylon, have been ignored in favour of a system which, by overlooking the existence of communal differences and conflicts, is not only bold and imaginative but also has the merit of simplicity.

In so far as this note of optimism is valid, the Alliance Party deserves some of the credit for having facilitated the success of the electoral system. Because communal co-operation was the best way to maximize its own power (and, before 1957, the only way of achieving independence), it had every reason to want to make the system workable and realistic.

If the success of the first two elections is to continue, it is necessary that inter-communal co-operation should be more alluring to political parties than the profits to be gained from communal campaigns.

## CHAPTER SEVEN

# COMMUNALISM AND THE POLITICAL PROCESS

THE communal divisions within the Malayan society have been discussed,[1] and reference has been made to some of the factors which have facilitated political unification.[2] In the light of the preceding study, two additional factors may now be suggested as having facilitated the creation of political unity.

First, there is the influence exerted by the electoral system. By not recognizing communal differences, it may be said to have given valuable scope for inter-communal politics, particularly by having encouraged inter-communal parties. At least up to the present, this has helped to avoid the hardening of communal tensions witnessed in British India (where there were communal rolls) and Ceylon (where the electoral system gives tacit recognition to communal divisions).

The success of the electoral system thus far may partly be attributed to the fact that it was put to the test at a time when the independence movement demanded national unity. It is possible that this success may prove to be only temporary, since present disagreements, if allowed to continue, might progressively reduce the incentive for inter-communal politics among Malays and non-Malays alike.

The second unifying factor has been the effort made by the present ruling *élite* to forge inter-communal partnership. The Alliance has conducted an extensive campaign (especially during elections) against communalism, and has met with some success in convincing the electorate that inter-communal politics is the best solution for everyone, that communal politics is irresponsible politics. It may thus be suggested that the Alliance (helped by other inter-communal parties) has facilitated extra-constitutional solutions to the country's communal problem. It should, however, be realized that inter-communal politics, besides being important for smooth administration (and besides having

1. See especially pp. 1–6. 2. See pp. 19–23.

been a vital prerequisite for independence), has also been necessary for the success of the Alliance.[3]

It may be argued that the process of unification has been helped by the fact that the non-Malays are not all concentrated in any particular part of the country. Had there been such concentration (particularly in the case of the Chinese), it is possible that efforts to foster non-Malay interests would have been much stronger, since the feeling of distinctiveness would, in all likelihood, have been increased. Experience suggests that minorities[4] which are territorially concentrated do not compromise as easily as those which are fairly evenly dispersed.[5]

It is only natural that communal divisions should tend to complicate the political process. It is not unusual for different sections of a population to have different needs and preferences, but in a multi-racial society, communal identification tends to result in a certain compartmentalization of these differences: people, acting in groups, not only have different preferences but also different values and different sets of considerations. In such societies, it may thus be necessary that some of the basic concepts and values commonly attributed to democratic government should be reconsidered.

Furnivall has defined a 'plural society' as one comprising two or more communal groups 'living side by side, but separately, within the same political unit'.[6] Since communal groups are usually less 'flexible' than most other social groupings, the central problem in such societies arises from the absence of a unified political community. In the case of representative government (to take an example), this restricts the scope for gaining popular support.

It may now be asked how the limitations thus imposed can best be minimized without unduly endangering the prospects for democracy. The choice appears to be between two alternatives. Should the different communities be unwilling to coalesce into a

3. As already mentioned, the Alliance owes a great deal of its success to the fact that it has adapted itself to local political realities; as far as communalism is concerned, its own interests coincide with those of the country.

4. The non-Malay communities are here being regarded as the minorities in Malaya.

5. In Ceylon, for example, Singhalese-Tamil relations would probably have been quite different had the latter been more widely distributed. The position of the French-speaking Canadians is also a good example.

6. J. S. Furnivall, *Colonial Policy and Practice*, p. 304.

common nation, an attempt may be made to segregate them politically, to such extent as may be found necessary or desirable;[7] in this way the exerting of communal interests could continue as an effective basis for competition, and the roots of democracy need suffer no fatal injuries. If, on the other hand, a solution is sought for the communal problem, it will be necessary for the different communities not only to respect each other's special characteristics but also to accept them as politically irrelevant. Each community should therefore make a conscious attempt to minimize the implications of its own particularism.

In view of the fact that a solution is being attempted in the Federation of Malaya,[8] it is vital that certain basic concessions be made by both the Malay and the non-Malay communities. The former would be most realistic if they acknowledged that they are no longer the 'owners' of the country and that, particularly in view of the economic role played by the non-Malays and the political outlook fostered by them,[9] it would be not only just but also expedient to give them a fair share of political power.[10] The non-Malays, for their part, should (notwithstanding their own claims of loyalty and allegiance) concede that the Malays have a stronger claim in the country than anyone else (for historical reasons, if nothing else), and recognize that this must have political consequences.[11] These conditions, however, should not be interpreted too rigidly for fear of producing a system of apportionment of political power, which would not only confirm the divi-

7. The introduction of communal rolls is an example of such segregation.
8. For example, most political parties advocate the establishment of some form of multi-racial government.
9. It will be remembered that a vast majority of the Chinese and Indians in the country now claim to be Malayans first and foremost, and hence entitled to a bigger share in the country's political life.
10. As indicated in the preceding chapters, the non-Malays have, in progressive measures, been given wider rights since the War. The fact that they are now allowed to become citizens, get admitted to the Civil Service, and play a crucial role in representative government, is clear indication of this. It should, however, also be realized that certain sections of the Malay community resent this increase in non-Malay rights.
11. In the light of what has been said in earlier parts of this study, these 'political consequences' may broadly be identified as comprising the 'special position' of the Malays, the preservation of Malay institutions (such as the Sultanate), the establishment of Islam as the State religion, and the recognition of Malay as the national language. While it is only natural that non-Malays should want to improve their rights, little good can come out of demands for complete equality.

sions present in the country and thus restrict the scope for their gradual eradication, but might also lead to endless disputes over the manner in which power is allocated.

In most plural societies, conditions such as these no doubt render popular government difficult. It is only too easy for one to forget some of the coarser facts and assert idealistically that 'it is the role of the official power holders to harmonize the conflicting interests of the communal groups which they represent for the common benefit of the entire community'.[12] Where different communal groups are not adequately integrated into a single political community, only too often these 'official power holders' (who, naturally, would be elected to represent communal interests) place sectional before national considerations. Should they go very far in placing national considerations over communal ones, they might not be able to retain power.

It has been the purpose of this study to examine the extent to which communalism has influenced the political process in the Federation of Malaya. In this connexion, it must be observed that the relationship between political behaviour (voting, for example) and membership in any particular community is neither direct nor automatic, but determined by the existence of certain rather practical considerations. The Malays, for example, do not behave (politically) in a certain manner simply because they happen to be Malays or because there happen to be Chinese and Indians in the country, but because certain practical considerations have encouraged them to do so (such as the fact that they were protected by the British for a considerable period of time and are now left to fend for themselves; the consideration that the cultural foundations of their own community might be relegated to a secondary position *vis-à-vis* the cultures of the other communities; and the economic superiority of the Chinese).

It is thus clear that the relationship between communal identity and political behaviour in Malaya is far from being the outcome of prejudice, pure and simple. The 'communal problem' has arisen not merely by virtue of the presence of three different communities in the country; communal identification has become a significant variable in the political behaviour of the Malayan society only because circumstances have rendered it politically relevant.

12. K. Lowenstein, *Political Power and the Governmental Process*, p. 346.

Generally, the communal framework of political activity in a plural society tends to act as a force preventing national and ideological considerations from exerting their usual influence; this results from the channelling of support to meet the demands of particular groups rather than of general issues not closely connected with communal interests. With reference to Malaya, one writer has observed:

> The hope has been expressed that under the influence of free institutions communal would quickly give way to class divisions and thus create a consciousness of Malayan nationality. This has not been the experience of India, Pakistan, Ireland, and Czechoslovakia; in all of them conflicts based on religion or race created unbridgeable divisions. In Malaya these differences reinforce one another and the gulf is widened. The first pre-requisite for a successful democracy is that the people shall be sufficiently homogeneous to feel that the causes of division are less important than the reasons for union.[13]

Considering that the most urgent political problem facing the Federation of Malaya today is that of integrating the different sections of the population into a single political community, it would be interesting to examine how communal differences can best be minimized so as to enable the emergence of such a community.

In view of the deep cultural divisions which still prevail in the country, the impossibility of eradicating social plurality within any reasonable period of time will first of all have to be taken for granted; the social distances between the different communities are too great to allow much collective life.[14] Thus the main hope is that it will be possible to overcome political plurality while social plurality continues to exist. For this to be possible, it will be necessary for any change of hands in political power (determined, say, by the number of seats in Parliament held by members of a particular community) to be commonly interpreted as being more a power-shift within the same supra-communal group than a shift from one community to another.

For the time being, however, the possibility of gradually

13. L. A. Mills, *Malaya: A Political and Economic Appraisal*, p. 74.

14. It will be some time before the unifying effect of national schools becomes evident (assuming that an appreciable measure of social unification does eventually take place).

reducing political plurality will have to depend on certain practical considerations, such as the fact that no political party campaigning on a purely communal platform can hope to win a majority in Parliament. The continued relevance of these considerations could result in a common assumption that political dilution is possible without social dilution, and that the former is not a necessary index of the subjection of one community by another. This will be possible as long as there is a common awareness that the presence of group differences (be they of class, ethnic, racial, or religious origin) need not necessarily impede the achievement of democratic goals, since the recognition of varying interests (and even the conscious furthering of contradicting aims and values) is implicit in democratic government.

It is, however, most vital that inter-communal rivalries should be contained within certain limits so as to guarantee an absence of violence and legislative reprisals as means of accommodating differing aims and values; there will have to be some assurance that the basic consensus of the Malayan society (meaning, particularly, the common desire for peaceful government) is not placed in jeopardy.

It is quite possible that these views are somewhat over-optimistic. It has to be admitted that the eradication of political plurality under present circumstances might, for the most part, be more artificial than real. It will not be possible to rid politics completely of its communal element as long as the different communities remain concerned over where they stand with regard to each other, and thereby continue to speculate on the future of their own positions. Communal politics is inevitable as long as each community is uncertain of the real motives of the others. It is thus necessary that culturally-inspired political differences are first of all settled; only then will it be possible to have a unified political community.

Turning now to party politics, the fact that no community forms a majority of the population could lead to interesting developments. Assuming (as has been done) that communal considerations will continue to be politically relevant for some time in the future, it is likely that there will be a continuing tendency for inter-communal parties to be formed.[15] The origins and the

15. This, no doubt, assumes the continued success of parliamentary democracy; a few unsuccessful elections may be enough for a breakdown.

growth of the Alliance may give some valuable indictions in this respect.

Before 1952, the U.M.N.O. and the M.C.A. were purely communal organizations which dedicated themselves solely to furthering the interests of their respective communities. They were trusted champions of communal demands, and each had convinced its own community of its stern dedication. Thus the Malays and Chinese were convinced that the founding of the Alliance was purely meant to ensure their respective interests. Also significant is the fact that the decision to form the Alliance was very much influenced by a common distrust and fear (among U.M.N.O. and M.C.A. leaders) of the I.M.P., a non-communal party which had set itself the task of serving national and not communal interests.

It was not long, however, before the U.M.N.O. and the M.C.A. realized that the Alliance could not be sustained if they continued to remain communal themselves. Each had to concede a certain amount to the other if a common policy were to be evolved and if better understanding were to be established. The need for mutual concessions became particularly pronounced after the Alliance became the elected Government in 1955; it then became necessary for the party not only to set its own house in order but also to work out suitable policies for the country's administration. With each new problem new concessions had to be made; the U.M.N.O. and the M.C.A. gradually began to lose their original communal flavour. As was inevitable, sections of the Malay and Chinese communities became dissatisfied with the manner in which these two parties were representing their interests; and this contributed very substantially to the increased support received by communal parties during the 1959 elections.

Other parties may, in the future, join hands to challenge the supremacy of the Alliance. To be successful, not only must such alliances have sufficient funds and manpower to organize themselves effectively and contest as many seats as possible,[16] but the partners must to a certain extent be communal organizations, for only then will they be able to convince their own communities of their sincerity.

Should another successful alliance be formed, it is unlikely that

16. Up to now, many Alliance candidates have been returned unopposed, especially at State and local council elections.

the problems now faced by the Alliance Party will be completely evaded. Thus, as long as communalism persists, it is possible that the experiences of the Alliance may be repeated over and over again.[17] There is nothing particularly discouraging about this: it will be the best way in which communal interests can be catered for while endorsement is given to the need for inter-communal partnership; furthermore, in the face of communalism, alliances of this nature are necessary to make the electoral system (which is optimistic in that it ignores communal divisions) workable. One must, at the same time, be aware that if political plurality is not gradually reduced (and especially if it is allowed to become more pronounced), elections may very well take on the character of auctions, with votes going in blocs to those who make the highest bid on behalf of their own communities. Should this occur, the prospects for parliamentary democracy will indeed be discouraging.[18] The ideal, of course, would be the development of a two-party system where both parties would be initially inter-communal, but would ultimately become non-communal.

It was earlier observed that such unity as exists today is partly the result of the efforts made by the present ruling *élite* towards inter-communal partnership. In thinking of unity in the future, however, it must be emphasized that common aims and mutual understanding at the 'top level' alone are far from sufficient, because there is no guarantee that the propaganda of this *élite* will continue to be successful. It is quite possible that the 'top level' may change, and that those who succeed may have different ideas of the type of unity to be desired and the way in which it should be encouraged. Thus, if some measure of political unity is to be firmly established, it is essential that the need for inter-communal partnership should become clearly understood by all sections of the population. At the same time, it is also important that the policies of the present ruling *élite* should not be too optimistic to accommodate the more gradual rate at which the general population is likely to accept partnership; otherwise inter-communal politics might very well lose its appeal before it has had a chance to establish deep roots.

17. It is of course possible that, despite its present difficulties, the Alliance may continue to be the strongest party in the country for some time to come.
18. Up to the present, however (as explained in the last chapter), election results have mostly been encouraging.

# APPENDIX I

*Federation Proposals, 1948: Recommendations concerning the Composition of the Federal Legislative Council*

(a) *Recommendations of the Working Committee*

The Working Committee recommended a Council of 48 with 14 Official and 34 Unofficial members.

*Officials:*

(High Commissioner as President)
*Ex-officio* members (Chief Secretary, Attorney-General, and Financial Secretary) .. .. .. .. .. .. 3
Nominated Officials (persons holding office of emolument under the Federal Government—e.g. the Directors of the various Government Departments) .. .. .. .. .. 11

Total 14

*Unofficials:*

(i) State and Settlement Representatives:
The *Mentris Besar* of the Malay States .. .. .. 9
Representatives from the two Settlement Councils, to be selected by members of the respective Councils .. .. 2

(ii) 'Functional' Representatives:
Labour (1 Chinese and 1 Indian) .. .. .. .. 2
Planting (1 European and 1 Chinese) .. .. .. 2
Mining (1 European and 1 Chinese) .. .. .. 2
Commerce (1 European, 1 Chinese, and 1 Indian) .. 3

(iii) Other Unofficials:
Representative of Educational and Cultural Interests .. 1
Representative of the Eurasian Community .. ..
Unallocated (outstanding person, from any community, to be appointed by the High Commissioner) .. .. .. 1
Representatives of Malay Interests (Malay associations in each area were to recommend suitable names through the U.M.N.O.; any other Malay body which the High Commissioner thought fit to consult could also recommend. Final selection was to be made by the High Commissioner) .. 9

| | |
|---|---|
| Chinese representatives, one from each Settlement, to be appointed by the High Commissioner .. .. .. | 2 |
| Total Unofficials | 34 |

In presenting the communal distribution of the Unofficial members, the Working Committee somehow separated the 9 State and 2 Settlement members from the remaining 23, thereby presenting a distribution of:

| | |
|---|---|
| Malays .. .. .. .. .. .. .. .. | 9 |
| Chinese (Labour, Planting, Mining, Commerce, 2 from Settlements) .. .. .. .. .. .. .. .. | 6 |
| Europeans (Planting, Mining, Commerce) .. .. .. | 3 |
| Indians (Labour, Commerce) .. .. .. .. .. | 2 |
| Eurasians .. .. .. .. .. .. .. .. | 1 |
| From any community: | |
| (a) Educational and Cultural Interests .. .. .. | 1 |
| (b) Unallocated .. .. .. .. .. .. .. | 1 |
| Total | 23 |

(With the 9 *Mentris Besar*, the Malays would actually have had 18 Unofficial members. Furthermore, the Settlement members could also have been Malay.)

(b) *Recommendations of the Consultative Committee*

The Consultative Committee recommended a Council of 75, with 23 Official and 52 Unofficial members.

*Officials:*

| | | |
|---|---|---|
| *Ex-officio* | same as recommended by the Working Committee | 3 |
| Nominated Officials | | 11 |
| *Mentris Besar* .. .. .. .. .. .. .. | | 9 |
| | Total | 23 |

(Thus the Consultative Committee felt that the *Mentris Besar* should actually be classified as Officials. The Settlement representatives, however, were left as Unofficial members.)

*Unofficials:*

The Committee recommended that the number of Unofficial members be raised to 52; it was felt that this would facilitate a better distribution between the different communities. The 52 Unofficials were to comprise:

| | |
|---|---|
| Labour | 4 |
| Planting | 4 |
| Mining | 4 |
| Commerce | 5 |
| Malays | 20 |
| Eurasians | 1 |
| Educational and Cultural Interests | 1 |
| Nominated Indians | 2 |
| Ceylonese | 1 |
| Nominated Chinese (2 from the Settlements and 5 others) | 7 |
| Nominated Europeans | 1 |
| Settlement Representatives | 2 |
| Total Unofficials | 52 |

The above would have given a communal distribution of:

| | |
|---|---|
| Malays | 20 |
| Chinese (Labour 2; Planting 2; Mining 2; Commerce 2; Nominated by the H.C. from the Settlements 2; Others nominated by the H.C. 5) | 15 |
| Europeans (Planting 2; Commerce 2; Mining 2; nominated by H.C. 1) | 7 |
| Indians (Labour 2; Commerce 1; nominated by H.C. 2) | 5 |
| Ceylonese | 1 |
| Eurasians | 1 |
| From any community: | |
| (i) Educational and Cultural Interests | 1 |
| (ii) Representatives from Settlement Councils | 2 |
| Total | 52 |

(c) *Minority Proposals* (made by Col. H. S. Lee and Mr. Leong Yew Koh, the two Chinese members of the Consultative Committee):

*Officials:*

| | |
|---|---|
| *Ex-officio* | 3 |
| Nominated | 11 |
| Total | 14 |

*Unofficials:*

Col. Lee and Mr. Leong Yew Koh recommended that the *Mentris Besar* of the Malay States should be included among the 20 Malay Unofficials. Thus, as compared to the majority recommendations, theirs would have reduced Malay strength in the Council by 9.

The total strength of the Council recommended by the Minority Proposals was thus 66, with an Unofficial majority of 38 (14 Officials to 52 Unofficials).

(d) *The Final Proposals*

The final proposals provided for a Council of 75, of which 50 were Unofficial members. (The High Commissioner was to be President.)

| | |
|---|---|
| *Ex-officio* (Chief Secretary, Attorney-General, and Financial Secretary) .. .. .. .. .. .. .. .. | 3 |
| *State and Settlement Members* (the 9 Presidents of State Councils and 1 representative from each of the Settlement Councils) .. | 11 |
| *Official Members* (persons holding office of emolument under the Federal Government or under the Crown, to be appointed by the High Commissioner either by office or by name) .. .. | 11 |
| Total | 25 |
| *Unofficials:* | |
| Labour .. .. .. .. .. .. .. .. | 6 |
| Planting .. .. .. .. .. .. .. .. | 6 |
| Mining .. .. .. .. .. .. .. .. | 4 |
| Commerce .. .. .. .. .. .. .. | 6 |
| Agriculture and Husbandry .. .. .. .. .. | 8 |
| Professional, Educational and Cultural interests .. .. | 4 |
| Settlements .. .. .. .. .. .. .. .. | 2 |
| States .. .. .. .. .. .. .. .. | 9 |
| Eurasian community .. .. .. .. .. .. | 1 |
| Ceylonese community .. .. .. .. .. .. | 1 |
| Indian community .. .. .. .. .. .. .. | 1 |
| Chinese community .. .. .. .. .. .. | 2 |
| | 50 |
| Total | 75 |

As can be seen, the final proposals followed the example set by the Working Committee, of presenting the *Mentris Besar* and Settlement Council representatives as a group distinct from the other Unofficials. This enabled the Malays to get 9 additional Unofficial seats (the 9 seats reserved for the 'States'), while the non-Malays could get only 2 ('Settlements').

# APPENDIX II

*1955 and 1959 General Elections: Cases of Non-communal Voting*

(i) *1955 Elections*

(All. stands for Alliance; Neg. for Party Negara; N.A.P. for National Association of Perak; Lab. for Labour Party of Malaya; P.M.I.P. for Pan-Malayan Islamic Party; P.P.P. for Perak Progressive Party; P.M.L. for Perak Malay League; and Indep. for Independent candidates.

It should be remembered that in all the constituencies mentioned here the Malays formed the majority of the electorate.)

*Wellesley South* (Penang):

Tay Hooi Soo .. Chinese .. All. .. .. 15,697 votes
Haji Zabidi bin Haji Ali .. Malay .. P.M.I.P. 3,523 votes

Total electorate .. .. .. .. .. 24,320
Percentage of registered electors voting (turn-out) 80%

*Malacca Central* (Malacca):

Tan Siew Sin .. Chinese .. All. .. .. 17,104 votes
Abdul Karim bin Bakar .. Malay .. Indep. .. 3,194 votes

Total electorate .. .. .. .. .. 25,511
Turn-out .. .. .. .. .. .. 81·3%

*Larut and Matang* (Perak):

Dr. Cheah Khay Chuan .. Chinese .. All. .. 15,407 votes
Abu Bakar bin Said .. Malay .. P.M.L. .. 4,453 votes
Wan Zara Zillah bin Wan Haji Ismail .. Malay
N.A.P. .. .. .. .. .. .. .. 3,437 votes
Dr. Puran Singh .. Indian .. Lab. .. .. 761 votes

Total electorate .. .. .. .. .. 30,454
Turn-out .. .. .. .. .. .. 81·7%

*Kinta Utara* (Perak):

V. T. Sambanatham .. Indian .. All. .. 7,900 votes
Chik Mohamed Yusuf bin Sheik Abdul Rahman
Malay .. N.A.P. .. .. .. .. .. 1,832 votes
K. R. R. Choudhary .. Indian .. Lab. .. 357 votes
Mohamed Ramly bin Abdullah .. Malay .. P.M.L. 214 votes

Total electorate .. .. .. .. .. 12,304
Turn-out .. .. .. .. .. .. 85·9%

*Kinta Selatan* (Perak):

Too Joon Hing .. Chinese .. All. .. .. 11,611 votes
Mohamed Baki bin Haji Daud .. Malay .. N.A.P. 1,689 votes
Mohamed Idris bin Hakim .. Malay .. Indep. 401 votes
Zaharie bin Hassan .. Malay .. P.P.P. .. 273 votes

Total electorate .. .. .. .. .. 16,216
Turn-out .. .. .. .. .. .. 87·3%

*Kuala Lumpur Barat* (Selangor):

Ong Yoke Lin .. Chinese .. All. .. .. 4,667 votes
Abdullah bin Ibrahim .. Malay .. Neg. .. 1,371 votes
Tan Tuan Boon .. Chinese .. Lab. .. .. 1,018 votes

Total electorate .. .. .. .. .. 8,862
Turn-out .. .. .. .. .. .. 80·1%

*Kuala Lumpur Timor* (Selangor):

Cheah Ewe Keat .. Chinese .. All. .. .. 6,790 votes
Mohamed Salleh bin Hakim .. Malay .. Neg. 2,431 votes
Abdul Wahab bin Abdul Majid .. Malay ..
Indep. .. .. .. .. .. .. 1,003 votes

Total electorate .. .. .. .. .. 13,184
Turn-out .. .. .. .. .. .. 78·8%

*Selangor Tengah* (Selangor):

Lee Eng Teh .. Chinese .. All. .. .. 5,652 votes
Zulkifli Mohamed .. Malay .. P.M.I.P. .. 1,711 votes
Atan Chik bin Lengkeng .. Malay .. Neg. .. 813 votes

Total electorate .. .. .. .. .. 9,465
Turn-out .. .. .. .. .. .. 88·5%

*Johore Selatan* (Johore):

Dr. L. H. Tan .. Chinese .. All. .. .. 21,581 votes
Kassim bin Awang Chik .. Malay .. Neg. .. 2,318 votes

Total electorate .. .. .. .. .. 29,090
Turn-out .. .. .. .. .. .. 83·7%

*Johore Tengah* (Johore):

Teo Chze Chong .. Chinese .. All. .. .. 7,100 votes
Haji Anwar bin Haji Abdul Malik .. Malay ..
Neg. .. .. .. .. .. .. 1,068 votes

Total electorate .. .. .. .. .. 11,737
Turn-out .. .. .. .. .. .. 71·7%

*Batu Pahat* (Johore):

Chelvasingam MacIntyre .. Indian .. All. .. 18,968 votes
Dato' Haji Syed Abdul Kadir bin Mohamed ..
Malay .. Neg. .. .. .. .. .. 2,717 votes

Total electorate .. .. .. .. .. 27,323
Turn-out .. .. .. .. .. .. 80·4%

*Muar Selatan* (Johore):

Tan Suan Kok .. Chinese .. All. .. .. 23,580 votes
Dato' Mahmud bin Mohamed Shah .. Malay ..
Neg. .. .. .. .. .. .. 4,108 votes

Total electorate .. .. .. .. .. 34,321
Turn-out .. .. .. .. .. .. 81·9%

*Alor Star* (Kedah):

Lee Thian Hin .. Chinese .. All. .. .. 27,897 votes
Haji Salim bin Haji Mohamed Rejab .. Malay
Neg. .. .. .. .. .. .. 1,700 votes

Total electorate .. .. .. .. .. 35,261
Turn-out .. .. .. .. .. .. 85·5%

*Kedah Selatan* (Kedah):

Lim Teng Kuang .. Chinese .. All. .. .. 21,050 votes
M. Salleh bin Haji Shafie .. Malay .. P.M.I.P. 1,563 votes

Total electorate .. .. .. .. .. 25,917
Turn-out .. .. .. .. .. .. 88·7%

(ii) *1959 Elections*

(All. stands for Alliance; P.M.I.P. for Pan-Malayan Islamic Party; S.F. for Socialist Front; P.P.P. for People's Progressive Party; M.P. for Malayan Party; and Indep. for Independent candidates.

As stated in footnote 65 on p. 205, the victories scored by Indian candidates belonging to the P.P.P. is essentially misleading in terms of inter-communal politics: they were in fact returned on a Chinese communal vote.)

*Sungei Siput* (Perak):

Total electorate .. .. .. .. .. 17,157

Malays .. .. .. .. .. .. 5,962
Chinese .. .. .. .. .. .. 8,427
Indians .. .. .. .. .. .. 2,768

V. T. Sambantham .. Indian .. All. .. .. 7,317 votes

K. Annamalai .. Indian .. P.P.P. .. .. 4,514 votes
Choy Kok Kuan .. Chinese .. Indep. .. 148 votes

Turn-out .. .. .. .. .. .. 70%

*Ipoh* (Perak):

Total electorate .. .. .. .. .. 30,370

Malays .. .. .. .. .. .. 3,378
Chinese .. .. .. .. .. .. 23,214
Indians .. .. .. .. .. .. 3,778

D. R. Seenivasagam .. Indian .. P.P.P. .. 12,242 votes
Dr. Chang Hoey Chan .. Chinese .. All. .. 6,531 votes
Yoon Too Thong .. Chinese .. S.F. .. .. 1,452 votes

Turn-out .. .. .. .. .. .. 67%

*Menglembu* (Perak):

Total electorate .. .. .. .. .. 33,597

Malays .. .. .. .. .. .. 3,866
Chinese .. .. .. .. .. .. 27,925
Indians .. .. .. .. .. .. 1,806

S. P. Seenivasagam .. Indian .. P.P.P. .. 14,338 votes
Wong Kok Weng .. Chinese .. All. .. .. 6,292 votes
Mohamed Dahan bin Khatib .. Malay .. S.F. 1,283 votes

Turn-out .. .. .. .. .. .. 65%

*Seberang Selatan* (Province Wellesley):

Total electorate .. .. .. .. .. 15,920

Malays .. .. .. .. .. .. 6,999
Chinese .. .. .. .. .. .. 5,869
Indians .. .. .. .. .. .. 3,004

V. Veerapan .. Indian .. S.F. .. .. .. 5,077 votes
Tay Sooi Soo .. Chinese .. All. .. .. 4,313 votes
Haji Jais bin Sudin .. Malay .. P.M.I.P. .. 3,093 votes

Turn-out .. .. .. .. .. .. 79·2%

*Malacca Tengah* (Malacca):

Total electorate .. .. .. .. .. 23,495

Malays .. .. .. .. .. .. 16,000 (approx.)
Chinese .. .. .. .. .. .. 6,000 (approx.)
Indians .. .. .. .. .. .. 1,000 (approx.)
Tan Siew Sin .. Chinese .. All. .. .. 13,635 votes

Haji Abdul Majid bin Haji Hussin .. Malay ..
P.M.I.P. .. .. .. .. .. .. 4,655 votes

Turn-out .. .. .. .. .. .. 78%

*Segamat Utara* (Johore):

Total electorate .. .. .. .. .. 15,155

Malays .. .. .. .. .. .. 6,416
Chinese .. .. .. .. .. .. 7,319
Indians .. .. .. .. .. .. 1,420

Haji Abdullah bin Haji Mohamed Salleh .. Malay
All. .. .. .. .. .. .. 6,572 votes
Lim Meng Shee .. Chinese .. Indep. .. 4,948 votes
Syed Mohamed bin Abdullah Al Kherd .. Malay
P.M.I.P. .. .. .. .. .. .. 917 votes

Turn-out .. .. .. .. .. .. 83·39%

*Johore Bahru Timor* (Johore):

Total electorate .. .. .. .. .. 15,918

Malays .. .. .. .. .. .. 7,154
Chinese .. .. .. .. .. .. 7,639
Indians .. .. .. .. .. .. 1,125

Dato' Haji Noah bin Omar .. Malay .. All. .. 7,771 votes
C. C. Yong .. Chinese .. S.F. .. .. 4,236 votes

Turn-out .. .. .. .. .. .. 77·62%

*Alor Star* (Kedah):

Total electorate .. .. .. .. .. 25,540

Malays .. .. .. .. .. .. 17,684
Chinese .. .. .. .. .. .. 6,104
Indians .. .. .. .. .. .. 1,721

Lim Joo Kong .. Chinese .. All. .. .. 10,730 votes
Abdul Malik bin Abdul Rahman .. Malay ..
P.M.I.P. .. .. .. .. .. .. 4,212 votes
Teoh Ah Thow .. Chinese .. S.F. .. .. 2,289 votes

Turn-out .. .. .. .. .. .. 68%

*Daman Sara* (Selangor):

Total electorate .. .. .. .. .. 19,760

Malays .. .. .. .. .. .. 2,755
Chinese .. .. .. .. .. .. 12,452
Indians .. .. .. .. .. .. 4,553

Kaher Karam Singh .. Indian .. S.F. .. 9,026 votes
Lee Eng Teh .. Chinese .. All. .. .. 5,653 votes

Turn-out .. .. .. .. .. .. 75%

*Bungsar* (Selangor):

Total electorate .. .. .. .. .. 36,100

Malays .. .. .. .. .. .. 4,000
Chinese .. .. .. .. .. .. 27,000
Indians (includes 'Others') .. .. .. 5,000

V. David .. Indian .. S.F. .. .. .. 9,734 votes
Koh Pooi Kee .. Chinese .. Indep. .. .. 6,821 votes
Law Joo Kooi .. Chinese .. All. .. .. 5,036 votes
Ong Yeow Kay .. Chinese .. P.P.P. .. .. 2,388 votes

Turn-out .. .. .. .. .. .. 68%

*Setapak* (Selangor):

Total electorate .. .. .. .. .. 22,494

Malays .. .. .. .. .. .. 7,482
Chinese .. .. .. .. .. .. 12,525
Indians .. .. .. .. .. .. 2,484

Ahmad Boestamam .. Malay .. S.F. .. .. 6,901 votes
Che Aisha binti Ghani .. Malay .. All. .. 4,805 votes
Yap Kim Swee .. Chinese .. Indep. .. .. 3,853 votes

Turn-out .. .. .. .. .. .. 70%

# APPENDIX III

## *Biographical Notes*

The purpose of these brief notes is to give a rough idea of the careers of some of those who have come within the limelight of Malayan politics. The following selection comprises the leading figures in the more prominent parties, and is intended to give a cross-section of the country's leading politicians.

*Tengku Abdul Rahman*[1]

Born in 1903, Tengku Abdul Rahman is the son of the late Sultan Abdul Hamid Halim Shah of Kedah and his Siamese wife. Educated at Cambridge University and the Inner Temple, London, where he qualified as a barrister at the age of forty-six, he joined the Federal Legal Department in 1949 as a Deputy Public Prosecutor. In 1951, he became the leader of the United Malays National Organization following the resignation of Dato' Onn. His political career since then has indeed been most impressive. He has retained his position as head of the U.M.N.O., and has also been the leader of the Alliance since it was founded in 1953. The Tengku became the Federation's first Chief Minister in 1955, and was one of the chief architects of independence. He resigned his premiership for a short time before the 1959 parliamentary elections, to help strengthen the Alliance election machinery. Following his party's return to power, he was sworn in once again as Prime Minister on 22 August 1959. Currently, he also holds the portfolio for Foreign Affairs.

*Che Ahmad Boestamam bin Raja Kechil*

Born in 1920, Che Ahmad Boestamam received his education in Malay and English schools. A journalist by profession, he has been very active in the Malay left-wing since the end of the Second World War. A founder-member of the Malay Nationalist Party, he was also the leader of the *Angkatan Permuda Insaf* before it was declared a subversive organization in 1948. He was detained for his 'extreme' political views under the Emergency Regulations in 1948, and returned to national politics as the leader of Party Ra'ayat in 1955. In 1961, he decided not to stand for re-election as the chairman of the Socialist Front (an alliance between Party Ra'ayat and the Labour Party), a position which he had held since the organization was

1. For a detailed study of Tengku Abdul Rahman's life, see H. Miller, *Prince and Premier* (London, Harrap, 1959).

founded in 1957, explaining that he needed more time to organize and strengthen Party Ra'ayat. Che Boestamam represents a Selangor constituency in the Federal Parliament, having won his seat at the 1959 elections.

*Dr. Burhanuddin Al-Hemy*

Dr. Burhanuddin was born in 1911 in Kota Bahru, Kelantan, and was educated in Malay, Arabic, and English schools. A free-lance journalist by profession, he has been a prominent figure in the pro-Malay cause for the best part of the last twenty years. During the War, he was one of the leaders of the movement to unite Malaya with Indonesia; soon after it, he became the president of the Malay Nationalist Party, and was also the general adviser of the *Pusat Tenga Ra'ayat*. He is now the president of the Pan-Malayan Islamic Party, and is a member of Parliament representing a Trengganu constituency which he won in 1959.

*Dato' Onn bin Ja'afar*[2]

Dato' Onn was born in 1895. Like his grandfather, father, and two elder brothers, he was also a *mentri besar* (chief minister) of Johore, a post which he resigned in 1951. Although he is no longer in the limelight of Malayan politics, it was not so long ago that Dato' Onn was the unquestioned leader of the Malay community. Having been a member of the nominated Johore State Council before the War, he emerged as the foremost figure in Malayan politics during the immediate post-war years. It was he who led the highly organized Malay opposition which resulted in the withdrawal of the Malayan Union scheme in 1947. The founder-president of the U.M.N.O., he left the party in 1951 to form the I.M.P., having failed to persuade the former to open its doors to non-Malays. The I.M.P., a non-communal organization, did not prove a happy venture. Following its dissolution Dato' Onn formed another party, Party Negara, which is strongly pro-Malay. He is still the leader of this party and is its sole representative in the Federal Parliament, having won his seat in a Trengganu constituency at the 1959 elections. At the 1955 elections his party suffered a crushing defeat at the hands of the Alliance, losing all the seats it contested. It has never quite recovered from this, nor has it looked like doing so.

Dato' Onn has held high government appointments. Among other things, he was the 'Member' for Home Affairs in the nominated Federal Legislative Council and the Chairman of the Rural Industrial Development Authority.

2. See Ishak bin Tadin, 'Dato' Onn, 1946–1951', *Journal of Southeast Asian History*, Vol. 1, No. 1, Singapore, March 1960, pp. 62–99.

*Mr. D. R. Seenivasagam*

Born in 1921 in Ipoh, Perak, Mr. Seenivasagam went to the Inne Temple, London, after the War where he was called to the Bar. He has been practising as an advocate and solicitor since 1949. It was as a member of the P.P.P., of which he is now the leader, that Mr. Seenivasagam first entered active politics. He was elected the party's Vice-President in 1953, and became its Secretary-General in 1955. Elected to the Ipoh and Menglembu Town Council in 1954, he lost his deposit in that constituency at the 1955 General Elections. At the by-election held there in 1956, however, he won a convincing victory. Ipoh and Menglembu have now become his party's strongholds: at the 1959 parliamentary elections both he and his brother, Mr. S. P. Seenivasagam, won very handsome victories there. Mr. Seenivasagam's success in Ipoh may largely be attributed to the manner in which he and his party have played up to Chinese dissatisfaction with the policies of the Alliance Government.

*The late Dato' Sir Cheng-lock Tan* (*Tan Cheng Lock*), b. 1883: d. 1960[3]

A Straits Chinese, Dato' Sir Cheng-lock Tan belonged to a family which traces its settlement in Malaya back several generations. Having started life as a schoolmaster, he entered the rubber industry in 1908, becoming a large proprietary rubber planter. He was made a Justice of the Peace in 1912, and was invited in the early '30s to serve on the Straits Chinese Consultative Committee, set up to advise the Governor on Chinese Affairs. In the '30s, he also served in the Legislative and Executive Councils of the Straits Settlements. During the period of Japanese occupation Dato' Sir Cheng-lock lived in India where he led the Oversea Chinese Association, a body which carried on extensive correspondence with the British Colonial Office on the question of Malaya's political future. Returning to Malaya after the War, he soon became the foremost political figure in the Chinese community. He was the Chairman of the All-Malaya Council of Joint Action, the founder-President of the Malayan Chinese Association, a member of the Communities Liaison Committee, a founder-member of the Independence of Malaya Party, and Joint-Chairman of the Alliance National Council.

Mr. Tan Siew Sin, the present Minister for Finance, is the son of Dato' Sir Cheng-lock Tan.

3. A fairly detailed account of Dato' Sir Cheng-lock's career is given in: Soh Eng Lim, 'Tan Cheng Lock—His Leadership of the Malayan Chinese', *Journal of Southeast Asian History*, Vol. 1, No. 1, Singapore, March 1960, pp. 34–61.

# BIBLIOGRAPHY

*Books and Pamphlets*

Allen, G. C., and Donnithorne, A. G. *Western Enterprise in Indonesia and Malaya.* London, Allen and Unwin, 1957.

American Institute of Pacific Relations. *The Development of Self-Rule and Independence in Burma, Malaya, and the Philippines* (Part II, on *Malaya*, by Patricia G. Barnett). New York, Amer. Institute of Pacific Relations, 1948.

Awberry, S. S., and Dalley, F. W. *Labour and Trade Union Organization in the Federation of Malaya and Singapore.* Kuala Lumpur, Government Printing Office, 1948.

Ball, W. M. *Nationalism and Communism in East Asia.* Melbourne, Melbourne University Press, 1956.

Bow Group. 'Malaya: A Nation in Embryo', *Race and Power.* London, Bow Group, 1956.

Brimmel, J. H. *A Short History of the Malayan Communist Party.* Singapore, Donald Moore, 1956.

Carnell, F. G. *Malayan Citizenship Legislation.* Institute of Colonial Studies, Oxford University. (Reprinted from *The International and Comparative Law Quarterly*, October 1952.)

Carrington, C. E., assisted by H. L. Rowland and A. S. B. Olver. *Malaya and Singapore.* London, Royal Institute of International Affairs, 1956.

Chelliah, D. D. *A History of the Educational Policy of the Straits Settlements, with Recommendations for a New System based on Vernaculars.* Kuala Lumpur, Govt. Printing Office, 1948.

Corry, W. C. S. *Malaya Today.* London, Longmans Green (for the Royal Empire Society), 1955.

Dodd, E. E. 'Reconstruction in Burma and Malaya' (in *Four Colonial Questions*). London, Fabian Colonial Bureau, 1944.

Elsbree, W. H. *Japan's Role in Southeast Asian Nationalist Movements 1940–1945.* Cambridge, Mass., Harvard University Press, 1953.

Emerson, R. *Malaysia: A Study in Direct and Indirect Rule.* New York, The Macmillan Co., 1937.

Emerson, R. (with supplementary chapters by Elsbree, W. H., and Thompson, V.). *Representative Government in Southeast Asia.* Cambridge, Mass., Harvard University Press, 1955.

Emerson, R., Mills, L. A., and Thompson, V. *Government and Nationalism in Southeast Asia.* New York, Institute of Pacific Relations, International Secretariat, 1942.

Firth, R. *Malay Fishermen: Their Peasant Economy*. London, Kegan Paul, Trench, Trubner & Co., 1946.

Furnivall, J. S. *Colonial Policy and Practice*. Cambridge, Cambridge University Press, 1948.

Ginsberg, N., and Roberts, C. F., Jr. *Malaya*. Seattle, University of Washington Press, 1958.

Gullick, J. M. *Indigenous Political Systems of Western Malaya*. London, Athlone Press, 1958.

Hanrahan, G. Z. *The Communist Struggle in Malaya*. New York, Institute of Pacific Relations, 1954.

Hansard Society. *Problems of Parliamentary Government in Colonies*. London, Hansard Society, 1953.

Harrison, B. *Southeast Asia*. London, Macmillan, 1954.

Ho Seng Ong. *Education for Unity in Malaya: An Evaluation of the Educational System in Malaya with Special Reference to the Need for Unity in its Plural Society*. Penang, Malayan Teachers' Union, 1952.

International Bank for Reconstruction and Development, Report of Mission organized by. *The Economic Development of Malaya*. Baltimore, Johns Hopkins Press, 1955.

Jones, S. W. *Public Administration in Malaya*. London, Royal Institute of International Affairs, 1953.

Josey, A. *Trade Unionism in Malaya*. Singapore, Donald Moore, 1954.

King, F. H. H. *The New Malayan Nation*. New York, Institute of Pacific Relations, 1957.

King, J. K. *Southeast Asia in Perspective*. New York, The Macmillan Co., 1956.

Lakeman, E. *Report on Malaya: the Relevant Facts and Opinions*. The McDougal Trust, 1952.

Lim Tay Boh. *Problems of the Malayan Economy*. Singapore, Donald Moore, 1956.

Miller, H. *Menace in Malaya*. London, Harrap, 1954.

Miller, H. *Prince and Premier*. London, Harrap (in association with Donald Moore, Singapore), 1959.

Mills, L. A. *Malaya: A Political and Economic Appraisal*. Minneapolis, University of Minnesota Press, 1958.

Peet, G. L. *Political Questions of Malaya*. Cambridge, Cambridge University Press, 1949.

Purcell, V. *The Chinese in Modern Malaya*. Singapore, Donald Moore, 1956.

Purcell, V. *The Colonial Period in Southeast Asia*. New York, Institute of Pacific Relations, 1953.

Purcell, V. *Malaya*. New York, Nelson, 1948.

Purcell, V. *Malaya: Communist or Free?*. London, Gollancz, 1954.

Purcell, V. *The Position of the Chinese in Southeast Asia.* New York, Institute of Pacific Relations, International Secretariat, 1950.

Pye, L. W. *Guerrilla Communism in Malaya: its Social and Political Meaning.* Princeton, Princeton University Press, 1956.

Rees-Williams, D. R., and Others. *Three Reports on the Malayan Problem.* New York, Institute of Pacific Relations, International Secretariat, 1949.

Robinson, J. B. P. *Transformation in Malaya.* London, Secker and Warburg, 1956.

Silcock, T. H. *The Economy of Malaya.* Singapore, Donald Moore, 1956.

Silcock, T. H., and Aziz, A. 'Nationalism in Malaya'—in Holland, W. L. (ed.), *Asian Nationalism and the West.* New York, The Macmillan Co., 1953.

Sington, D. *Malayan Perspective.* London, Fabian Publications, and Gollancz, 1953.

Smith, T. E. *Population Growth in Malaya: An Analysis of Recent Trends.* London, Royal Institute of International Affairs, 1952.

Swettenham, Sir F. *British Malaya.* John Lane, The Bodley Head, 1929.

Tan Cheng Lock. *Malayan Problems.* Singapore, G. H. Kiat, 1947.

Tan Cheng Lock. *The Reorganization of the Malayan Chinese Association, etc.* Singapore, Tiger Press, 1952.

Thayer, P. W. (ed.). *Nationalism and Progress in Free Asia.* Baltimore, Johns Hopkins Press, 1956.

Thompson, V., and Adloff, R. *Minority Problems in Southeast Asia.* California, Stanford University Press, 1955.

Wight, M. *British Colonial Constitutions, 1947.* Oxford, Clarendon Press, 1952.

Wight, M. *The Development of the Legislative Council; 1606–1945.* London, Faber and Faber, 1947.

Winstedt, Sir R. *Britain and Malaya: 1786–1941.* London, Longmans Green, 1944.

Wiseman, H. V. *The Cabinet in the Commonwealth: Post-War Developments in Africa, the West Indies and Southeast Asia.* London, Stevens, 1958.

*Articles*

Adloff, V. T. 'Opposition in Malaya', *Far Eastern Survey*, Vol. 16 (1947), pp. 130–1.

Bauer, P. T. 'Nationalism and Politics in Malaya', *Foreign Affairs*, Vol. 25, No. 3 (April 1947), pp. 503–17.

Benson, W. 'Labour Problems in Malaya', *Pacific Affairs*, Vol. 16 (1943), pp. 389–96.

'Britain Faces a New Malaya', *Amerasia*, Vol. 11, No. 1 (Jan. 1947), pp. 11–15.

Carnell, F. G. 'British Policy in Malaya', *Political Quarterly*, Vol. 23 (1952), pp. 269–81.

Carnell, F. G. 'Communalism and Communism in Malaya', *Pacific Affairs*, Vol. 26 (1953), pp. 99–117

Carnell, F. G. 'Constitutional Reform and Elections in Malaya', *Pacific Affairs*, Vol. 27 (1954), pp. 216–35.

Carnell, F. G. 'The Malayan Elections', *Pacific Affairs*, Vol. 28 (1955), pp. 315–30.

'Complications of Union in Malaya', *The Round Table*, Vol. 36 (Dec. 1945–Sept. 1946), pp. 238–46.

Cooper, E. 'Urbanization in Malaya', *Population Studies*, Vols. 5–6 (1951–3), pp. 117–31.

Creech-Jones, Rt. Hon. A. 'The Asian Crisis and the Malay Peninsula', *International Journal*, Vol. VI, No. 1 (Winter 1950–1), pp. 29–41.

Dobby, E. H. G. 'Malayan Prospect', *Pacific Affairs*, Vol. 23 (1950), pp. 392–401.

Finkelstein, L. S. 'Prospects for Self-Government in Malaya', *Far Eastern Survey*, Vol. 22 (1952), pp. 9–17.

Fletcher, W. 'Malaya', *United Empire*, Vol. 40, No. 1 (Jan.–Feb. 1949), pp. 3–8.

Gamba, C. 'Government in Malaya', *Public Administration* (Australia), Vol. 12, No. 1 (New Series), March 1953.

Gamba, C., and Aziz, A. 'R.I.D.A. and Malayan Economic Development', *Far Eastern Survey*, Vol. 19 (1950), pp. 123–6.

Gammans, L. D. 'Crisis in Malaya', *The Spectator*, Vol. 176 (14 June 1946), pp. 601–2.

Hawkins, G. 'Marking Time in Malaya', *International Affairs*, Vol. 24 (1948), pp. 76–88.

Ishak bin Tadin. 'Dato' Onn, 1946–1951', *Journal of Southeast Asian History*, Vol. 1, No. 1 (March 1960), pp. 62–99.

King, J. K. 'Malaya's Resettlement Problem', *Far Eastern Survey*, Vol. 23 (1954), pp. 33–40.

Lim, H. B. 'Malaya's "Constitution" ', *Labour Monthly*, Vol. 28, No. 12 (1946), pp. 380–3.

Mackenzie, W. J. M. 'Representation in Plural Societies', *Political Studies*, Vol. 11 (1954), pp. 54–69.

Morrison, I. 'Aspects of the Racial Problem in Malaya', *Pacific Affairs*, Vol. 22 (1949), pp. 239–53.

Nicholson, M. 'A Problem in Colonial Government', *Political Quarterly*, Vol. 20 (1949), pp. 160–71.

Palmer, J. N. 'Trade Unions and Politics in Malaya', *Far Eastern Survey*, Vol. 24, No. 3 (March 1955), pp. 33–39.

Peterson, A. D. C. 'The Birth of the Malayan Nation', *International Affairs*, Vol. 31 (1955), pp. 311–16.

Purcell, V. 'After Merdeka: The Constitutional Outlook in Malaya', *Pacific Affairs*, Vol. 10 (4), pp. 388–96.

Purcell, V. 'Overseas Chinese and the People's Republic', *Far Eastern Survey*, Vol. 19 (1950), pp. 194–6.

'Races and Parties in Malaya', *The Round Table*, Vol. 42 (1951–2), pp. 234–9.

Rees-Williams, D. R. 'The Constitutional Position in Malaya', *Pacific Affairs*, Vol. 20 (1947) pp. 174–8.

Sadka, E. 'Constitutional Changes in Malaya: A Historical Perspective', *Australian Outlook*, Vol. 11 (3), (September 1957), pp. 17–30.

Seitelman, M. 'Malaya in Transition', *Far Eastern Survey*, Vol. 16 (1947), pp. 109–11.

Silcock, T. H. 'Forces for Unity in Malaya', *International Affairs*, Vol. 25 (1949), pp. 453–65.

Silcock, T. H. 'Policy for Malaya, 1952', *International Affairs*, Vol. 28 (1952), pp. 445–57.

Soh Eng Lim. 'Tan Cheng Lock—His Leadership of the Malayan Chinese', *Journal of Southeast Asian History*, Vol. 1, No. 1 (March 1960), pp. 34–61.

Tinker, I. 'Malayan Elections: Electoral Pattern for Plural Societies?', *Western Political Quarterly*, Vol. 9 (1956), pp. 258–82.

Tregonning, K. G. P. 'Malaya, 1955', *The Australian Quarterly*, Vol. XXVII, No. 2 (June 1956), pp. 20–35.

Vlieland, C. A. 'The 1947 Census of Malaya', *Pacific Affairs*, Vol. 22 (1949), pp. 59–63.

*Newspapers*

Federation of Malaya, Department of Information, *Daily Press Summary of Vernacular Papers*, 1956–1959.

*The Malay Mail*, Kuala Lumpur, 1946–1959.

*The Singapore Standard*, Singapore, 1951–1959 (discontinued in July 1959).

*The Straits Echo*, Penang, 1957–1959.

*The Straits Times/Straits Budget*, Singapore, 1946–1961.

*Official Publications*

del Tufo, M. V. *Malaya 1947 Census*. London, Crown Agents, 1949.

Federated Malay States. *Proceedings of the Federal Council* (1924–1933). Kuala Lumpur, Government Printing Office.

Federation of Malaya. *Annual Reports* (1948–1957). Kuala Lumpur, Government Printing Office.

Federation of Malaya. *Annual Report on Education, 1957*. Kuala Lumpur, Government Printing Office, 1958.

Federation of Malaya. *Constitutional Proposals for Malaya. Report of the Consultative Committee, together with Proceedings of Six Public Meetings, Summary of Representations Made and Letters and Memoranda Considered by the Committee*. Kuala Lumpur, Government Printing Office, 1947.

Federation of Malaya. *Federation of Malaya Agreement, 1948*. Published in Federation of Malaya, *Government Gazette*, 5 February 1948. Kuala Lumpur, Government Printing Office, 1948.

Federation of Malaya. The Report of a Commission Invited by the Federation Government to Study the Problem of the Education of Chinese in Malaya: *Chinese Schools and the Education of Chinese Malayans*. Kuala Lumpur, Government Printing Office, 1951.

Federation of Malaya. *Report of the Committee on Malay Education*. Kuala Lumpur, Government Printing Office, 1951.

Federation of Malaya. *Report of the Education Review Committee, 1960*. Kuala Lumpur, Government Printing Office, 1960.

Federation of Malaya. *Report on the Introduction of Elections in the Municipality of George Town, Penang, 1951*. Kuala Lumpur, Government Printing Office, 1953.

Federation of Malaya. *Report of the Committee to Consider Financial Aids to Non-Government Islamic Religious Schools*. Kuala Lumpur, Government Printing Office, 1957.

Federation of Malaya. *Report of the Committee Appointed to Examine the Question of Elections to the Federal Legislative Council*. Kuala Lumpur, Government Printing Office, 1954.

Federation of Malaya. *Report of the Education Committee, 1956* (Razak Report). Kuala Lumpur, Government Printing Office, 1956.

Federation of Malaya. *Report of the Constituency Delineation Commission*. Kuala Lumpur, Government Printing Office, 1954.

Federation of Malaya. *Summary of Revised Constitutional Proposals Accepted by His Majesty's Government, 24th July, 1947*. Kuala Lumpur, Government Printing Office, 1947.

Federation of Malaya. Central Advisory Committee on Education. *Report on the Barnes Report on Education and the Fenn-Wu Report on Education*. Kuala Lumpur, Government Printing Office, 1951.

Federation of Malaya. Department of Information. *Communist Terrorism in Malaya*. Kuala Lumpur, Kee Meng Press, 1952.

Federation of Malaya, Federal Ordinances, No. 23 of 1952. *The Federation of Malaya Agreement (Amendment) Ordinance, 1952*. Kuala Lumpur, Government Printing Office, 1952.

Federation of Malaya, Legislative Council. *Official Report of Debates*, 1950–1959. Kuala Lumpur, Government Printing Office.

Federation of Malaya, Legislative Council. *Report of the Committee Appointed on July 11, 1951, to Examine and Report to the Legislative Council on the Federation of Malaya Agreement (Amendment) Ordinance, 1951* (Papers to be laid before the Legislative Council, No. 19 of 1952). Kuala Lumpur, Government Printing Office, 1952.

Federation of Malaya, Legislative Council. *Resettlement and the Development of New Villages in the Federation of Malaya* (Papers to be Laid Before the Legislative Council, No. 33 of 1952). Kuala Lumpur, Government Printing Office, 1952.

Federation of Malaya, Public Relations Department. *How the Constitution Works* (A Series of Talks Broadcast by Radio Malaya). Kuala Lumpur, Government Printing Office, 1949.

Federation of Malaya, State Enactments Passed During the Year 1952, No. 2 of 1952. *State Nationality Enactments, 1952* (Enacted individually by each State). Kuala Lumpur, Government Printing Office, 1952.

Fell, H. *Federation of Malaya 1957 Census* (Reports by States). Kuala Lumpur, Government Printing Office, 1959.

Great Britain, Central Office of Information. *Malaya—The Making of a Nation.* Ref. Pamphlet 3600, London, H.M.S.O., May 1957.

Great Britain, Central Office of Information. *Malayan Record.* London, H.M.S.O., 1957.

Great Britain, Central Office of Information. *Towards Self-Government in the Federation of Malaya and Singapore.* Ref. Pamphlet 3492, London, H.M.S.O., 1957.

Great Britain, Colonial Office, Colonial Reports—Annual. *Malay States, Federated.* 1923–1933.

Great Britain, Colonial Office. Colonial Reports—Annual. *Malay States, Unfederated.* 1923–1933.

Great Britain, Colonial Office. Colonial Reports—Annual. *Straits Settlements.* 1923–1933.

Great Britain, Colonial Office. *Constitutional Proposals for the Federation of Malaya.* London, H.M.S.O., 1957, Cmnd. 210.

Great Britain, Colonial Office. *Federation of Malaya—Summary of Revised Constitutional Proposals.* London, H.M.S.O., 1947, Cmd. 7171.

Great Britain, Colonial Office. *Malayan Union and Singapore—Statement of Policy on Future Constitution.* London, H.M.S.O., 1946, Cmd. 6724.

Great Britain, Colonial Office. *Malayan Union and Singapore—Summary of Proposed Constitutional Arrangements.* London, H.M.S.O., 1946, Cmd. 6749.

Great Britain, Colonial Office. *Report by the Federation of Malaya Constitutional Conference.* London, H.M.S.O., 1956, Cmd. 9714.

Great Britain, Colonial Office. *Report of the Federation of Malaya Constitutional Commission*. London, H.M.S.O., 1957, Colonial No. 330.

Great Britain, Parliament, House of Commons. *Official Report of Debates*. London, H.M.S.O. Relevant debates from 1945 to 1957.

Great Britain, Parliament, House of Lords. *Official Report of Debates*. London, H.M.S.O. Relevant debates from 1945 to 1957.

Great Britain, United Kingdom Information Service, Background Note No. 19. *Malaya, a New Nation*. Toronto, 1957.

Great Britain, United Kingdom Information Service. *Malaya, the Facts*. Ottawa, 1952.

Great Britain, Colonial Office. *Report of Brigadier-General Sir Samuel Wilson, G.C.M.G., K.C.B., K.B.E., Permanent Under-Secretary of State for the Colonies on his Visit to Malaya, 1932*. (Cmd. 4276), London, H.M.S.O., 1933.

MacMichael, Sir H., G.C.M.G., D.S.O. *Report on a Mission to Malaya, October 1945–January 1946*. London, H.M.S.O., 1946. Colonial No. 194.

Malayan Union. *Annual Report, 1947*. Kuala Lumpur, Government Printing Office, 1947.

Malayan Union. *Constitutional Proposals for Malaya: Report of the Working Committee Appointed by a Conference of His Excellency the Governor of the Malayan Union, Their Highnesses the Rulers of the Malay States and the Representatives of the United Malays' National Organization*. Kuala Lumpur, Malayan Union Government Printing Office, 1946.

Nathan, J. E. *British Malaya 1921 Census*. London, Crown Agents, 1922.

Smith, T. E. *Report on the First Election of Members to the Legislative Council of the Federation of Malaya*. Kuala Lumpur, Government Printing Office, 1955.

Straits Settlements. *Proceedings of the Legislative Council of the Straits Settlements, 1928–1933*. Singapore, Government Printing Office.

Vlieland, C. A. *British Malaya 1931 Census*. London, Crown Agents, 1932.

*Miscellaneous*

Malayan Forum, United Kingdom. *Merdeka Conference Pamphlets*. 1957.

*People's Constitution for Malaya*. (Constitutional Proposals submitted by the *Pusat Tenga Ra'ayat*—All-Malaya Council of Joint Action coalition for the consideration of the British Government, 1947).

*Political Party Manifestos*. 1955 and 1959 Elections.

# INDEX